Walking the Stations

Walking the Stations

Fourteen Way Stations on a Christian Pilgrimage

DONALD HEINZ

CASCADE Books • Eugene, Oregon

WALKING THE STATIONS
Fourteen Way Stations on a Christian Pilgrimage

Copyright © 2025 Donald Heinz. All rights reserved. Except for brief quotations in critical publications or reviews, no part of this book may be reproduced in any manner without prior written permission from the publisher. Write: Permissions, Wipf and Stock Publishers, 199 W. 8th Ave., Suite 3, Eugene, OR 97401.

Cascade Books
An Imprint of Wipf and Stock Publishers
199 W. 8th Ave., Suite 3
Eugene, OR 97401

www.wipfandstock.com

PAPERBACK ISBN: 979-8-3852-0356-7
HARDCOVER ISBN: 979-8-3852-0357-4
EBOOK ISBN: 979-8-3852-0358-1

Cataloguing-in-Publication data:

Names: Heinz, Donald, author.

Title: Walking the stations : fourteen way stations on a Christian pilgrimage / Donald Heinz.

Description: Eugene, OR: Cascade Books, 2025 | Includes bibliographical references.

Identifiers: ISBN 979-8-3852-0356-7 (paperback) | ISBN 979-8-3852-0357-4 (hardcover) | ISBN 979-8-3852-0358-1 (ebook)

Subjects: LCSH: Spiritual formation—Christianity. | Ethics—Christianity.

Classification: BV4511 H45 2025 (print) | BV4511 (ebook)

New Revised Standard Version Bible, copyright 1989 National Council of the Churches of Christ in the United States of America. Used by permission. All rights reserved worldwide

Hymns by Carolyn Winfrey Gillette used by permission. All rights reserved.
She Suffered Twelve Long Years c2015
God Of the Women c1998
That Woman in the Crowd c2016
Christ Would Not Cast the Judgment Stone c2013

"Will you come and follow me" c 1987 Iona Community, WGRG, Iona Community, Glasgow, Scotland.

"*Walking the Stations* offers an innovative, but also a challenging way of delving more deeply into what it means to be a follower of Christ. While many study guides encourage applying Christ's life to our own, our contemporary culture too often focuses that effort on our private personal growth. For those of us who hope to make a difference in the world, this book's message should be one that we incorporate into our practice."

—Robert Wuthnow, professor emeritus of sociology, Princeton University

"Heinz invites us not only to read about but to create a meaning-filled, twenty-first-century Christianity by encountering the surprising Jesus of the Gospels. Historical and contemporary, informed and informing, the book asks us to rethink "our" Jesus on a pilgrimage with Scripture and tradition and in a grand company that includes Francis, Hildegard, Augustine, Luther, Wesley, Dorothy Day, Martin Luther King Jr., and Anne Lamott. As the book and familiar song remind us—we want to be in that number."

—Eileen Elrod, professor of English, Santa Clara University

"So many are asking the question famously posed by Dietrich Bonhoeffer: 'Who is Christ, actually?' In such times Spirit draws us to hear the testimony of the Gospels anew as it brings life and meaning to our contemporary lives. Donald Heinz offers us in *Walking the Stations* a practical and transformative way of entering the first century to walk in the footsteps of Jesus and contemplate the relevance of his life and ministry for our own."

—Conrad A. Braaten, former senior pastor, Church of the Reformation (ELCA), Washington, DC, and co-founder, The Forgotten Luther Project

"If Don Heinz's *Mathew 25 Christianity* was a rich appetizer, *Walking the Stations* is the four-star feast that follows. Heinz invites Christians (and seekers) to walk with the Gospel Jesus through fourteen 'stages' of his life, listening, observing, following, and exemplifying the full incarnation of God in human experience. On this pilgrimage we, too, can hear God proclaim that we, like Jesus at his baptism, are 'sons and daughters in God's family, beloved, and well-pleasing.' We, too, see our own great life challenges in the three temptations of Christ. And so on through the whole adventure to the cross and empty tomb. *Walking the Stations* is an exhilarating and profoundly true account of Jesus' life that offers an authentic Christian faith from the center: Jesus himself. It is the powerful, and perhaps only, antidote to both anemic and toxic representations of Christianity in our culture—and in many of our churches as well."

—DAVID W. GILL, professor of ethics, retired, author of *Workplace Discipleship 101: A Primer* and nine other books

"Many question whether following Jesus is possible, given current failures. So, Don Heinz invites us into communal participation in the life of Jesus by encountering him in the Gospels. He draws from Christian streams of sacramental, textual, experiential, social, and communal engagement, leading us to participation and formation that are neither passive nor activist, but follow Jesus to intimacy with God and engagement with the world God loves and sent Jesus—and us—into to restore. This book and this way are for anyone wanting a way to follow Jesus that is intimate, transformative, and hopeful."

—FRED BAILEY, senior field ministry director, InterVarsity Christian Fellowship, USA

To my family
    Will you come and follow me
        The way is made by walking
            May we walk together
                I want to be in that number

"Putting on Christ" in the New Testament

Come, **follow me,** *Jesus said (13 times). At once they left their nets and followed him.* MATTHEW 4:18–20

My sheep listen to my voice; I know them, and **they follow me.** JOHN 10:27

Put on the Lord Jesus Christ. ROMANS 13:14

For if we have been united with him in a death like his, we shall certainly be united with him in a resurrection like his. ROMANS 6:5

All of us who have been baptized into Christ Jesus were baptized into his death. Therefore we have been buried with him by baptism into death, so that just as Christ was raised from the dead by the glory of the Father, so we too might walk in newness of life. ROMANS 6:3–4

As many of you as were baptized into Christ have clothed yourself with Christ. GALATIANS 3:27

Clothe yourselves with a new self, created according to the likeness of God in true righteousness and holiness. EPHESIANS 4:24

Contents

Foreword xi
Preface xxi

PART ONE: PREPARING FOR A WALK WITH CHRIST

Expectations: Mining Jesus' Life as Treasure in a Field 3

Christian Pilgrimage: The Setting for Walking the Stations 6

From "Fourteen Stations of the Cross" to Fourteen Stations of Jesus' Entire Life 14

Fourteen Stations in Jesus'—and the Believer's—Life 21

An Anthropological View of How Religion Works 25

Establishing and Embellishing the Religious Practice of Walking the Stations of Jesus' Life (and Our Own) in the Life of the Church and Its People 29

PART TWO: WALKING 14 STATIONS ALONG THE CHRISTIAN WAY

WAY STATION 1: Jesus Is Born Into the Human World and Our World—*Will We Meet Him There as We Are Born Again?* 39

WAY STATION 2: Jesus Is Baptized, Opens His Life to God, and Engages a World of Temptation and Possibility—*Have We Been Mostly Clueless About the Implications of Our Own Baptism?* 47

WAY STATION 3: Jesus Inaugurates His Vocation by Proclaiming the Arrival of the Kingdom of God with a Jubilee Message—*Will We Recognize God's Reign When We See It? Will We Proclaim Jubilee?* 59

Contents

Way Station 4: Jesus Is Calling and Making Disciples—*How Do We Answer? Do We Consent to Be Made New?* 66

Way Station 5: Jesus Teaches Us to Pray, with the Lord's Prayer as a Model—*Could We Learn to Pray? Are We Paying Attention to the World Around Us When We Pray?* 74

Way Station 6: Jesus Eats and Drinks with Outsiders and the Excluded—*Could We Learn Christian Table Manners?* 83

Way Station 7: Jesus Offers Healing Amidst Human Brokenness—*Could the Church Become a Field Hospital and We Its Chaplains?* 93

Way Station 8: Jesus Preaches Sermons That Reveal a Gospel from God for All Peoples—*Do We Hear a Gospel That Sounds Like This Every Sunday and Preach It in the Midst of a World Longing for Good News?* 99

Way Station 9: Jesus Welcomes Women and Outsiders, and Calls Us to Do the Same—*How Do Women and Outsiders Fare in Our Congregations?* 104

Way Station 10: Jesus Teaches Wisdom in Parables That Open up Alternative Worlds with Space for God—*Will We Walk Into That Space and Learn to Live In It?* 116

Way Station 11: Jesus Rides Into Jerusalem, Challenging the Religious and Political Establishment—*Do We Dare to Speak Nonconforming Truths as Communities of Resistance?* 126

Way Station 12: Jesus Washes the Disciples' Feet, Dispenses a New Love Commandment, and Offers His Own Body to the World in His Last Supper—*Can We Learn "Christian Yoga" as Our Servant Discipline, Justice as the Social Form of Life, and the Eucharist as Our Weekly Refreshment for a Difficult Journey?* 132

Way Station 13: Jesus Dies the Most Famous Death in History—*Can Christians See in It a Messianic Enthronement and Their Salvation with God?* 140

Way Station 14: Jesus Rises from the Dead, Signaling the Triumph of God's Love and the Reconciliation of the World—*Do Christians Spend Their Lives Following in the Train of Their Risen Lord?* 155

Appendix 165
Bibliography 181

FOREWORD

A Personal Note to Readers from the Author—
Now That You Have This Book in Your Hands, What Are You Going to Do With It?

How did you happen to pick this book? Interesting title? Catchy? You're interested in the idea of pilgrimage? You're familiar with the idea of "stations"? You're ready for a new step in your own spiritual journey? You see yourself as a seeker? Or you just felt like reading a book on religion or Christianity?

Or, did someone present you with this book? Did you ask them what they had in mind, what hopes they have for you? What was the occasion? Your adult baptism? Confirmation? Your first day at college? Graduation? Marriage? Your first house, and a hint for a home altar to display this book? Your firstborn child? Your first serious depression? A bout of spiritual anorexia? Your church group's pilgrimage to the Holy Land? Your first trip to Europe and its holy sites? A pre-op moment for a serious medical intervention? First day in a nursing home?

Do you keep a journal? Do you have a "writing life"? Is your life a book that needs writing? Which chapter will provide ultimate meaning for all the others?

What is your setting in life? What does the world look like in your neighborhood? (A modern paraphrase of the Bible turns John 1:14, "The Word became flesh and lived among us," into: "And moved into the neighborhood.") What kind of world is in your imagination? What is your sense of religion in America? What's right or wrong with your local church? Do you find yourself in the midst of a religious community? Or wish you did?

Foreword

Will you tuck this book into your backpack for an important journey? Wait, do you ever do important journeys? Do you ever plan for them but not carry on? Do life-opening journeys have a place in your imagination? Your bucket list?

If you are placing this book in your backpack, or giving it pride of place on your desk, you might be interested to know that it comes with two earlier books preceding it. I've not exactly written a trilogy. I didn't have all three books in mind when I set out to write three books, but I think they come out of the same disposition, a common idea about God's challenges to American Christians. Or a pressing agenda for our times. The first book, written a couple years ago, was called *After Trump: Achieving a New Social Gospel*. So that book wasn't so much an attack on Trump, or on the prevailing view of society from Reagan to Trump, as it was a proposal for what a good society, a just social system, should look like, *After Trump*. "Social Gospel" refers to the idea that Christians who hear the good news from God inside their churches are obligated to take that message out the door and into society. Not just to "witness to" people who are not yet Christian but to work to achieve the kind of human community the Bible envisions. To get more specific, to provide a "prooftext," my next book was called *Matthew 25 Christianity: Redeeming Church and Society*. The last story in the twenty-fifth chapter of the Gospel of Matthew is a manifesto about how Christians should be responding to "the least of these" in society—namely the unhoused, the hungry, the thirsty, the sick, the lonely. In all such people were the disciples of Christ able to see Jesus himself, Jesus about to be enthroned as a king on a cross? Or did they mostly go through life clueless and indifferent to needy people all around? Or, in the language of the Old Testament, were they oblivious to the "holy trinity" of widows, orphans, and immigrants? Now this book, the one in your hands just now, wants to deepen and quicken your walk with God, to suggest a certain discipline to your discipleship. It does this by laying out a lifelong Christian pilgrimage (a very old idea in Christianity) that, as I see it, consists of fourteen "way stations" on which Jesus' eventful life and now yours meet, come together, become a thoughtful conversation and meditation. Just imagine all those "stops" on the journey of your life.

So do you dream of really taking off to somewhere? A journey that might change your life? Worth careful packing for in preparation? Do you need to feed your imagination to quicken your resolve? Do any of the

A PERSONAL NOTE

following literary evocations get you going, as they did for me when I first came across them? Are they the kind of thing that could get you packing?

At the turn of the twentieth century some Christian scholars had set out on a "quest for the historical Jesus." Who was he, and what was it like in those days? The German Albert Schweitzer led the way and closed his *Quest for the Historical Jesus* with these haunting words: "He comes to us as One unknown, without a name, as of old, by the lake-side, he came to those men who knew Him not. He speaks to us the same word: Follow thou me! And sets us to the tasks which He has to fulfill for our time. He commands. And to those who obey, whether they be wise or simple He will reveal Himself in the toils, the conflicts, the sufferings which they shall pass through in his fellowship, and, as an ineffable mystery, they shall learn in their own experience Who He is."

Do you ever aspire to create "stories to live by"? Might your life *be* the story? The countercultural pastor Nadia Bolz-Weber, with no grandiosity, admonishes the first step: *Just show up.* Like Mary Magdalene! Like her, think of the witness you could be. Don't just settle for an "immanent frame" for your camera, no higher than the next building. Prepare yourself for a macro-story. A steep adventure. With trees that reach the sky. The exodus story in the Old Testament is such a story. To deliver the children of Israel to become a new community, God calls the prophet Moses to lead them from their bondage in Egypt to a new life. But first they must flee across the Red Sea, with Pharaoh's armies chasing them. When you now, familiar with this epic story, find yourself at the edge of a great sea you must cross, how do you respond? First say a prayer, a modern rabbi admonishes. Do you hear and heed an answer: Put your foot in the water, take the first step, move in the direction of a new life? After that first step comes a total immersion, and then the arrival in a new land.

Consider what St. Augustine was able to see with his imagination in the fourth century when the Christian movement was struggling to escape the persecution and rejection of the Roman Empire and imagine a new world waiting to be created. He wrote: "That very cross on which he was derided, he has now imprinted on the brows of kings." Augustine's imagination lasted medieval Christianity for a thousand years. And grounded Luther and the Reformation as well.

Ever since my junior year in college I have been inspired by Longfellow's poem "A Psalm of Life":

> Tell me not, in mournful numbers,
> Life is but an empty dream! –
> For the soul is dead that slumbers,
> And things are not what they seem.
> Life is real! Life is earnest!
> And the grave is not its goal;
> Dust thou art, to dust returnest,
> Was not spoken of the soul.
>
> Not enjoyment, and not sorrow,
> Is our destined end or way;
> But to act, that each to-morrow
> Find us farther than to-day.
> Art is long, and Time is fleeting,
> And our hearts, though stout and brave,
> Still, like muffled drums, are beating
> Funeral marches to the grave.
>
> In the world's broad field of battle,
> In the bivouac of Life,
> Be not like dumb, driven cattle!
> Be a hero in the strife!
>
> Trust no Future, howe'er pleasant!
> Let the dead Past bury its dead!
> Act, —act in the living Present!
> Heart within, and God o'erhead!

Or consider, on our own shores, the timely exhortations of James Russell Lowell, which became a well-known hymn:

> Once to every man and nation comes the moment to decide,
> In the strife of Truth with Falsehood, for the good or evil side;
> Some great cause, God's new Messiah, offering each the bloom or blight,
> Parts the goats upon the left hand, and the sheep upon the right,
> And the choice goes by for ever 'twixt that darkness and that light.

As this poem turned into a beloved Protestant hymn this verse appeared:

> By the light of burning martyrs,
> Christ, Thy bleeding feet we track
> Toiling up new Calv'ries' eve
> With the cross that turns not back

A Personal Note

New occasions teach new duties,
Time makes ancient good uncouth,
They must upward still and onward,
Who would keep abreast of truth.

But perhaps we should begin our trek more modestly and less grandly. (Great poetry sometimes leads me to grandiosity!) Our old backpacks may not be fit for too much weight. Each epoch finds its own thoughts, its own burdens, its own adventures, its own pilgrimage. An important theme of this book is to make "Walking the Stations" a communal walk, with companions with their own backpacks, and things to do, and ponderous discussions to be made at each way station, each stop on the journey. In his *Canterbury Tales*, Chaucer had his band of pilgrims engage in storytelling contests on their way to a famous pilgrimage site. Very suggestively, Chaucer saw this motley band of pilgrims became a joyful community, along their way.

So the Christian life can become a parade through life, attracting new sign-ons along the way. Small groups can create great festivals, new opportunities for leading marches, performative liturgies, banners, music, in homes, and from church to town. My family back in Dubuque, Iowa turned every Christmas Eve into an inspiring event—first the Heinz children playing starring roles in the Sunday school pageant, then a powerful sermon and even more stirring music, and then, when it all seemed nearly over, my father took us on a tour through town to see all the lights, all the creches, all the celebrations. And then home where each of us four children could open one present, anticipating Christmas morning.

One last point. As I was choosing a title for this book, I fixed on: *Walking the Stations: Way Stations on a Christian Pilgrimage*. Are you curious about what stations you've already gone through in your own religious life?

I also considered as my title *The Way Is Made by Walking*. This is an old and insightful idea that emerged from pilgrimage walks, such as the Camino de Santiago, the most famous of all European pilgrimage walks that begins in southern France and then moves westward across all of northern Spain until it reaches its destination in Galicia, where a cathedral in honor of St. James the early Christian martyr climaxes the walk. But it's a long, challenging pilgrim's walk, with a certificate of achievement when you finally complete it. What to do to get started on such a daunting trip? "The way is made by walking." Showing up and getting started takes care of itself.

Foreword

Composing a (Christian) Life was another tempting title. Margaret Mead's daughter, Mary Catherine Bateson, wrote a book with this provocative title. She told the story of how she and several other women put their lives together with the materials at hand that challenged modern women. I imagined that the "stations" in Jesus' life that I have enumerated could become chapters in Christian autobiographies. I was also moved by C. S. Lewis's idea that every book needs at least one chapter which, if missing, evaporates the deep meaning of it all.

Finally, I have loved to sing along with *I want to be in that number* from "When the Saints Go Marching In." This suggests that a parade of the saints through life, through history, can become a compelling invitation. You just have to join it. Please do.

AUTHOR AND AUDIENCE: WHO AM I AND WHO ARE YOU

I am a professing Christian writer whose teaching career has been in a religious studies department (Bible, history of Christianity, social ethics, sociology of religion, death and dying) in a public university (California State University, Chico) where I also became a champion of the liberal arts, including religion, as dean of humanities and fine arts.

During my teaching time I became alert for *religious seekers* and welcoming to Christian students looking for a new identity in religious studies. I found many. I was intrigued by students moving beyond the "education vs. religion" dichotomy, and I intended to embellish and deepen their lives as carriers of Christian life in community. I sought to provoke students approaching graduation to open themselves to Christian callings in life after college, a mission the Protestant Reformers urged on those moving from monasticism out to the streets. As a Lutheran I did not hope to isolate them in sectarian enclaves but embed them in trajectories where the life of the mind, and life in community, and lives seeking engagements with social justice, would come together as fully developed Christian callings. With St. Paul, I hoped that in college they would begin the practice of "putting on Christ." Some students hoped to change the world as young adults.

Several years ago I began writing this *book that moves deliberately beyond walking the Good Friday "stations of the cross" to walking fourteen way stations that fully sum the entire life of Christ and could constitute the composition of a life of discipleship, a serious practice of pilgrimage, and even*

A Personal Note

become a contemporary religious movement. I was always imagining as my audience both a public of spiritual seekers and church-based Christians. I hoped to attract student initiates, new Christians seeking entry into the tradition, and all Christians who are looking to practice theology, Bible study in community, and discipleship (Jesus and Justice is a recent Inter-Varsity Christian Fellowship model). I imagined social activists coming together on a pilgrimage towards becoming *Matthew 25 Christians,* the subject of my last book. I imagined an audience that might come to exemplify that 10 percent of social activists in any given moment that could change the world. *I am impressed by the statistic that a third of adult believers became Christian during their youth, with college as a window of opportunity.* This book would also appeal to all those who seek "Jesus but not the church."

I am intrigued by and not fearful of *altar call* questions that might evoke *altar answers* as people drop everything and "come forward," like: Which Jesus are you following and to what end? What kind of relationship with Jesus Christ, beyond doctrinal affirmations, do you imagine? Do Christian creeds and catechisms help you think about what you believe? Consider this question as well: *What in each station in Jesus' life subverts normal assumptions*—of oneself and of fellow Christians and of the culture I live in? Is there room in my world for walking these stations, or must I create new worlds in order to make room for God? Will these way stations alter the God-picture I normally carry in my wallet? Must I change direction (repentance) in my own life?

In an era of unjust social systems, both Catholic and liberal Protestant theologians have lately made **social justice** central to their understanding of Christianity, and have also appealed to the Old Testament idea of **Jubilee** (forgiveness of debt, recovery of ancestral lands) as a central manifestation in Jesus' own ministry and a way of appealing to the modern age. Is this working? Jubilee has not yet quite become a central theme in sermons. Or in churchly literature. This book will weave Jubilee as a new Christian calling into some of the stations to be walked, especially station #3.

For some moderns, making one's own bucket list of events chosen from the life of Jesus could become a new thing, even fashionable, and certainly heuristic. Let me see, what scenes from Jesus' life impress me the most?

For college students seeking to meet and *pledge* Jesus over one semester, this could be a guide book, with one chapter for each week of the semester.

FOREWORD

The sum of these stations could become a necessary and inviting handbook for adult instruction and initiation classes, and the center of religious retreats, both Catholic and Protestant, that become an introduction to theology, Bible study in community, discipleship, and networking.

OVERVIEW OF WHAT'S COMING

In a time when Catholic piety is often fixed on the Good Friday "stations of the cross," and evangelical piety is associated with an imaginary "what would Jesus do," and much of Protestant religion has slimmed Jesus down from the fully dimensioned Christology of the Gospels, and contemporary Christianity misses a Christ who has "moved into the neighborhood" and fully engaged the world and its peoples, and touring liberals tout how little a Christian actually needs to believe and still be a Christian, *this book chooses fourteen episodes from Jesus' entire life and makes them "way stations" on a pilgrimage on which we gather to meet Jesus in person, share him in community, and follow him to a fully realized discipleship.* Such way stations may recall the medieval imitation of Christ or the notion of a Christian pilgrimage during which we "make the way by walking." Historically, marching pilgrims are meant to evoke "I want to be in that number." Yet identifying these stations is fully congruent with contemporary New Testament scholarship, whether contemporary liberal or historically orthodox.

The significance of this book is that it sets forth a process of adult Christian education today that is rich with all the dimensions of Jesus' life, from birth to death and resurrection, with all the happenings in between. And most important, it turns adult Christian education into a compelling **Bible study in community**, and one that attracts participation like walking a labyrinth together. Through such engagement it recovers for lively practice today the mostly forgotten medieval **imitatio Christi** and inserts this into the nearly forgotten but once vividly realized practice of **pilgrimage,** overdue today as a way of imprinting the Christian walk onto the culture and onto individual believers and their communities. Finally, it follows contemporary Gospel scholarship back to the **historical Jesus**, imagining visionary Holy Land tours and inviting a modern walking the way stations that constitute Jesus' own life and our immersion in it that would constitute **true discipleship.** Along the way, we tell stories and *become the stories we tell,* an old Anabaptist aspiration.

A Personal Note

The burden of this book, then, is to propose an **entirely new approach** to Bible study, discipleship, and the construction of a Christian presence in the world. The point of adopting the "stations" trope is to make fourteen stations a comprehensive and graduating enactment of Jesus' entire birth, life, death, and resurrection—a curriculum readers could own as his followers. A fully adequate portrayal of Christ would stimulate a kind of preaching in which every great moment in the life of Christ, even for example including his interactions with women and foreigners, would become kerygmatic—so that stories, easily ignored or forgotten, are taken seriously enough to open one up to the arrival of the kingdom of God, where we weren't expecting it, in contemporary experience.

These fully adequate way stations in the life of Christ would open the churches to storytelling as theological construction, to the medieval imitation of Christ, to discipleship as faith formation, to spirituality as the inner pilgrimage that engages through meditation and moral action each great vignette in Jesus' life. Altogether these fourteen stations constitute a labyrinth that serious Christians walk together as a communal exercise and surprise themselves meeting each other in the wholeness of the journey.

PREMISE

It is a compelling agenda for the modern church to retrieve Jesus' entire life as good news from God and a call to a discipleship that traces the ways of Jesus' own earthly journey. A book such as this could attract active believers, contemporary spiritual seekers, and the ever larger number of Christians who have disaffiliated with the church but who tell researchers they could be lured back under the right circumstances. (This is the argument of a recent book, *The Great Dechurching*.)

Claiming stations in Jesus' life as one's own to follow replicates the theology of story and the "narrative quality of experience" and turns one into a *waymaker and wayfarer* in life. The early church saw its own experiences of discipleship, especially in the lives of its saints, as *incarnational deposits* that mark the Christian way and encourage others on the journey—bread crumbs scattered along pilgrimage routes, where Christians track their calling.

There is a predilection among many comfortable middle-class Christians to spiritualize Jesus away from everyday eating and drinking, away

Foreword

from rough neighborhoods, to locate Jesus in one's heart but not in the public square, to make following Jesus a prim moral walk more than a neighborhood demonstration. But *the New Testament connects God, through the rough life and death of Jesus, to a gritty earth.* That is where the reign of God, proclaimed by Jesus, takes up space on earth (as Calvinists like to emphasize). *So stations refers to all the places where Jesus stopped*, and established his presence, and where one could even now pause to meet him and to consider joining the pilgrimage on which we make the way by walking. Stations are stops in the life of Christ where the modern church is meant to fill out its own life and also take on passengers.

Again, the concept of "stations" of course comes from the historic Good Friday "stations of the cross" in Catholic piety. But this book makes of stations a comprehensive enactment of Jesus' entire birth, life, death, and resurrection. So every great moment in the life of Christ can become part of gospel proclamation (kerygma), part of Jesus' call to discipleship, part of the church's life-together-in-Christ a dimension of Christ's presence on earth.

There is something else attractive about choosing fourteen stations to sum up Jesus' life. It invites communal reflection and discussion—something like a fraternity or sorority *initiation* at the beginning of a semester. It also suggests the heuristic question, Which fourteen stations would *you* choose for your own "bucket list"? All these stations awaken the moral imagination of the Christian pilgrim who "wants to be in that number." Fourteen stations could become fourteen chapters in a book I am writing, to be called *Composing a (Christian) Life.*

PREFACE

Opening an Invitation

THIS BOOK IS AN invitation and a guidebook for *walking the stations* of Jesus' life. What are these stations? How many are there? Where do you find them? Do you get to them by meditation or by train ride to each stop? A station is in fact an opportune stop, a way station for pious reflection or group retreat, or a place to pause and "put on Christ," as St. Paul admonishes.

The language of "fourteen stations" comes down to us from the "fourteen stations of the cross" in medieval Catholicism. The artistic and spiritual stimulation for "walking the stations" occurs in every Catholic church in the world, in which religious seekers pause before fourteen artistic depictions of Good Friday events as they make their way on a pilgrimage up and down the aisles of their church. In the Catholic tradition "walking the stations" happens every Good Friday, and often many times during Lent, and even throughout the church year.

While acknowledging and honoring this ancient tradition, this book proposes pilgrimages through fourteen different stations of Jesus' *entire life, and adoptable by all Christendom,* and not just an evocation of events on Good Friday in a Catholic setting. The point is that walking fourteen stations of Jesus' *life* is a fuller and more adequate immersion in the entire life of Christ and not just one concentrated on his death. Jesus' entire life is New Testament proclamation of the good news of the gospel. And a call to discipleship. The medieval *imitatio Christi* can be an *evocation of everything Jesus did and said.* The pious believer puts on the entirety of Christ's life, and wears it like Christian clothing.

A difficult journey opens up to us once we *show up* and begin it. This book is a call to become pilgrims who will walk selected way stations of

Preface

Jesus' whole life, from birth to death and resurrection, and through much of his sayings and doings in between. To add mystery and magnitude to Christian pilgrimage, consider a myth that arose during the Middle Ages, far above the road to Compostella, namely: the Milky Way is a product of the dust raised on the journey by millions of pilgrims through the ages! For those who still seek, the heavens point the way! There is a Protestant call to such a journey as well. It famously occurs in John Bunyan's bestseller, *Pilgrim's Progress: From This World to That Which Is to Come*. He wrote it from prison, at the beginning of the sixteenth-century Puritan revolution in England.

So walking the stations is inevitably a pilgrim's road. Pilgrims pause for meditation and pious conversation and fellowship at each of the stations. These stations along the way become a time to "put on the Lord Jesus Christ and make no provision for the flesh," as Paul urges in Romans 13:14. Would it be too much to suggest that at each station the church practices dressing up as the bride of Christ (Ephesians 5:22–32)? At each station, as at a theatrical site, the church, which is to say the totality of believers, stops to practice *improvisational theater*, as "indrafts of meaning" are drawn to the stage. At each of the stations of Jesus' life as theater, it can happen that members of the audience are drawn from their seats to join Christ on the stage. The point is to become an actor in Christ's play. Gerard Manley Hopkins wrote: "*Christ plays in ten thousand places*, Lovely in limbs, and lovely in eyes not his. To the Father through the features of men's faces."

At each of the stations, by ourselves or in concert with other believers, there is opportunity to write Christ's walk into our own life stories, themes and variations in the music of our own lives. University students could *pledge* to write Jesus into their evolving curriculum vitae each semester. Walking the fourteen stations can become a Rite of Christian Initiation for Adults, the Catholic name for what Protestants call confirmation, for all those being formed into a new people, the church, the body of believers. Just as the pilgrims who walked to Compostela got their journey certificates stamped at their conclusion, the resumes of modern pilgrims could be stamped with their accumulating stations from Jesus' life!

One of the loveliest themes on the way to a Christian curriculum vitae, a comprehensive Christian resume, is "Fashion Me a People," Maria Harris's title of her book that imagines God calling for the construction of a lifelong Christian curriculum, a lifelong practice of Christian education replete with community, service, worship, proclamation, and formation of

Opening an Invitation

all members of the church from birth to death. What might all this look like? Imagine fourteen stops on a Christian labyrinth on which Christian believers meet each other while making their way together to practice the presence of Christ. All the while we are *mapping Jesus' life onto our own.* The life of Christ becomes habit-forming. By walking the stations we compose a Christian life!

Finally, in the mystical imagination, is it possible that the stations Christians walk could be imagined as *Ancestry.com?* (Spit in a cup and send the evidence in.) The first chapter of the Gospel of John calls Jesus the incarnate Word, indeed the Word first spoken at creation, the Word now giving new life to the world, the Word that cannot be extinguished by darkness. From creation and the garden of Eden until now, there comes a steady succession of divine appearances, of divine presence. Do Christians who now pause at Jesus' genome appearing at each station find God's DNA expressing itself in their own human lives? Would the expression of the divine gene, as evolutionary biology suggests, become the process by which encoded information is turned into modern functions? Are we adapting to the holy living to which God calls us?

Is this book for you, then?

But wait, before turning the page to study the table of contents, which outlines my proposed fourteen stations. Have *you* ever thought to "count the ways" of following Jesus' teachings and life?

Also before you set out, ask yourself: What kind of spiritual journey would walking the stations be? Do we literally walk the stations, or is it an esoteric mystical or spiritual exercise? When many Christians think of mysticism or spirituality, they conjure up images of difficult prayer techniques: workshops with meditation gurus, intense weekend retreats. Spirituality begins to seem a matter of tutoring by professionals.

Don't be intimidated. Walking the stations could be like *ordinary spirituality.*

In fact, many books on spirituality or mysticism have *ordinary* in their titles. Look up such books on Amazon and see what ordinary might mean for you. Consider this: In her books on Clare of Assisi, St. Francis's sister who was active in the first half of the thirteenth century, Joan Mueller, a contemporary Franciscan Sister of Joy, shares how Clare of Assisi taught her version of Franciscan prayer, that holy immersion in a material Christ. Remember Francis setting up manger scenes in small villages so the common people could take their place in them?

Preface

Franciscan piety is, after all, a spirituality of the people. The largest order of Franciscans is made up of lay people, and both Francis and Clare chose a quasi-lay lifestyle over the monasticism of their time. Neither Francis nor Clare participated in prayer workshops, nor did they have extensive monastic training, and yet both experienced profound union with God. What was their secret?

Although we have prayers that were written by St. Francis, it is St. Clare, in her fourth letter to St. Agnes of Prague, who explains what is meant by Franciscan prayer. In this letter, written on her deathbed, Clare wants to teach Agnes to make a habit of daily prayer. This daily practice of prayer, however, is not an esoteric task as Clare explains it. Clare suggests that we "consider the midst of Jesus' life, his humility, his blessed poverty, the countless hardships, and the punishments that he endured for our redemption." Here Clare is asking us simply to reflect on the public life of Christ and immerse ourselves in it.

Medieval Christianity demonstrated remarkable roads to spirituality and meditation. When a cathedral or local church was being frescoed, an artist would come to town and the subjects for the paintings that were being commissioned for the church's walls and ceilings would be decided. But whom would the painter use for his artistic models? Most often, he wandered the local streets, interacted with the villagers, and decided whose faces he might portray. One day you might go to church and find yourself in a fresco on the wall listening to Jesus preach. Maybe your face would represent one of the disciples, or one of the women who cared for Jesus. Perhaps one of your children would be listening to Jesus teach. In any case, you would be placed right in the midst of the gospel; your own face would actually be central to the story.

This is what St. Clare is asking us to do. Take the gospel for the day, a Gospel from Sunday's Common Lectionary or the liturgy of the hours, or a Gospel passage from a daily devotional, and imagine yourself in the midst of the story. Who would you be most comfortable portraying? What are you hearing, seeing, smelling, tasting? Clare asks us to spend a few minutes really entering into the Gospel story of Jesus' public life and imagining what it would be like to be there, to become what is happening, to wear the life of Jesus like a garment. Which is to say, to walk the stations.

Finally, as you contemplate walking the stations, ask yourself which Jesus you have been following in your mind before you began. Could you count the ways in which Jesus comes to you, who Jesus is, and what he says

Opening an Invitation

when he knocks at your door? Of course you're not the first to walk the stations. There is a long tradition of discipleship, imitation, pilgrimage. And it can happen in community settings, in which there is a mutual walking of the stations together.

Consider this possibility: Some pilgrims seek to literally walk the stations, "where Jesus walked" or to visit holy places. And like Hindu pilgrims, they may feel commissioned to bring back souvenirs to display in their hometowns and churches, and place on their home altars. Water from the Jordan River could be poured out in the streets of the village, or used at the next baptism. Might every station yield "treasures in a field," as Jesus once suggested, for those with sufficient imagination? And a readiness to dig in? To begin?

To get ready, go to YouTube on your TV or Google on your computer. Type in "Will you come and follow me?" You will see this is a contemporary hymn, beloved by both Catholics and Protestants. You will see the lyrics, below, and several different performers singing their own arrangements of this hymn, which will enter your heart and charm your imagination:

> Will you come and follow me
> If I but call your name?
> Will you go where you don't know
> And never be the same?
> Will you let my love be shown,
> Will you let my name be known,
> Will you let my life be grown
> In you and you in me?
>
> Will you leave yourself behind
> If I but call your name?
> Will you care for cruel and kind
> And never be the same?
> Will you risk the hostile stare
> Should your life attract or scare?
> Will you let me answer prayer
> In you and you in me?
>
> Will you let the blinded see
> If I but call your name?
> Will you set the prisoners free
> And never be the same?
> Will you kiss the leper clean,

Preface

And do such as this unseen,
And admit to what I mean
In you and you in me?

Will you love the "you" you hide
If I but call your name?
Will you quell the fear inside
And never be the same?
Will you use the faith you've found
To reshape the world around,
Through my sight and touch and sound
In you and you in me?

Will your summons echoes true
When you but call my name?
Let me turn and follow you
And never be the same.
In your company I'll go
Where your love and footsteps show.

PART ONE

Preparing for a Walk with Christ

Expectations: Mining Jesus' Life as Treasure in a Field

"The kingdom of heaven is like treasure hidden in a field, which someone found and hid; then in his joy he goes and sells all he has and buys that field."
—MATTHEW 13:44.

THE BURDEN OF THIS book is to propose the idea not of "fourteen stations of the cross" but to make of "fourteen stations" a comprehensive enactment of Jesus' entire birth, life, death, and resurrection. This portrayal of Christ would stimulate a kind of preaching in which every great moment in the life of Christ, even for example including his interactions with women and foreigners, would become kerygmatic—that is, proclaiming the arrival of the reign of God as good news for humanity in every story about Jesus. *All together these constitute the whole of the reign of God and the life of Christ as treasure in a field.*

When Christians have sold everything to buy that field, they will make the most of the treasure discovered there. They experience an all-encompassing call to discipleship. They become pilgrims. They take new initiatives in Christian preaching and teaching and living. They aspire to come together as a people, Catholics and Protestants, liberals and conservatives, rich and poor, who are called together as one, holy, catholic, and apostolic church. Gradually, they practice walking the way stations in the life of Christ. They are opened up to storytelling as a way of owning and rehearsing the full life of Christ and passing it on. They practice the medieval *imitation of Christ,* which is to say discipleship as faith formation and the composing of a Christian life. They aspire to spirituality as the *inner pilgrimage* that engages through meditation each great vignette in Jesus'

Part One: Preparing for a Walk with Christ

life. Perhaps whimsically and perhaps diligently, Christians who mine the treasures in a field, as in a Holy Land visit, dig up souvenirs and take them home as permanent treasures. What souvenirs might be just right for your home altar, stimulations to your family's piety? Water from the River Jordan for the next baptism at your church?

So could fourteen stories, fourteen events, fourteen way stations be adequate to represent the treasures of the kingdom, adequate summaries of the life of Christ to seekers coming by? Could fourteen stories constitute a pilgrim's way? Could fourteen stories sufficiently decorate Christmas and Lent and Easter and Pentecost, and baptism and communion, and then also the second half of the church year that the liturgy calls "ordinary time"? All these together become quite a Christian walk.

How do I love you, God? Am I like the prodigal son who "came to himself" and, in fact, to the Father? What do I do to find redemption and a new life with treasures in a field? Fourteen stations of Jesus' life count the ways in which we construct our own lives and offer them up to God—in response to divine grace and justification, Luther would hasten to add. Bookended by incarnation and resurrection, Christmas and Easter, all the stations together give evidence of what the reign of God looks like on earth. And what we could look like in a community on whom the reign of God has touched down. A life of Jesus is not merely the story of a great teacher. The kingdom of God is not merely a location in the believer's heart, but whole neighborhoods newly inhabited by the "Word become flesh." The Gospel stories as theological proclamation are meant to be good news to follow, to provoke unending decisions for God. As Martin Luther kept saying, altogether they constitute lives in which we keep "seizing the promises" made at our baptisms. (Could walking the stations be like a prolonged baptism?)

In his earthly life Jesus encountered and immersed himself in the midst of socioeconomic stratifications, the isolation and exclusion of the poor and the hungry and the unhoused, the outcasting of the ritually impure, the prophetic longing for social justice, the world of empire and the colonized, and a religious establishment that failed in its mission to be God's good news to everyone. Affinities between Jesus' audience and the audience that must hear the modern church's proclamation and walk the stations are waiting to be noticed and embraced. Those newly awakened while walking the stations then want to awaken the world.

What is God like, seekers wonder?—perhaps "the spiritual but not religious" who show up in polls. Can one meet God at the stops along the way of Jesus' life? The New Testament proclamation is that God looks like and acts like Jesus. If what is said of Jesus can be said of God, then we are seeing in the pages of the New Testament God suffering persecution because God will not bend to the inexorable evil so characteristic of the human condition. A new exodus and a restored covenant are afoot. Jesus' life aligns with our lives, and his crucifixion gives evidence of the willingness of God to suffer and to die with and for us. His resurrection is the assurance of the tenacity of God's involvement with the world.

While the historic fourteen stations *of the cross* are unique to Jesus, and so each one is not likely to be duplicated in the life of the Christian believer, the fourteen way stations in this book mean to sum the entire life of Christ, which can be grasped by us wayfarers. *Jesus made the way; we follow the way.* We are called to walk where Jesus walked, staying close to his ground. The goal is to acquire the disposition to think and act like Jesus in all things.

All of this together fulfills the admonition of the apostle Paul to "put on the Lord Jesus Christ," or to live one's life "in Christ." As you walk through life, pause at stations that strike you, drive a stake in the ground, and say, "I claim this territory for Jesus as Lord." Paul saw clearly that the Lordship of Christ, which he and early Christianity confessed, meant acknowledging Jesus as Lord of all, not that other lord—Emperor Caesar, not the gods of the age we know so well today, not the free market, not the American way of life, not a compromised following. Paul radicalizes the Christian ethic into a life of *subversive, nonconforming obedience to the love command.* Properly expanded, the love command comes to mean social justice. That is what you aspire to when you have sold all for treasure in the field. Christian love is not a mere sentimentality.

How would the imitation of Christ proceed today? Paul and John's horizontal ethic of love to the neighbor, once one is vertically grounded by the grace of God, must find its way into ever changing situations—throughout the land where some misguided Christians lately call *social justice* nothing more than cultural Marxism. The Protestant Reformation "secularized" the Christian religious calling into the everyday world. Reformation Christians left the monasteries and followed God's call into the streets. But where do such roads lead? Walk the stations and find out.

Christian Pilgrimage: The Setting for Walking the Stations

RECOVERING THE WHOLE CHRIST of the Gospels by identifying fourteen way stations for wayfarers to follow him, and then making of this a religious exercise for individuals and groups, and then composing a whole life out of this, lends itself to the historic Christian language of pilgrimage, which is to say walking all the steps toward God in the Christian life. Following fourteen stations of Jesus' life can become a way-making in which we try to compose and construct our own lives by means of a lifelong walk, a pilgrimage through earth to heaven, as the Puritan John Bunyan depicts it in his perennial bestseller, *Pilgrim's Progress*.

Bookended by incarnation and resurrection, Jesus' entire life gives evidence of what the reign of God in our lives could look like if it touched down on earth, and what we should look like as disciples. A life of Jesus is not merely the good story of a great teacher. The Gospel stories as theological proclamation are meant to freely bestow God's righteousness upon us, and then to call us to follow. The Gospels are not first of all complicated cognitive statements about divinity that demand an abstract faith from us. They are calls to meet and relate, and then to follow. The point of Christianity is more a relationship to Christ than a cognitive belief in Christ. And it can happen through identifying with and imitating many stations along the way. As Luther would say, we may experience these as both law and gospel, convicting news and then good and freeing news and then heeding the Ten Commandments as service to our neighbor.

Just as the modern pilgrimage route to Compostela in Western Spain still draws many seekers (and a movie!) and not just convinced believers, so the growing number of "nones" who acknowledge no denominational Christianity might be drawn to a pilgrimage that tries out fourteen stations of Jesus' life. For any Christian, or any spiritual seeker, these fourteen stations suggest a way to compose a life—putting it all together by assembling the materials of Jesus' life as pieces of a grand puzzle that you embrace for yourself. If your religious life were to resemble writing a book, these fourteen stations could be the chapters in a story of grace and faith. If you wanted to form your faith into a mature edifice, even a thing of beauty, these could be the building blocks, the elements of a perfect vision. If you wanted to construct a life of Christian discipleship, just as in the Gospels, these would be the steps and challenges along the way—as Dietrich Bonhoeffer imagined in his commentary on the Gospel of Matthew.

Consider this somewhat abstract meditation from philosopher Gotthold Ephraim Lessing:

> *If God were to hold all Truth concealed in his right hand,*
> *and in his left only the steady and diligent drive for Truth,*
> *albeit with the proviso that I would always and forever err in the process,*
> *and to offer me the choice,*
> *I would with all humility take the left hand, and say: Father,*
> *I will take this one—the pure Truth is for You alone.*

Or consider this challenging poem "Flame of God" by the Irish Christian missionary to India, Amy Carmichael:

> *From prayer that asks that I may be*
> *Sheltered from winds that beat on Thee,*
> *From fearing when I should aspire,*
> *From faltering when I should climb higher*
> *From silken self, O Captain, free*
> *Thy soldier who would follow Thee.*
> *From subtle love of softening things,*
> *From easy choices, weakenings,*
> *(Not thus are spirits fortified,*
> *Not this way went the Crucified)*
> *From all that dims Thy Calvary*
> *O Lamb of God, deliver me.*
> *Give me the love that leads the way,*
> *The faith that nothing can dismay*
> *The hope no disappointments tire,*
> *The passion that will burn like fire;*
> *Let me not sink to be a clod;*
> *Make me Thy fuel, Flame of God.*

Regrettably, the idea of pilgrimage is mostly a distant memory in the contemporary Christian tradition, barely echoing John Bunyan's bestseller, or evoking glimmers from Compostela or Canterbury. Mostly it is not a part of the contemporary lingua franca. Where did it go? Was it too demanding, no longer a favorite trope, lacking the living superstructure of the Christian tradition, absurd in a modern age of self-congratulation and self-aggrandizement?

But Christian pilgrimage remains the ultimate setting for walking the way stations Jesus walked, a path of discipleship for followers of Jesus, a way of thinking about where we by faith are going. In this view of the Christian life *Jesus is the way-maker and we are the wayfarers*. And this is the wisdom and the language of pilgrimage: The way is made by walking. Pilgrimage as a Christian practice began with journeys to Jerusalem in the fourth century, in which pilgrims from afar believed they were walking in the very steps of Jesus on the *Via Dolorosa*, the sorrowful way to the cross that Jesus once walked. In his fourteenth-century *Canterbury Tales*, Chaucer depicts pilgrims on their way to the Canterbury Cathedral to honor the memory of St. Thomas Becket, the archbishop of Canterbury murdered in his cathedral by knights of King Henry II during a contest between church and crown. Although the ultimate pilgrimage destination was still Jerusalem, within England Canterbury became a popular destination. Or, pilgrims would journey to cathedrals that preserved relics of saints, believing that such relics held miraculous powers. Wonderfully, Chaucer's seminal work in middle English depicts how diverse pilgrims turned into an *accidental community* while making their way. In the background are a weakening of the high stature of the church because of the Black Death and the rise of Lollardy, a movement led by John Wycliffe advocating that the church should help people to live a life of evangelical poverty and imitate Christ. This was to become a pre-Reformation critique of the medieval church.

Lately a movie was made that chronicles the great variety of people walking the *camino* in Spain: the devout, seekers, nonbelievers, mourners, newly divorced or estranged from family, penance-makers, bicycle riders, etc. To be sure, the premier pilgrimage destination for all of Europe, and existing to this day, became the Camino de Santiago de Compostela. Pilgrimage was understood to begin at home and head toward a pious destination, a lifelong exercise of faith. In this case that destination was imagined as the far western land's end (*finisterrae*) of Spain, where it was believed the martyred apostle James had been buried. An entire mythology grew up around this site. Pilgrims claimed the Milky Way was raised from the dust of pilgrims and thus pointed the way at night. A scallop shell was carried by all pilgrims to signify their identity and was also mounted on signs to show the way to Compostela. The shell enhanced the camaraderie of pilgrims and assured them they were on the right track. What signs would you look for to keep you on the way? The apostle James, it was believed, had been a missionary to Spain, then saw a vision of the Virgin Mary and returned to Jerusalem, where he was martyred in 44 AD. His body was shipped back to Spain. But following a shipwreck on the way his body washed ashore covered in scallops. His own bodily course reminded Christians of the evocation of Christians as pilgrims in this world in Hebrews 11:13–14: "All of these died in faith without having received the promises, but from a distance they saw and greeted them. They confessed that they were strangers and foreigners on the earth, for people who speak in this way make it clear that they are seeking a homeland."

The way toward Compostela saw hospitals and hostels rise along the way for poor pilgrims. When pilgrims reached Compostela they laid their hands on a pillar inside the great door of the cathedral, until gradually they wore away that stone. Compostela became a famous European cultural route and in our day a UNESCO world heritage site. St. James Day was celebrated on July 25. For many, the pilgrimage became a form of penance. It even came to mean freedom for one prisoner each year who went there under guard. After the Black Death and the Protestant Reformation, pilgrimage to Compostela shrank to mere hundreds, but then grew again to 300,000 a year by 2017.

These days pilgrims come by foot, bicycle, or bus. They all carry a credential (a pilgrim's passport) with a stamp from each site along the way, and also offering discounts at hostels. The arrival at Compostela acquires a certificate of completion. "The Chapter of this holy apostolic and metropolitan Church of Compostela, guardian of the seal of the Altar of the blessed Apostle James, in order that it may provide authentic certificates of visitation to all the faithful and to pilgrims from all over the earth who come with devout affection or for the sake of a vow to the shrine of our Apostle St. James, the patron and protector of Spain, hereby makes known to each and all who shall inspect this present document that [Name] has visited this most sacred temple for the sake of pious devotion. As a faithful witness of these things I confer upon him [or her] the present document, authenticated by the seal of the same Holy Church." It was marked as given at Compostela on the day of the month in the year of the Lord. The Deputy Canon for Pilgrims verified it was done for religious reasons, and that at least the last one hundred kilometers had been done by foot or the last

Part One: Preparing for a Walk with Christ

two hundred kilometers by bike. The pilgrim's passport would show stamps from along the way. *By no means was pilgrimage a letter of indulgence bought and paid for as a ticket to heaven, but a visible testimony to a life of faith made possible by the grace of God calling.*

In *Divine Comedy* Dante's closing affirmation of "the love which moves the sun and the other stars" locates the individual experience of pilgrims and the collective faith of the church in an all-embracing vision of the ultimate harmony between the cosmos with its creator. With five hundred biblical allusions, Dante's great work was a three-part allegory on the soul's journey toward God, beginning with the recognition and rejection of sin in the *Inferno*, followed by the penitent Christian life in *Purgatorio*, and concluding with the soul's ascent to God in *Paradiso*.

The Christian life as a pilgrimage walk is by no means unknown to Protestantism. I have already mentioned John Bunyan's *Pilgrim's Progress*, a Christian allegory written from prison in 1678 by a devout Puritan and regarded as one of the most significant works of religious fiction in English literature, one that became the most popular book after the Bible. The protagonist, Christian, is an everyman character. The plot centers on his journey from his hometown to the Celestial City atop Mt. Zion. Christian is weighed down by the great burden of his sin, from which he seeks deliverance. He meets Evangelist, who directs him to a place to begin his deliverance, which he at first cannot see but which he is guided to see. Eventually he *reaches his destination but then returns to bring his family along as well.* A closing passage that thrilled me when I first read it in college was when Pilgrim reaches the end of his earthly journey on one side of the great river. He pronounces "Death where is thy sting?" and "Grave, where is thy victory" and then as he passes over, *"All the trumpets sounded for him on the other side."*

I believe that pilgrim bands can turn into vibrant communities. *Individual Christians can become parades that turn into nonconforming resistance movements calling out to onlookers along the way.* One of the fathers of sociology, Emile Durkheim, famously posited *collective effervescence* as the essential element in the emergence of religion, what can happen when groups come together and experience a unifying transformation and transportation from their profane worlds into a sacred reality. Anthropologist Victor Turner paid considerable attention to the capacity of rituals to cross thresholds and carry participants into liminal states, betwixt-and-between stages in which ambiguity, dislocation, and boundarylessness stir the imagination of new worlds. Turner was sure that in religious ritual "the gods come down and ride human horses."

Pilgrims don't always band together. Lately, as in gay pride or women's marches, there are contentious arguments over who gets to be in the parade. I wonder whether readers of this book, summoned to pilgrimage, coaxed to walk fourteen stations of Jesus' life, could get along. What kind of readers would they be and what would they be looking for? Could they all dig together when they arrived at places that promised treasure in the fields—an idea Jesus once bespoke. I thought about writing multiple versions, each with a different cover and pitched to a different audience, each in their own silos. A version for evangelical patriots and for neo-evangelical progressives, another for mainstream Protestants and Catholics, another for a distinctive Christian Left, another for spiritual seekers of a New Age, and certainly one for closed-minded leftists who cannot put radical and religion together in the same sentence. Lutherans would be carrying signs testifying to the centrality of the gospel and justification by faith in any and every parade. I thought each version could have chapters that spoke only the language of its intended readers, eliciting happy aha's from them. The heavy stuff from other groups' rhetoric would not be bothersomely present. But shouldn't all these readers have to meet eventually? Shouldn't there be an ecumenical launch party? Shouldn't they have a Pentecostal experience in which they all hear each other's tongues speaking simultaneously? And even understand?

I hope some readers will be willing to wager, for the sake of a new world, that other pilgrimages to other destinations also beckon. That new futures appear to those who dream, that they arrive as epiphany gifts. I never have out of mind the statistic that if 10 percent of people seize a truth and act on it, they can change the world. I write to attract that 10 percent, wherever you may now, in exile, be. As Luther did.

I have also tried to keep remembering all those in this country and abroad who have never been invited to a messianic banquet, on whose backs the feast is enriched, and, frankly, in whose faces the banquet hall bespeaks its closed privileges. With such in mind, and in view of Jesus' last judgment story in Matthew 25, I knew I could not exclude a theology of hope, a determined pilgrimage that would, by grace, reach "the least of these." If the New Testament echoes as one "takes and reads" (as Augustine once did), then existing domination systems erected to exclude the poor

Part One: Preparing for a Walk with Christ

must fall. My last book was written in the promise of a new movement of *Matthew 25 Christians* who would sponsor good news to "the least of these."

I have recently been fascinated by responses to the new interloping sculpture of the *fearless girl* who faces down the long-standing rival sculpture of the *bull of Wall Street* on his own territory. The artist who sculpted the original bull is angry and protests the unfairness of a rival arrival. My statue alone is meant to *occupy Wall Street,* he insists. "My bull and I own the symbolism of this site." The fearless girl should go somewhere else where tourists are not lined up snapping oppositional selfies. But bands of pilgrims keep arriving to stand with the defiant young girl, to occupy Wall Street themselves, and to take a class picture of themselves as new pilgrims. To take another example, every time I find myself in Berlin I find an excuse for making my way to the central railroad station where there is a moving and disturbing group of statues that depict children desperate to escape the reach of Nazis and have their way made to London on a *Kindertransport*. I look at little suitcases of things they are trying to take along, and I cry to myself—not letting this moving sculpture cheer me up too much. I think of Jews these days long after the holocaust becoming resentful of those who want to make Anne Frank the patron saint of optimism and good cheer. And what will the holy space of the stations of Jesus life offer today's seekers? Discovery, revelation, repentance, a new life with holy meaning?

This book then carries a distinctive agenda—calling together individual pilgrims to discover themselves in community, colonies of heaven, activists in a great religious movement, instruments in a great parade through history—walking the stations of Jesus' life and making them their own—in the face of a secular society, one which erases Jesus' stations. While pilgrims want to become preoccupied with what lies ahead, they should first take note of where they are standing at the start. At this point in history, the starting point could look like this—to those who have eyes to see:

1. Heading into the third millennium invites a Christian cosmology that positions God at the becoming of the universe and humans as the original desire of God's heart and the continuing objects of God's long coming. The Old and New Testament portray this God as liberating, loving, and reconciling, climaxing in a divine incarnation that made earth capable of heaven. (This happens to be Station #1.)

2. The continuing *deposit of the incarnation* is the Christian church as the body of Christ. Being the church means parading Christ through the world, inviting onlookers to wager on God, and living as strangers and aliens who mediate a commonwealth between God and humans. Will you let this parade pass you by? Are you already in this parade?

3. As American Christianity finds its bearings, it must answer the call of a new "errand into the wilderness," turning contemplation and action into a parade back to the commons with a public theology up to the task, and moving from the thoughtful case for God to an ambitious plan for the presence of God in social justice for all. Life in the commons reveals considerable PTSD, bankrupt values, and the demonic power of a ruthless economic system, but *the church as field hospital can leverage hope, perform the reconsideration of the human project, and re-enchant the earth.*

The end gradually appears in our social imaginary—a collaborative eschatology that envisions God on the road ahead and joins God's arriving with the church's becoming into the grand effort of the Universe Becoming. This may seem burdensome language, but I write it so that pilgrims do not imagine that Jesus is confined to their own hearts and they are on a personalized journey to heaven independent of all others.

From "Fourteen Stations of the Cross" to Fourteen Stations of Jesus' Entire Life

I HAVE SELECTED FOURTEEN stations of Jesus' entire life to honor the historic fourteen stations of the cross, and to move beyond them to achieve a much fuller portrait of Jesus' life.

The origins of a Good Friday piety that follows Jesus' steps on the way to the cross lie in Christian pilgrimages to Jerusalem begun around the fourth century, on Friday, the day of his crucifixion, accompanied by the prayers and meditations of the faithful. The stations of the cross grew out of imitations of the Via Dolorosa in Jerusalem, which is believed to be the actual path Jesus walked to Mount Calvary. The objective of the stations is to help the Christian faithful make a spiritual pilgrimage by contemplating the passion of Christ. Many sites feature a series of fourteen images arranged in numbered order along a path or around the inner walls of a church building. The faithful walk from image to image, in order, stopping at each station for selected prayers and reflections. This is done individually or in a communal procession most commonly during Lent, especially on Good Friday, and practiced by many Catholics.

But the aim of the true pilgrim is not to see Jerusalem, but to see Jesus. So centuries ago, a Via Dolorosa (way of sorrows) would sometimes be constructed in European villages, so that everyone, not just those who could attempt long pilgrimages, could participate in this devotion. Eventually, stations of the cross were installed in most Catholic churches.

The original fourteen stations suggest Jesus' own pauses on the way to the cross, providing our own places to stand on the journey to see God, a pause for spiritual reflection en route to heaven. During Lent, many Catholic Christians walk the stations of the cross, alone or in groups. Here are the original fourteen stations of the cross, defined for Catholic piety by the

Fourteen Stations of Jesus' Entire Life

early eighteenth century but which stem from a much longer tradition that ranged from five to thirty scenes. The scenes below marked with * were not actually from the Bible:

1. Jesus condemned to death
2. Jesus handed his cross
3. Jesus falls for the first time*
4. Jesus meets his mother*
5. Simon of Cyrene enlisted to help carry Jesus' cross
6. Veronica wipes the face of Jesus*
7. Jesus falls a second time*
8. Jesus meets the women of Jerusalem
9. Jesus falls a third time*
10. Jesus is stripped of his clothes
11. Jesus is crucified
12. Jesus dies on the cross
13. Jesus' body is taken down from the cross*
14. Jesus' body is placed in the tomb

The earlier set of seven scenes usually included numbers 2, 3, 4, 6, 7, 11, and 14.

In 1731, Pope Clement XII standardized the number of stations at fourteen. Then in the late twentieth century Pope John Paul II slightly altered these stations so that all are based directly in the Gospel accounts. These new additions from the Gospels are marked below with *.

1. Jesus prays in Gethsemane*
2. Jesus is betrayed by Judas*
3. Jesus condemned to death
4. Jesus denied by Peter*
5. Jesus judged by Pilate*
6. Jesus scourged and crowned with thorns*
7. Jesus carries his cross*

Part One: Preparing for a Walk with Christ

8   Jesus helped by Simon of Cyrene

9   Jesus meets women of Jerusalem

10 Jesus is crucified

11 Jesus' promise to good thief*

12 Jesus and his mother below*

13 Jesus dies on the cross

14 Jesus placed in the tomb

Sometimes "Jesus rises from the dead" becomes a fifteenth station of the cross.

The stations of the cross have sedimented into Catholic piety and also entered the material culture of Catholicism with depictions that are painted, engraved, carved, or sculpted in stone, wood, or metal. They appear in every Catholic church. Popular devotions and the stations can sometimes be found in some Protestant churches, including Anglican, Methodist, and Lutheran. Though far less common in evangelical traditions, this piety is also capable of migrating there as well. In 2012, a 58,000-member Baptist church in Houston, Texas initiated a stations of the cross experience in which thousands of people touched a crown of thorns, smelled bottles of spices, held pieces of silver, and nailed their sins to a large cross—effective embellishments to Catholic practice.

No one doubts the value of this form of piety. We are embodied creatures, and moving through the physical stations of the cross engages heart, soul, and ritualized bodily movement. (*A common critique of rituals, especially in Protestantism, is that they are not performative but just wordy.*) It helps Christian believers think about their lives as a performance of discipleship that imitates Christ. Christians are engaged in a pilgrimage through life, a journey towards God. Visual arts dress this performance and rivet the stations to earth. *The way is made by walking it.*

Even given the historic power and practice of these original stations of the cross, they do not try to achieve a full portrait of Jesus' entire life. These are a religious map that does not cover all the territory. *It may seem to reduce the meaning of Jesus' life to the day of his death.* Across the entire spectrum of Christian theology today, there is vigorous debate concerning how to interpret and proclaim Jesus' life, death, and resurrection. It is not just a matter of getting the cross right, but also of getting Jesus' entire life right. Liberal and conservative, Catholic and Protestant scholarship has begun to reclaim the entire life of Jesus as essential New Testament proclaimed gospel. But the piety and discipleship of the church, not to mention its art and music, would have very much catching up to do. *Fourteen stations of Jesus' life, the proposal of this book, could open new journeys to spiritual formation and radical discipleship,* while suggesting new modes and topics for the catechumenate and stimulating a more comprehensive new art and music. These fourteen stations would surely become a call to new hymns and art forms.

But why hold on to the stations at all? We are embodied creatures. While Christianity has the highest theology of embodiment of any religion, primarily because of the doctrine of the incarnation, it has a relatively low level of embodied spiritual practice—especially Protestants who may confine the faith, and Jesus himself, to the interior space of their hearts. Moving through these proposed stations of the cross, just as we move Thursday through Sunday of Holy Week, engages heart, soul, mind, and body—especially if *lectio divina* (communal meditation while reading biblical texts), art, praying, poetry, hymns, and story are involved. It helps Christian believers think about their lives as a pilgrimage through life, in union with Christ, a journey towards God that follows Jesus' own.

Let us then consider these fourteen new stations that try to encompass Jesus' entire life, with all its profound significance for our own spiritual walk. You can review the original fourteen stanzas of compelling prayer, art, and music fully accessible on YouTube, and much additional information can be Googled. Very remarkable on YouTube is the CRS (Catholic Relief Services) Rice Bowl Digital Retreats, which pair each station of the cross with Catholic teaching on social justice. This is a remarkable combination of visual art and guided meditation, combining the stations of Jesus' way to the cross with the opportunities for Christian reflection, repentance, resolve, and action.

Almost everyone knows stories from the life of Christ. While Christmas and Easter top the list, many Christian traditions give special weight to Jesus' suffering and death on the cross. The Lutheran J. S. Bach wrote a St. John and a St. Matthew Passion, which became pinnacles of choral music in the Western tradition. For many centuries Catholics have given the stations of the cross central place in their Holy Week devotions, and an entire material culture arose to mark those stations with Christian art in every Catholic church around the world and also in much medieval Christian art. Evangelical preachers have emphasized Jesus' death for our sins in their calls to repentance and conversion. As people came forward at Billy Graham rallies, the choir always sang: "Just as I am without one plea/but that thy blood was shed for me/and that thou bidst me come to thee/O Lamb of God, I come, I come."

A station is a place to stand on the way to God, en route to heaven. *Station* means an embarkation point or a transition stage for a traveler, or a resting place on a journey, an opportunity to take in an entire journey with a thoughtfulness that makes it unlikely one is merely going through the motions and scarcely recognizing what should be seen as a pilgrimage—from earth to heaven. In Christian parlance station refers to each of a number of holy places to be visited on a pilgrimage, or a special service or respite for pilgrims. (On the radio a *station break* is a pause to identify whom you're listening to.) A station is a place to stand while contemplating the view of God, a pause to consider the far country, to review the way to heaven. When connected specifically to Jesus' suffering and death, the fourteen stations of the cross rehearse the way that Jesus went, the way we follow.

Here I am proposing fourteen stations that are to be proclaimed, contemplated, embraced, emulated—in the overall context of the New Testament gospel, God's good news for humanity. The context then and now is the appeal for faith, the crisis of decision triggered by the reign of God, the call to discipleship, and the birth of the church. It is a compelling agenda for the modern church to retrieve *Jesus' entire life as gospel.* Indeed, the kerygma of the life of Christ is much more likely to attract the attention of the world than ontological assertions and intellectual fideism and especially the too-certain proclamations of the Christian Right that get Jesus flat wrong or the anemic ventures of many progressive Christians who pride themselves on how little they actually believe while still identifying as Christians.

I have wanted to set up as direct *parallels* (in a way not possible if limited to fourteen stations *of the cross*) the road Jesus' life follows and the road the Christian life of discipleship exemplifies today. I have been emphasizing that station means "stand" or "stop," like a bus stop or train station on the way to a destination. A pause that refreshes! *A station is a place to stand on the way to God, en route to heaven.* I also have in mind the medieval imitation of Christ, the Reformation sense of calling to *faith active in love* in the world, the Jesuit adoption of spiritual exercises and formation, the contemporary evangelical model of Bible study that replicates monastic *lectio divina*, the ancient and contemporary notion of religious pilgrimage and being "on the way," and even Mary Catherine Bateson's lovely title for an autobiography, *Composing a Life*—in her case that of several modern women struggling to put everything together in order to achieve their potential.

Altogether, and as evidenced especially in the popular apologetic work of Marcus Borg and Brian McClaren, this approach makes discipleship and Christlike presence in the world the point of Christianity, a relationship first, not just a matter of cognitive belief. As such, this then can function as an invitation to all the "nones" out there, and indeed to rank secularists, who find institutional Christianity a difficult pill to swallow but the life of Jesus potentially compelling, or at least intriguing and worth another examination. McClaren cleverly imagines pilgrims moving towards a *Christianity 2.0*, which is to say a modern update or significant improvement from the previous version.

Stations also suggest *pause*, a pilgrim's rest and reflection. Where and when that occurs, the arts spring up—images and poetry and hymns and prayers and communal exercises. This book will invoke classical Christian art but also notice new efforts and invite more, including readily usable digital art and PowerPoints, to sediment the stations of Jesus' life, and of the Christian life, in a new and renewed Christian material culture—precisely at a time when religious art is in almost total eclipse, or has been reduced to kitsch. God is the answer to many a Google search! Music and certainly selected hymns of the church will follow. Based on my own worship experience, I would guess that many more new than old Christian hymns will illuminate precisely the stations of Jesus' life here presented. The fact that the classic hymns are more likely to speak to death and resurrection and the newer Christian poetry to the many other dimensions of Jesus' life, for example "open commensality" and healing and prophetic justice and the inclusion of women, suggests this new approach is consonant with contemporary theological trends and human needs and interests.

It may also be true that fuller reflection on the stations of Jesus' life will bring the modern hearer and observer closer to the situation of Jesus' own earthly ministry and thence to its hitherto unnoticed parallels with the contemporary period, and not just in the third world. Jesus encountered and immersed himself in the midst of socioeconomic stratifications, the isolation and exclusion of the poor and the hungry and the unhoused, the outcasting of the ritually impure, the prophetic obsession with social justice, the world of empire and the colonized, and a religious establishment

Part One: Preparing for a Walk with Christ

that fails in its mission to be God's good news. Affinities between Jesus' audience and the audience that must hear the modern church's proclamation and walk the stations are waiting to be noticed again and embraced.

In Jesus God seems to be announcing God's own gentleness and vulnerability and compassion for the lowly. God really does head straight for the marginalized, once arriving on earth. God really does evince a compassionate love for all, a grace-drenched new life with no proof of having earned it. A true treasure in a field.

Fourteen Stations in Jesus'— and the Believer's—Life

Before we get to my proposed fourteen stations it may be worth considering whether you have your own "bucket list." Bucket lists of "to do" things before you die were popularized by Morgan Freeman and Jack Nicholson in the film of that name. Maybe you could think of your own bucket list of scenes and events in Jesus' life you would like to immerse yourself in before you die! Think of the selfies you could produce and save on your computer or send to your friends: Here's an image of me and my friends from church and Jesus sitting together at a table with strangers and outcasts. Here's me getting my feet washed at the Last Supper. Look at me at the cross with my eyes fixed on the suffering Savior. You could turn your choices into a communal walk, with companions and things to do, and suggestive storytelling. Both conservative and liberal Christians have lately adopted the practice of walking together, praying together, studying the Bible together. Now they would be agreeing to meet each other at the stations, on a spiritual retreat. What aftereffects and legacies might you leave if you followed such an example? What you do when you stop at a station is more important than getting the list of stations right. I would hope that studying my list might stimulate readers to produce their own.

The bulk of this book, in Part Two, will be the exposition of each of the fourteen stations proposed here, each getting a chapter, complete with accoutrements like theological meaning, connection to our discipleship, and decorated with visual art, hymns, poetry, prayers, stories, and proposals for communal exercises and pilgrimage. The theological exposition will depend on current scholarship on the Gospels and contemporary Christian theology, while also self-consciously grounding in historic Christianity. Of course there will be the relevant citations from the Gospels, tables

Part One: Preparing for a Walk with Christ

of correlation in the appendix with the three-year lectionary cycles used in many liturgical traditions, and references to historic and contemporary Christian visual art. The presence of these stations of Jesus' life and their relevance to historic liturgies, to Christmas, Lent, and Easter, and to Baptism and Eucharist will also be displayed.

So can fourteen stories adequately summarize the life of Christ? Are fourteen stories sufficient for making the "way" of the pilgrim? Can fourteen stories summarize the New Testament proclamation of the reign of God? Can fourteen stories cover all the ground, with Christmas and Easter, Baptism and Eucharist as bonuses? *Are these the fourteen you would choose?* More important than agreeing on precisely fourteen, or which fourteen, is the finding among nearly all historical Jesus scholarship, left and right, liberal and conservative, Catholic and Protestant, that it is long past time to reclaim the entire life of Jesus as essential New Testament theological proclamation.

While all the fourteen stations of the cross are unlikely to be duplicated precisely in the life of the Christian believer, or of anyone who finds Jesus compelling, fourteen stations that sum up the entire life of Christ may and should apply directly to the lives of Christians. Disciples are called to follow their master, as also, for example, in Buddhism's "mindfulness." The grace of Christ gradually infuses the character of the believer. The goal is to acquire the disposition to think and act like Jesus in all things.

Having spent all this time preparing the reader for moving on from the historic stations of the cross to adequate "stops" in Jesus' life, I at last offer my list—for your consideration and critique. These are "stops" or "stations" of Jesus' life that could become congruent with the lives of all Christians, dimensions of their inner pilgrimage as well as their walk in the world. These could become parts of "composing a life," part of discipleship, part of the imitation of Christ, part of Christian pilgrimage, the means of God fashioning for himself a people. Here they are:

1 Jesus is born into the human world—

   Will we meet him there as we are born again?

2 Jesus is baptized, opens his life to God, and engages a world of temptation and possibility—

   Have we been mostly clueless about the implications of our own baptism?

Fourteen Stations in Jesus'—and the Believer's—Life

3. Jesus inaugurates his prophetic vocation and proclaims the arrival of the kingdom of God—

   Will we recognize God's reign when we see it? Will we proclaim Jubilee?

4. Jesus is calling and making disciples—

   How do we answer? Do we consent to be made new?

5. Jesus teaches us to pray, with the Lord's Prayer as a model—

   Could we learn to pray? And are we paying attention to the world around us when we pray?

6. Jesus eats and drinks with outsiders and the excluded—

   Could we learn Christian table manners?

7. Jesus heals physical disease and social illness—

   Could the church become a field hospital and we its chaplains?

8. Jesus preaches sermons that reveal a gospel from God for all peoples—

   Do we hear a gospel that sounds like this every Sunday and preach it in the midst of a world longing for good news?

9. Jesus welcomes women and outsiders and calls us, in his name, to do the same—

   How do women and outsiders fare in our congregations?

10. Jesus teaches wisdom in parables that open up alternative realities in which God can appear—

    Will we walk into that space and learn to live new lives in it?

11. Jesus rides into Jerusalem and challenges the religious and political establishment—

    Do we dare to speak nonconforming truths as communities of resistance?

12. Jesus washes the disciples' feet, gives a new love commandment, and offers his own body to the world in his Last Supper—

    Can we learn "Christian yoga" as our servant discipline, justice as the social form of love, and the Eucharist as our weekly refreshment for a challenging journey?

Part One: Preparing for a Walk with Christ

13 Jesus dies the most famous death in history—

Can Christians see in it a messianic enthronement and their salvation with God?

14 Jesus rises from the dead and signals the triumph of God's love—

Do Christians spend their lives following in the train of their risen Lord?

As you imagine walking one or more stations, pause to prepare yourself, asking the following questions about following Jesus: *What in this station subverts normal assumptions—of me and of fellow Christians and of the culture I live in? Is there room in this world for walking these stations, or must I create new worlds in order to make room for them? Will this walk alter the God-picture I normally carry around? Must I change direction (repentance) in my own life? Which stations will find me kicking and screaming?*

An Anthropological View of How Religion Works

PERHAPS TO HELP UNDERSTAND yourself as you go on a religious quest, I suggest you pause to consider the kinds of questions and observations a contemporary anthropologist asks concerning what is happening when people practice religion.

Before that analysis, however, I offer the advice of the provocative Lutheran pastor Nadia Bolz-Weber: *Just show up.* This is the obvious first step, one many Christians do not always get around to. But here are some ideas about what is happening when religious people are seeking and encountering God—from anthropologist T. M. Luhrman, in her recent book, *How God Becomes Real: Kindling the Presence of Invisible Others.* In this, as well as in her earlier book, *When God Talks Back: Understanding the American Evangelical Relationship with God*, this mostly a-religious scholar demonstrates a remarkable ability to join unusually devout evangelical and Pentecostal communities as a "participant-observer" and actually hear and witness to their religious practice. She practices putting on their piety and gives it names and categories.

Luhrman sees that Christians are made not born. For this to happen they *must create a new world to live in.* Of course all her advice is not necessarily congruent with Christian practice and experience, because she has stepped back from religious immersion to a somewhat distancing observation of how it seems to her to work. The technical, theoretical apparatus she offers to help account for religion and her understanding of how it works will not be useful to everyone, but some people setting out to walk the stations and reflect on what is happening, what is opening up to them, may find all this helpful. Meeting and "putting on" Christ will after all become the entire meaning of their life pilgrimage, and so it may be worth meta-thought.

Part One: Preparing for a Walk with Christ

Luhrman sees religion as an effort to *make contact* with an invisible other. Religious people are looking for change, and are determined to experience *how God becomes and remains real to people.* People believe because they worship; they shift from abstraction to "real-making," to making God matter in the here and now. Inner awareness is their committed focus. The capacity to imagine, Luhrman thinks, is what makes religion possible. She likes to use the word *kindling (what it takes to start a fire)* to account for acts of *real-making.*

Her theme is God being made real for people, and this real-making shifts attention from what is in one's life to what could be. This is not easy. Talent and training matter. The way one thinks about mind also matters. The sense of response to God must be kindled from the tinder of practicing attentiveness. Prayer practices change the way people attend to their inner thoughts. But Luhrman observes people changing when God is made real and turns into a relationship.

Believers must first practice a *faith frame,* which is to say a sustained, intentional, deliberative commitment to the idea that there are invisible beings that can become involved in human life in life-changing ways. Faith can be seen as a shift in attention that *re-frames,* allowing one to enter another mode of thinking about what is real. Faith and the sacred have a play-like quality; the faith-frame is different from the reality-frame. The believer interprets the world through a special way of thinking, expecting, remembering. Church becomes the place to change people's mental habits. Christians do not believe, they know; they don't think, they believe. In religious ritual people are reminded that God matters. They practice the reversal of the Enlightenment's contention that nature is non-agentic, objective, and free of human intention.

Her next concept for understanding religion is *paracosm,* which is to say a private but shared imagined world. Religious people achieve a world in which God responds, via words and details and substantial experiences. They achieve a Tolkien-like Middle Earth that is vividly real. Practicing religion comes to mean remaking the world as one's own. Vivid narratives—like the fourteen stations—enable one to enter into different ways of experiencing the world: think how an avid reader looks up from a book just finished and sees differently, actually sees a different world, even awaiting to meet characters she has just met in her book. Religion trains people in detached credulity, the ability to imagine and then see alternative worlds.

The Gospels, Luhrman thinks, are not first of all didactic, even if they impart information. They train readers to experience Jesus by suspending normal awareness, to be captured by the realness of evocative metaphors, to change the reader's sense of what is true. Faith traditions train believers in immediate sensory evidence; they come to know God first through stories about God. Successive, cumulative, serialized stories enlist engagement over time; they come in installments in the religious life. The more richly detailed they are, the more vividly they are reworked as one's own. *Rather than God entering our story, we enter God's.* When religious people "do God," God shows up.

People prepared to walk the stations, as they are presented in this book, must achieve and apply *talent and training*. They must learn to absorb and cultivate an inner sense of hearing God. They must learn to experience the world as responsive and alive—one they too can enter and live in. Luhrman quotes Jeremiah 1:4–6: "Before I formed you in the womb I knew you, sanctified you, ordained you." Religious people cultivate and come to see they have been cultivated by God. They come to acquire new skills, a new awareness, that can be taught and mastered. *They practice God, as in active daydreams.* They become open, receptive, "in the moment"—as Buddhist meditation practice also urges. Religious people score high on *absorption measures*, because they have grown accustomed to God speaking to them.

The seventeenth-century Parisian Carmelite monk, Brother Lawrence, became known for "practicing the presence of God." He imagined: I'm a piece of stone, waiting for a sculptor. I make the world of mind vivid; vividness leaks into my world. He taught his followers to achieve the capacity to imagine a world beyond the one before us.

Luhrman the anthropologist moves next to *how the mind matters*. She thinks faith is about the mind because God cannot be known through the senses—a questionable assertion. God comes as a thereness, more like an emotion than a belief. But this is not a citadel view of the mind, disconnected from reality. She thinks believers pick out certain thoughts as not their own but God's voice. People scoring high on absorption measures and praying actively are more likely to hear God speak to them.

She uses *kindling* to address how people experience God differently by the way they attend to their experience. Religion becomes shaped, habituated, fluent; goosebumps can be kindled as a learned response to the presence of God. Over time small sparks set fires burning. Attributing experiences to God can change the experience of events.

Prayer is paying attention in its purest form. It requires a mode of thinking she has called the faith frame. Religion involves the effort of practicing the way one thinks, the faith frame, plus the felt realness of God generated by kindling. Prayer changes people. A reciprocity is set in motion, as we speak and God responds. This means engaged prayer, not rote prayer.

Practicing religion becomes its own outcome. Expressing a sense of how things should be helps someone live with the world as it is. Prayer keeps changing the person who is praying. Luhrman mentions Anne Lamott's well-known summation of prayer: *help, thanks, wow*. Gratitude illustrates cognitive behavioral therapy; it alters the thoughts one thinks and functions more effectively than any other psychotherapy.

Asking is an assertion of hope. We make things real by making them external in public space, by giving them shape. Choosing to hope trains attention and makes hope external. Every day the religious address all of God within themselves, creating opportunities to be heard.

God's felt response comes to feel like a relationship, and this changes people, as they imagine themselves living up to God's expectations.

Luhrman concludes reflecting on her work by evoking an ontological turn in anthropology that *does not dismiss* strange claims as false beliefs but takes them to be real life events. Just focusing on "strange beliefs" misses the experiences underway. Noticing the faith frame discloses how feelings of realness are kindled, how God becomes real for people.

Establishing and Embellishing the Religious Practice of Walking the Stations of Jesus' Life (and Our Own) in the Life of the Church and Its People

IN HISTORIC CATHOLIC PRACTICE, especially during Lent, the faithful would enter their churches and slowly walk the fourteen stations of the cross, artistically displayed on the left and right sides of the nave. They might pause at each for pious reflection and perhaps pray assigned prayers at each. They might see this as a Lenten pilgrimage. The stations of the cross have a very long history in Catholic piety and practice. *Could the stations of Jesus' life similarly take root in the life of the church today?*

I want to propose a whole array of practices that could become attached to the fourteen stations of Jesus' life, whether in a church, or in group devotions, or communal spiritual retreats, or in private prayer and meditation, or in the practice of Christian pilgrimage over an entire life of discipleship and imitation of Christ. The richer the embellishments, the more powerful the practice of the stations become ingrained. The fourteen stations of Jesus' life could be practiced consecutively at one time. But I am urging their practice over an entire Christian year, and indeed a Christian life. Altogether, they would come to amount to the composing of a whole religious life. Other than the first and the last, they would not have to be practiced in order, since they *are not meant to be consecutive*, in the way the fourteen stations of the cross are.

Minimally, one may offer prayers while reflecting on and practicing each of the stations. These could be spontaneous prayers, made up at each time, but eventually the church may wish to provide more elaborate written prayers, perhaps printed in booklets meant to expand and empower these stations in the life of the church. And of course not limited to Lent. Perhaps they could be of special value during "ordinary time" in the church year, after Pentecost and before Advent. Such a book of prayers for the stations should become for pious Christians a *vademecum,* a handbook for constant use along life's way.

Over time, as you have come to observe each station repeatedly, you would have produced a record of your religious life, your pilgrimage, your imitation of Jesus' walk, your "putting on Christ." Eventually the church might produce the records of its more illustrious teachers and preachers and saints, and these could amount to evidence of the practice of the stations in the life of the church. All the saints would produce a far more ambitious reflection than that of any one Christian individual. The practice of discipleship, the imitation of Christ, would build up as one of the church's finest treasures.

In churches whose worship is enriched by liturgical practice, it makes sense to include the stations of Jesus' life in the liturgy, a great carrier and compilation of worship and sacraments and prayer and music. The individual chapters for each station will include, for example, correlations with the three-year lectionary cycle. (See the appendix.) Over a three-year period all the proposed stations of Jesus' life would appear in the appointed Gospel readings for each Sunday. *Liturgical inculturation* refers to embodying in liturgy the Christians' encounter with the world, imported from themes and acts in the dominant culture, while of course weekly liturgies are a priceless path for enriching regular worship. At least four of Jesus' way stations correspond to major events in the Christian calendar: Christmas, the Last Supper, Good Friday, and Easter—not to mention baptism into the life of the church. These are opportunities, not to be overlooked, for *performative liturgies,* banners, special music, and moving outside the church itself. The liturgical year can be seen as the annual performance of major events in Jesus' life and the great festivals that mark the Christian life. These may also, with care, become opportunities for the church to *parade* its faith and practice in the world outside the church, the world the church is called to sacramentalize. *Liturgy as performance* gives weight and motivation to the moving performance of stages of Jesus' life—and invites onlookers to come along.

Remember that *station* evokes train station or bus stop, a pause on the way to a far destination. Each could become a famous way station on the Christian pilgrimage, like Canterbury or Compostela or Rome or Jerusalem or Wittenberg or Geneva or Los Angeles (the birthplace of Pentecostalism). Although I am a Lutheran, I always visit Wesleyan sites in London because

Establishing and Embellishing the Religious Practice

I value Wesley's correctives to the Lutheran Reformation. And of course Catholic sites rich with material culture are scattered around the world. The weight of Christian practice could build up at such stations, artistic and devotional evidence of what previous Christians have left behind as mementos.

Various stations might accumulate souvenirs, takeaway objects and material memories from each station. Or perhaps individuals would find or produce such souvenirs that would remind them of their experience. Hindu pilgrims who practice the presence of God (*darshan* refers to where one saw God and was seen by God) on pilgrimage are expected to return to their home villages and pour out physical remembrances, like water from the Ganges. Evangelical Christians who have pilgrimaged to the Holy Land often bring back water from the Jordan River, which they may use for baptisms in their families—Protestant holy water. Catholics may return from such sites as Lourdes or Fatima or the Vatican with cherished souvenirs displayed on home altars. Hispanic Catholicism has a special liking for home altars, in which religious art can be displayed and prayers said. Pilgrims to Compostela will certainly bring back souvenirs, certainly their stamped certificates of journeys completed included.

Not many of us are poets, but some are. Might you, over time, compose a poem that goes with a station of Jesus' life? You may have been invited to a party in your life whose entrance admission required a self-composed *haiku*, that famous and often trite three-line poem of five/seven/five syllables—which all my students were required to bring to parties at my house each semester. Stop and try one right now. Of course the easier way is to find books and pamphlets and Google searches that offer famous poems that go with a station in Jesus' life. For my book *Christmas: Festival of Incarnation*, I took great delight in searching for and printing such evocative poems as these, which could go with station #1:

> George MacDonald: *"They all were looking for a king/To slay their foes and lift them high:/Thou cam'st, a little baby thing/That made a woman cry."*

> William Alabaster: *"How might this goodness draw our souls above/Which drew down God with such attractive Love."*

> Ruth Sawyer: *"And many children—God give them grace/Bringing tall candles to light Mary's face."*

Part One: Preparing for a Walk with Christ

John Donne: *"Thy Maker's maker, and thy Father's mother; Thou hast light in dark, and shutst in little room, Immensity cloistered in thy dear womb."*

William Butler Yeats: *"The terror of all terrors that I bore/The Heavens in my womb."*

Elizabeth Jennings: *"So from her ecstasy she moves/And turns to human things at last/(Announcing angels set aside)/It is a human child she loves/Though a god stirs beneath her breast/And great salvations grip her side."*

William Butler Yeats: *"What is this flesh I purchased with my pains/This fallen star my milk sustains/This love that makes my heart's blood stop/Or strikes a sudden chill into my bones/And bids my hair stand up?"*

Robert Southwell: *"The same you saw in heavenly seat/Is he that now sucks Mary's teat/the flowers looked up at him/And all the stars looked down."*

Charles Coffin: *"Shine forth and let your light restore/Earth's own true loveliness once more."*

Sedulius: *"The eastern sages saw from far/And followed on his guiding star/By light their way to Light they trod/And by their gifts confessed their God."*

Alice Meynell: *"Sudden as sweet/Come the unexpected feet/All joy is young and new all art/And he, too, whom we have by heart."*

You get the idea. Note it is the "coincidence of opposites" that attracts me to these poetic imaginations, God's awesome greatness coinciding with our humanness. I deliberately chose poetry that echoed the human side of Christmas and tried to capture the mystery and contradictions of the incarnation. Probably few readers of this book could manage the literary elegance and theological depth-in-simplicity of this poetry. Try it, when you put this book down. Then choose a station of Jesus' life and go looking for poetry that witnesses to it. You may find it through Googling.

Speaking of the poetic, consider these short meditations on the long Christian pilgrimage, not limited to Christmas:

We keep a troubled vigil at the bedside of the world. Howard Thurman

Establishing and Embellishing the Religious Practice

The church cannot have an inner life without having at the same time
A life which expresses itself outwardly as well
She cannot hear her Lord and not hear the groaning of the Creation.
Karl Barth

When we go before Him, God will ask
Where are your wounds? Allan Boesak

Go and make disciples of all nations. Matthew 28:19

There is not a square inch over which Christ does not intervene to say Mine. Abraham Kuyper

The church does not have a social ethic; the church is a social ethic. Stanley Hauerwas

Of course there are great hymns of the church too, often under organizing topics laid out in standard hymnals. Perhaps especially compelling for their relevance are those written by contemporary Christian hymn-writers. Christmas (station #1) and Easter (station #14) hymns, as well as hymns for baptism (station #2) and communion (station #12), are well known and widely available as historic treasures, and you may already know many by heart as part of your own spiritual repertoire. But it is unlikely that you know many hymns celebrating the other stations proposed in this book. It's interesting to pursue them on Google and then YouTube, where you will make interesting new discoveries and *hear the music* that goes with them.

Many themes from Jesus' life are depicted in Christian art. But contemporary art more likely mimics the eclipse of religion and the preoccupation with secular themes. Still, almost any great art still speaks. Books like *Christ for All People: Celebrating a World of Christian Art* are valuable because they pay attention to all regions of the world, not just Europe, demonstrating how broad the indigenous Christian imagination can be. Christ is "adopted" into exotic cultures. The World Council of Churches' *The Bible through Asian Eyes* is invaluable for its attention to Christian art mostly unknown in the West. Among a wide tradition, *Christ for All People* displays art relating to the stations of Jesus' life featured in this book, such as the incarnation and many Christmas themes, Jesus' baptism, prayer, calling of the disciples, the blessing of the children, Jesus relating to women, washing the disciples' feet, the Last Supper, and of course many on crucifixion and resurrection. For each of the fourteen stations you could choose a biblical image and also a modern image reminiscent of life in the Christian world of today—because Jesus is present there and now, too. Deeply resonant images of the fourteen stations could become memorable icons, adopted to stimulate the visual imagination and stimulate the Christian walk. The medieval *Books of Hours* includes models of religious meditation adorned with great art. On the opposite scale, Christian publishing houses might produce coloring books illustrating the stations of Jesus' life and waiting for children to color them in. On certain Sundays congregations could be invited to bring art from their homes and adorn the walls of their church.

An "art of the everyday" could be constructed if you occasionally illustrated various stations with images from newspapers and magazines, or photo clippings. (My wife has learned how to create images, via AI, to illustrate her anthropological writing.) Preachers were once admonished to read the newspapers to see how they should elaborate their biblical preaching. This could become a communal project if members of a meditative group brought together newspapers and magazines, not to mention Facebook and TikTok and Instagram in for discussion. What kind of T-shirts might pilgrims choose to wear congruent with the stations at which they pause on their way?

If you are a journal keeper, you might record your experience with the stations of Jesus' life. Or, responding to the stations, write stories to live by, stories to live in. Indeed, *you might become the story*. Over a long time you might find yourself creating worlds to live in. Sociologists speak of the constructed social realities in which religious people live (like the life of the church) as *plausibility structures,* within which you live out and test the realities you confess. Do they hold up? You could tell stories now which some day will become the stories told at your funeral. A recent Facebook admonition is to tell your funeral stories now, rather than waiting, so that your life becomes a preview of the good things to say about it.

Lately, "walking the labyrinth" has become an attractive form of Christian piety. This can be done inside a church along paths laid out in large fabrics placed on the church floor. Or on paths on the church grounds outside. Along the sometimes confusing and bewildering and circuitous path, shared with other pilgrims finding their way, you can meditatively create an inner narrative of your Christian walk—while running into fellow pilgrims along the way.

Establishing and Embellishing the Religious Practice

If walking along the stations of Jesus' life is a form of discipleship, of imitation of Christ, it also becomes a moral walk, a walk from the church into and through the world—where Jesus walked. In these days some Christians are discovering the call to justice, the social form of love, in society. Pilgrims can walk out of their inner devotions into a world where God's special love for the poor is followed and displayed. Luther scholars unfailingly comment on the Protestant Reformation's "secularizing" the Christian calling, so that the Christian walk unmistakably occurs in the world—from the monastery into the streets. There in the life of the world Christians would attend to the voice of God and look for their calling.

A much larger undertaking would be to search out significant works of literature that feature attempts to expand the imagination and reflection on great events in Jesus' life that might also be examples of the fourteen stations. For example, more than one great writer finds irresistible Jesus' addressing the devil's temptations that followed his baptism. In Dostoevsky's *The Brothers Karamazov,* a very famous short story appears called the "Grand Inquisitor." In this tale, Christ comes back to earth in Seville at the time of the Inquisition. He performs a number of miracles (echoing miracles from the Gospels). The people recognize him and adore him at the Seville Cathedral, but he is arrested by Inquisition leaders and sentenced to be burnt to death the next day. The Grand Inquisitor visits him in his cell to tell him that the church no longer needs him. The main portion of the text is devoted to the Inquisitor explaining to Jesus why his return would interfere with the mission of the church. It is of course bizarre to depict Jesus' return to earth as precisely an interference with the church's mission. In Nikos Kazantzakis's *The Last Temptation of Christ,* Jesus on the cross experiences his final temptations. In a famous film based on the book we see Jesus struggling with fear, doubt, depression, reluctance, and lust for Mary Magdalene! Perhaps many writers map the perils of the human condition, the stations of our lives, back onto Jesus.

Feminist scholars have been depicting Jesus' striking, and empowering, encounters with women, such as Mary Magdalene and the woman who towards the end of Holy Week anoints Christ for his burial. Elizabeth Schussler Fiorenza's *In Memory of Her* offers a feminist reconstruction of Christian origins in which New Testament women play major roles in the early development of Christianity. A striking piece of modern art depicts Jesus ministering to the woman taken in adultery as a hostile law-and-order policeman stands menacingly by with his billy club.

PART ONE: PREPARING FOR A WALK WITH CHRIST

It has been said that early Christian theologians sought a *language that would not collapse under the weight of what they believed.* Augustine wrote that "the very cross on which he was derided, he has now imprinted on the brows of kings." This would be an example of the stations of Jesus' life imprinting themselves on Christians—and the surroundings of non-Christians. In his daily columns the well-known Franciscan Richard Rohr meditates his way toward a cosmic Christology, in which Christ is mapped upon us and we are mapping the human way in the universe chocked full of God's goodness and invitations to works of mercy. Who knew the stations in Jesus' life could become cosmic—the ultimate stages of the Word spoken at creation, then incarnated in Jesus Christ, and now becoming the evolutionary meaning of the universe. How many Christians walking the stations could catch sight of this as they get in touch with the DNA they have inherited? It calls for a meditative posture of awareness in the face of life—as Buddhists also affirm. "Christ mysticism" is very evocative, even mind-blowing.

If you search Amazon books or on Google, or elsewhere, you will find books that facilitate connecting these fourteen stations of Jesus' life with great art, literature, poetry, and music. A particularly helpful book is Terry Glaspey's *75 Masterpieces Every Christian Should Know.* This book is not directly connected to the idea of fourteen stations of Jesus' life, but it does illustrate and comment on masterpieces of art, literature, music, and film as they interact with great Christian themes, especially from the life of Jesus himself.

PART TWO

*Walking 14 Stations
Along the Christian Way*

Way Station 1

*Jesus Is Born Into the Human World and Our World—
Will We Meet Him There as We Are Born Again?*

WHILE ALL FOUR GOSPELS proclaim the life, death, and resurrection of Jesus Christ, only Matthew and Luke tell stories about Jesus' birth, although John's "high Christology" sets Jesus' coming into the world as a continuation of the Logos spoken at creation. The "infancy narratives" locate the origins of epochal events and set the stage for them. Like an opera whose overture is written after the main acts are completed, these are stories read back from the present of Jesus' life and of the church's understanding to the beginning of God's new actions to reclaim the world. Another way of seeing these stories is as an epilogue, but now displaced from the end to the beginning, that names the significance of what all has occurred in the life, death, and resurrection of Jesus into an indispensable doctrine of early Christianity: the incarnation of God into the human story has become the prologue.

Matthew wants us to see a cosmic story of earthshaking significance, and so signals it with a star in the sky. But on the ground, Matthew's first readers will see not only the fate of Jesus—this refugee child driven by rough humans to unexpected destinations—but also the fate of early Christianity mirrored. Matthew wants his readers to see the theological disturbance caused when new initiatives from God come to a world that dominates, oppresses, marginalizes, and destroys. Jesus' birth is meant to unsettle everyday reality and to intimate God's revolutionary dreams. For those who think encounters with the biblical texts are best construed as a critical, objectifying historical investigation, Matthew means to be *formational, more* than *informational*. We are to reflect on what it means that God has broken into our world and joined us in the neighborhood. God is fashioning us as a new people. How will this story reshape us?

Luke intends to account for how all the events surrounding Jesus Christ—all these fourteen stations of a life—brought the Christian church into being and changed the world. Making John the Baptist the prophetic hinge, Luke writes of a new age dawning from an old. As with a Bach aria or religious devotion that follows a compelling narrative, Luke keeps pausing in his birth story to reflect on the larger meanings of his recitative. Luke's account is the best known story in the New Testament (Charlie Brown knows it by heart), and one could scarcely omit it from the stages of Jesus' life. It is the beginning of how the church came to wrest the titles *Savior* and *Lord* from the Emperor and reassign sovereignty to this new protagonist of God's reign.

As any "theology of story" would have predicted, generations of readers gradually turn into a community shaped by their founding narrative. As "reader response theory" suggests, this original story continually comes true among successive generations of readers. In new ways! We readers become the physical presence of Christ in the world today. This is what we are born for! And into. Our churches become visual signs of a Christian community. Luke's point is to transform theological announcement and proclamation into the movement that emerges to embody it.

In a modern age likely to decontextualize and disencumber primal stories, the first agenda of those who "walk the stations" is to return to original meanings, meditate on them, and then reclaim them for modern life by turning that station into the first step in the Christian's own pilgrimage. Consider Jesus' birth. Consider the birth of the church. Consider your birth. All are markers of God's plan for the world.

Amidst our rapture around manger scenes in Matthew and Luke, the Gospel of John invites us to contemplate a theology of incarnation. A Word spoken at creation now comes true in a populated world. And not merely to be hidden in our hearts. The well-known verse in John 1 about the "Word became flesh and dwelt among us" becomes in Eugene Peterson's provocative modern paraphrase: "The Word became flesh and blood and moved into the neighborhood."

We may pause at this first station to reflect on a *theology of incarnation*. The obvious first thing: the incarnation does not authorize maleness but humanness, an obvious conclusion Catholic and evangelical patriarchy, for example, does not get around to. That the Word "moves into the neighborhood" suggests that God was not content to live in our hearts, but intended to take up space in the world, including rough neighborhoods, as Matthew already suggests in his account of the holy family as refugees fleeing to another country. And how great is the impact of this child. From gentle Virgin Mary empowered by the angel Gabriel's annunciation comes an earthshaking song in the Gospel of Luke—the *Magnificat*, which, in the Old Testament Jubilee tradition, sings of God's putting down the mighty from their seats and exalting them of low degree, of filling the hungry with good things and sending the rich empty away. The church could not get enough of this song and so monks sang it for centuries in evening vespers, and so would all Christians in the liturgy for vespers. And because many Christians could not get enough of Mary she is prominent in Catholic piety and the stimulus for endless poetry, as I have demonstrated in a previous chapter.

I have alluded to God "fashioning us as his people." These three Gospel accounts of Jesus' coming into the world all appear in the Common Lectionary used in many churches. The function of liturgy is to become *didache*, the teaching, forming of a people who come to be shaped and made and completed by liturgy and worship. The Common Lectionary insures we are well-developed by a comprehensive biblical narrative, and not just by the pastor's favorite topics. Jesus is a model, as well as Savior. In him God acts as the master sculptor who wants to make us in his image. If we imagine Jesus as God's genotype, we might imagine that we who live as his heirs have inherited God's very DNA, the genome that appeared to the world in the incarnation.

In most of these stations of Jesus' life modern pilgrims will be called to make their own lives an imitation of this one paradigmatic life. Probably Christmas has not been an occasion for you to reflect on your own birth, or to invite family members to testify to it. But what could be the pilgrims' parallel to this first station, Jesus' birth? The prophet Jeremiah urged Israel to see itself as birthed in the intentions of God. Jeremiah 1:5 has God saying, "Before I formed you in the womb, I knew you." Similarly, Luther thought that the Christian's entire life should consist in a repeated return to baptismal seal and promises.

Some modern existentialists talk about a "thrownness" in human existence: we come into the world as some kind of projectile from somewhere in the universe. Thomas Aquinas wanted human life to be a story of grace compounding our nature and completing thereby the human agenda. John Calvin wanted us to claim our election, and Luther said we should cling to the promise in baptism that makes us new. A current evangelical bestseller encourages Christians to find and practice a "purpose-driven life." Already our own birth, at least retroactively (as also in Matthew and Luke), can be experienced as *vocation*. Christmas sets us in motion.

The Gospel of John does not offer an infancy narrative like those of Matthew and Luke. But for those who pause to reflect, John's birth narrative takes up the very Word God spoke to bring creation into being and now makes that Word incarnate in the coming of Christ.

> In the beginning was the Word and the Word was with God . . . the light shines in darkness and the darkness did not overcome it . . . the true light, which enlightens everyone, was coming into the world. He was in the world, and the world came into being through him; yet the world did not know him . . . To all who believed in his name he gave power to become children of God. . . . And the Word became flesh and lived among us, and we have seen his glory, the glory as of a father's only son, full of grace and truth. (John 1:1–5; 9–14)

John's "Logos Christology" imagines a cosmic evolution into which we all, if we reflect on it, fit. All the stations of a life, the means by which we "compose a life"—begin here, fit here. In a sermon preached in Athens, the apostle Paul says, "In him we live and move and have our being" (Acts 17:28).

As we will see with all the way stations, that of Christmas invites believers to interact with this station of Jesus' life and make it their own, connecting Jesus' birth to all human births. Even our own. The German theologian Jürgen Moltmann, in his book *The Living God and the Fullness of Life*, writes that every child is born into God's great yes to her life. He sees that in the incarnation, God accepts and embraces human life and interpenetrates it, reconciling and healing. Two movements cut across the frontiers of the world: God's incarnation into this human life, and the transformation of this human life into a life that is divine.

God's action and our reaction become themes in Christian life and the way a life of discipleship arises from walking the stations on Christian pilgrimage. Recent Catholic theology emphasizes the "offering of consent" as the human, the church's, response to the sacraments, to God's invitations. The Virgin Mary becomes, as it were, the patron saint of consent.

Way Station 1

At the Annunciation, the Virgin Mary said yes to the angel. The point is that God's action, whether Jesus' birth or great commission or "open commensality" in his welcome of strangers as guests at the table, invites and indeed requires a response from us. This is the whole point of walking the stations—to interact with Jesus' life and make his mission our own. Jesus and we are to coincide.

In the European tradition it was St. Francis who did his part to bring Christ down to earth, who winsomely invited humans to interact with God when he introduced the practice of manger scenes in villages and churches. They became a place of adoration and reflection.

A beloved down-to-earth Christmas song is Jester Hairston's "Mary's Boy Child" famously sung by Harry Belafonte. The great Lutheran hymnwriter Paul Gerhardt taught the church to sing:

> *Ere ever I began to be,*
> *Thou hadst for me appeared*
> *And as Thine own hadst chosen me*
> *Ere Thee I knew or feared.*
> *Before I by Thy hand was made,*
> *Thou hadst the plan in order laid*
> *How Thou Thyself wouldst have me.*

Far more familiar are such Advent and Christmas hymns as these—to sing while you walk the first station: "O Lord How Shall I Meet You?," "Hark the Glad Sound," "Come Thou Long-Expected Jesus," "O Come, O Come Emmanuel," "Joy to the World," Martin Luther's "From Heaven Above to Earth I Come," "Hark the Herald Angels Sing," "Away in a Manger," "O Little Town of Bethlehem," "Silent Night," "O Come All Ye Faithful," "What Child Is This?," and "The First Noel." Many readers, and wayfarers, could immediately begin singing many of these.

On the other end of the scale of accessibility to modern hearers is Bach's *Christmas Oratorio*, one of the great monuments of Western choral music (along with Bach's St. Matthew and Magdalenions) and a challenge to those who live outside the world of classical music. Find it on YouTube and see if it moves you. While Bach's music is not accessible to everyone, to those with full appreciation of classical music it is a wondrous adornment of the Christmas season with musical art. It consists of six separate cantatas assigned to six consecutive days of Christmas in the liturgy of that time, from Christmas Day (the birth of Jesus) to December 26 (annunciation to the shepherds), to December 27 (the adoration of the shepherds), to New

Year's Day (the circumcision and naming of Jesus), to the first Sunday after New Year (the journey of the magi), to Epiphany (the adoration of the magi). As such these cantatas are embedded in regular German Lutheran morning worship. Indeed, the *Christmas Oratorio* and the two Passions come replete with Lutheran hymns. But Bach also seems to have imagined the entire cycle performed in a single hearing three hours long in a concert setting, as is sometimes done today.

A remarkable dimension, and evidence of Bach's sophisticated appropriation of Luther's theology, is the Christmas use, twice, of the tune of a famous Good Friday hymn that was used repeatedly in Bach's St. Matthew Passion, "O Sacred Head Now Wounded." Strikingly, that tune, immediately recognized by Leipzig worshippers as alluding to Good Friday, is the last music to be heard in the *Christmas Oratorio*—connecting Christ's birth to the death of Christ which culminated his earthly story. Luther's beloved hymn "From Heaven Above to Earth I Come" also occurs three times in the *Oratorio*, a reference which any churchgoer would have recognized and cherished immediately.

Though this would only be known by music scholars, another dimension of the *Christmas Oratorio* is its repeated use of "parody"—a term that refers to the use of previous musical compositions, usually secular, in a new and now religious setting. Was this Bach's way of dressing an important religious event in the clothing of the everyday world—for example a work celebrating the birthday of an important person's child now being used to celebrate the birth of God's own child? But all children are God's children and Bach effortlessly, and perhaps deliberately, is making that point. He dresses the newborn baby Jesus both in profoundly religious but also everyday secular art. Just so, six cantatas for six church services can also be experienced as a "sacred opera" distinctively gracing any concert stage. (A remarkable fact of American life is that college choir students, who are by no means religious studies majors, inevitably come to experience religious texts abundantly built into much of the classical music in the Western choral tradition. Bach would have smiled at the fact that religion "owns" the tradition of great choral music.)

A very famous, and much more accessible work of art celebrating Christmas, is Charles Dickens's *A Christmas Carol*. Ebenezer Scrooge is visited by a ghost of Christmas past and undergoes a transformation into a much kinder and more generous human being. While some insist this is just a secular story with allusions to Christmas, there is much evidence that

Dickens was in fact a deeply religious man here making of Christmas the inspiration of a higher morality. Perhaps inadvertently, Dickens's extremely popular work contributed to the revival of Christmas celebration in his day, and since. Dickens opened the heart of a bitter old miser who despised Christmas to produce a heartwarming change of life.

REFLECTIONS WHILE WALKING THIS STATION

What are your favorite souvenirs (memorable objects) from Christmas and what do they mean to you? And how do they connect to Christmas?

Ask your family about your own birth. Do you ever connect your birthdays with the birth of Jesus, making the point that God foresaw you and brought you into the world? Is it too much to imagine yourself, and other newborns, as instances of God's presence and intentions taking root and shape in the human family?

Art history books that focus on religious art, recent books that go beyond Europe to world art, effortless Google searches, and the abundant images of the Getty Museum are readily available sources for the art of Christmas.

My book *Christmas: Festival of Incarnation* portrays the leading figures in the Gospels as the "cast" for a Christmas drama. I see the church as the "Festival House of Incarnation" and indeed the entire world as a theater of (risky) incarnation. Can we see Christian worship as theater and ourselves as the motley crew trying to make it happen? I have also decorated the stage with Christmas poetry (some of which appeared in Part I of this book). Indeed, the material culture of Christianity furnishes the stage, even as, with St. Francis, we find humble stages for traveling manger scenes. Of course, the Gospels are the original scripts, and Christian theology evokes continuing re-presentations. The question is whether we *show up* for the festival and, even more important, whether we will feel compelled to join the cast on the stage. That the whole world becomes a stage is a blessing and can be a curse. On the one hand, the whole world becomes enchanted. On the other, the world clutters Christmas with all manner of distracting artifacts.

I close with these observations about poets and poetry at Christmas. Artists are an "indicator species." What will happen to the rest of us first happens to them. They are sounding alarms, alerting the day, concentrating the mind, running away from sentimentality and distraction, chilling with irony, or warming with beauty. Wordsworth thought poets had a disposition to *be affected more than others by absent things as if they were present.* More, the poetic imagination operates most powerfully in the space of loss. Poetry is grief-work over the missing words. For an age that has lost the words, a poetry of incarnation makes the absent present to new celebration. Once a divine poem that was the nativity reprised humanity lost; the baby evokes the missing man and cries for companionship. Poetry illuminates the space where a lost God, a lost Christmas, and a lost humanity reassemble. Not knowing what he was foretelling, the pre-Christian poet Virgil wrote: "Now the virgin is returning . . . a new human race is descending from the heights of heaven."

Czelaw Milosz thought poetry "a word wakened by lips that perish." Like God at Bethlehem, Milosz would not leave the *thickness of the actual* without accolade. To adorn the everyday with incarnational awareness is to let the soul exceed its circumstance. A fifteenth-century poet wrote:

> *Lo, in the silent night*
> *A child is brought again*
> *That ere was lost or lorn.*
> *Could but thy soul, O man*
> *Become a silent night!*
> *God would be born in thee*
> *And set all things aright.*

And Thomas à Kempis wrote:

> *He sent no angel to our race*
> *Of higher or of lower place*
> *But wore the robe of human frame*
> *And to the world himself he came.*

All this mysticism may be more than most of us can abide. And so as we set out to walk this station, we sing Charles Wesley's hymn:

> *Mild he lays his glory by,*
> *Born that man no more may die,*
> *Born to raise the sons of earth,*
> *Born to give them second birth.*
> *Hark! The herald angels sing,*
> *Glory to the newborn King.*

Way Station 2

Jesus Is Baptized, Opens His Life to God, and Engages a World of Temptation and Possibility—*Have We Been Mostly Clueless About the Implications of Our Own Baptism?*

Contemporary Christians pausing at this station should notice the contest between Jesus and Satan. Are we always rooting for the right one?

A prayer that Christians around the world pray every Sunday of their lives, and perhaps every day, the Lord's Prayer, becomes the energy and direction of the Christian life: *"Thy kingdom come, Thy will be done*, on earth as it is in heaven." For those empowered by a corporate resurrection, in which we're all included, these words become revolutionary and anticipatory. God embraces us from out of the future and together with God we participate in God's ultimate plan in the present. No doubt when Paul says "You have been raised with Christ," he is implying "You should be living risen lives," pointing toward resurrection in the universe.

There's a funny thing about baptism, both Jesus' and ours. It's a two-part ritual. First Jesus resists the temptations from Satan that would derail his presence and mission in the world. Then he proceeds to announce the arrival of the kingdom of God and begins living its agenda. In our own Christian baptism we first renounce the world, looking backward out the door of the church. Then we do an about face and proceed into the church, where we are commissioned to return to the world with a new engagement, living out the kingdom of God. Our life may consist of renouncing—when I was a little boy in Dubuque my many Catholic friends would often act this out: "Cross your heart and spit to the devil." The other half is our baptismal commission and engagement.

The history of Christian baptismal liturgies is always working out an imitation of Jesus' own baptism. Newly baptized Christians momentarily turn their back on the world and renounce all its empty promises, as Jesus did in the temptation stories that follow his baptism in the Gospels of Matthew, Mark, and Luke. But then the newly initiated baptismal candidates turn around and seek engagement with the very world they are called to make new, where Christ's kingship is recognized as occupying real earthly territory.

Re-visioning baptism to include renunciation and counterculture commissioning brings me to Michael Knippa's surprising analysis of the unending shift from one to the other. In "Converted Citizens: From National Allegiance towards Heavenly Adherence" (*Word and World*, Fall 2017) he calls on the modern church to recover lost territory and influence. Likewise, William Cavanaugh's *Migrations of the Holy: God, State, and the Political Meaning of the Church* argues that in recent centuries the state has in fact *occupied the sacred* and, in many ways, replaced the cultural role of the church. Cavanaugh believes that the migration of the sacred from the church to the state diminishes the possibilities of a unique Christian culture, the possibilities of *resistance and nonconformity and insurgency* (does that sound like your church?). While many Christians do not pause to notice, the state increasingly demands first allegiance even from people who are religious. The very opposite is occurring in the Gospels, where Jesus yields no ground to worldly powers and customs. Permission not to participate in the absolutizing of the nation might, as Jehovah's Witnesses discovered, have to go all the way to the Supreme Court. Football players must not sit out the national anthem for any reason. The place of the state and of the secular world (like Black Lives Matter or other causes) has displaced the sacred space of the church. The state controls material life and its spaces, while privatized (and irrelevant?) space is conceded to religion.

Similarly, in *The Borders of Baptism: Identities, Allegiances, and the Church*, Michael Budde argues that since the Protestant Reformation, political and economic leaders have *fragmented the unity of the church in the interests of nationalism, capitalism, and individualism*. In the unacknowledged commitment to white racism, for example, many churches self-segregated for a long time. And so "the bonds of baptism were spiritualized and sidelined in favor of the blood and iron ties of patriotism and ethno-national solidarity." There lies the contemporary decline of moral and spiritual formation, which half-hearted and somewhat rare confirmation classes, or "rites of initiation for adults," cannot make up for. *The state and national culture become the undefined god, what the apostle Paul calls "principalities and powers."* Many Catholic and Orthodox moral theologians and Protestant ethicists have decried the formative and corrosive power of American nationalism upon the church (which is winning out today among evangelical *Christian nationalists*), the absolutizing even by Christians of national, ethnic, political, economic, and cultural values. Indeed, consider the readiness of the secular world to *call any movement towards a Christian culture an unacceptable and dangerous theocratic displacement of the state.* People who do not think this through, especially liberal Christians, are far too ready to make the state their default and to declare unacceptable any assertions from the church in public space. Do all baptismal vows silently include the caveat "except for the separation of church and state"? That phrase does not warn of the state's encroachments but the church's.

These modern examples call our attention to what we may have missed in Jesus' own resisting of the devil's temptations in the story of Jesus' baptism. These temptations have been the subject of abundant literary and theological reflection. In these recent studies, the long overdue resolve to renounce absolute demands of state and culture and economics in favor of the reign of God proclaimed by Jesus and claiming public space for the church are at the top of the baptismal agenda.

And let's not stop our analysis there. In recent decades New Testament scholars have come to see that the designation of Jesus Christ as Lord (*Kyrios*) was *political speech* directed in part as a rejection of the deification and worship of the Roman Caesars. Jesus' ride into Jerusalem on Palm Sunday, which we'll practice in a later station, might be seen as counter to the ceremonial ride-in of Roman troops. Richard Horsley was one of the early leaders of this scholarship, and he noted that St. Paul, a Roman citizen himself, was careful to root the ultimate citizenship of new Christians in the reign of God, not in the Roman Empire. Few contemporary Christians take any notice of these claims, except perhaps Anabaptists who were practicing resistance already in their sixteenth-century origins. Many Christian pastors and their congregations (often with national flags in their worship space) are pledged to "keep politics out of the pulpit"—*not noticing that all speech is political speech, all speech is occupied and situated speech, all speech is connected to power and part of a worldview, all speech and stories have a social location.*

I have wanted to surprise the reader by making all these demanding points first, because they are so often forgotten or ignored. But now—on to the story of Jesus' own baptism, his resistance to the world, and his proclamation of the reign of God. It's quite a story. Discuss it with your fellow pilgrims. To get you ready to seeing it's a big deal, consider these memorable New Testament verses:

> Go and make disciples of all nations, baptizing them in the name of the Father and of the Son and of the Holy Spirit. Teaching them to obey everything that I have commanded you. Remember, I am with you always, to the end of the age. (Matthew 28:19–20)

> You will be baptized with the Holy Spirit. (Acts 11:16)

> For all of you who were baptized into Christ have clothed yourselves with Christ. (Galatians 3:27)

> Having been buried with him in baptism, in which you were also raised with him through your faith in the working of God, who raised him from the dead. (Colossians 2:12)

> Baptism now saves you, as an appeal to God for a good conscience through the resurrection of Jesus Christ, who has gone into heaven and is at the right hand of God. (1 Peter 3:21–22)

Here are the instances in the Common Lectionary of the full biblical witness to Jesus' baptism by John the Baptist and the beginning of Jesus' public ministry and proclamation of the reign of God, reported in all four Gospels: Matthew 3, Mark 1, Luke 3, and John 1. In Orthodox Christianity, Jesus' baptism is commemorated on January 6, the feast of Epiphany. In the Roman Catholic Church, the Anglican Communion, the Lutheran churches, and some other Western denominations, Jesus' baptism is recalled in the week following Epiphany, the major festival following Christmas. In Roman Catholicism, Jesus' baptism is one of the "luminous mysteries" sometimes added to the rosary. It is a Trinitarian feast in the Orthodox churches.

Recalling the historic age of outspoken prophets, John the Baptist has gone out to the desert (where encounters with God are sought) and begins preaching repentance and practicing a baptism that heralds a new age. When he proclaims the forgiveness of sins, he seems to be working around the religious establishment in Jerusalem and breaking with religious routine. He is preparing a spiritual climate in which a new messenger from

God can be imagined. Nearly all European art depicts John with his hand outstretched and his finger pointing towards another—namely Jesus. John is the forerunner (does every evangelist, every Christian, play such a role?). Could Christians walking the stations imagine themselves moving through life with outstretched hands pointing to Jesus?

John the Baptist models the role of the church, holding up a banner and pointing to Jesus. Jesus models for the church the resistance to the world's temptations and the alert embrace of the reign of God. Eventually John was martyred by political powers. Jesus too.

When Jesus surprises John and accepts his baptism, he also takes up his vocation in the plan of God. God authenticates this by anointing Jesus with the Holy Spirit and commissioning him. The heavens open, a dove descends, and a voice pronounces: "This is my beloved Son."

In this teachable moment for us, Jesus begins to act out his vocation. In subsequent Gospel readings assigned to the season of Lent, Jesus is immediately beset by the temptations of the world—a dilemma every new believer knows. As rival Messianic ambitions present themselves, one by one, Jesus turns away from them and sides with God's intentions and God's devices for a new Israel. (In a wickedly ironic remark, the Anabaptist John Howard Yoder suggested that Calvinist engagement with the world is always one Christian temptation—consider the double meanings of that word *engagement*.)

The aftermath of baptism, then and now, is a contest between the reign of God and the beguiling claims made by worldly powers. In each case, Jesus declines the beckoning detours offered by pronouncing a counter-word from the Lord, drawn from ancient Israel's own exodus experience: Deuteronomy 8:3b; 6:16; 13. As we will see in the unfolding stations in Jesus' life, his whole ministry is one of conflict with the powers of darkness and triumph over them. (A very important three-volume work by Walter Wink opens the powers up and calls us to respond: *Naming the Powers, Unmasking the Powers,* and *Engaging the Powers.*)

Jesus' resistance to the powers and embrace of the reign of God is climaxed in the second-to-last station, his death on the cross. Eschatology in the New Testament alludes to "last things" and becomes a setting that gives weight to some of the stations in Jesus' life. His temptations now prefigure the great eschatological battle that ensues when the reign of God arrives with its claims. This dramatic contest at his baptism is just the opening salvo, the clarification and purification of his vocation. It's the same for us, and the replication of Jesus' temptations in our own lives has long fascinated novelists. What would you say are the most salient temptations in your own life, and those around you? Jesuit Daniel Berrigan is said to have challenged his students: "Name the seven deadly sins. And describe how you have gone about integrating them into your own life!"

Jesus' baptism may remind pious Christian pilgrims walking these stations of their own baptisms, first in a sentimental way but then in a much more radical understanding of baptism as Christian initiation than had previously been realized. When we fully identify with the New Testament setting, we may come to a countercultural understanding of the Christian life that opens our eyes to a vocation of resistance and breakthrough on behalf of the reign of God. Children who were baptized as babies may trigger searching family discussions by asking of their parents: What did you think you were doing when you brought me forward to be baptized? Whom did you choose as my sponsors and what did you expect of them? Did the minister or priest insist on a pre-baptism class in which all its significance was unpacked?

Like all rituals, the ritual of baptism becomes *a way of paying attention*. It opens us up to the claims of modern discipleship. For Protestants, baptism is one of two sacraments, and for Catholics one of seven. Sacraments can be understood as a *planned running into mystery*, a ritualized exchange between the world as religiously imagined and the world as commonly lived. It is common to hear today that Jesus Christ himself can be seen as the sacrament of God, the one who gave body to God's presence and God's claims on earth. Sacraments are something to receive, something to do, something to see by. They *perform God's ways* in the life of a religious community. *They require the community to participate, to "offer consent" to the movement of God.* Is everyone paying attention? It's never too late to take all this up when pausing at this station. And discussing it with fellow pilgrims.

John the Baptist, too, struggled with paying attention and worried about losing track. At a late point in his own ministry, according to an account in Matthew 11:2–6 read in an Advent Lectionary, John, now in prison, sends some of his own disciples to Jesus, asking, "Are you the one who is to come or are we to wait for another?" Jesus answers, in words from the prophet Isaiah: "Go and tell John what you hear and see: the blind receive their sight, the lame walk, the lepers are cleansed, the deaf hear, the dead are raised, and the poor have good news brought to them." When people

Way Station 2

ask you why you are baptized, tell them how you have come to expect the presence of Jesus in worldly life.

Seen in John's eschatological setting, baptism becomes the inauguration of a life of resistance, under the sign of God who calls us to bury the old life and begin a new one. At some times and in some places in the history of Christianity (e.g., the American Jesus Movement of the 1970s), baptism was played as guerrilla theater in public waters, a ritual of initiation into a distinct counterculture, "before the watching world," sometimes covered by the media while the Christian community already baptized cheers from the sidelines. When baptism is practiced in the more staid environment of a church building, the congregation is asked if they will welcome and support the newly baptized into their Christian life in community. That new life is seen through the prism of baptism.

But the modern church has mostly tamed this radical reorientation exercise and made it a smooth transition from human culture to an American Christian culture that threatens no one. In secular Europe baptism can mean as little as being recognized as a new citizen of the European Union! Birth certificates and baptismal certificates run together in the archives of Europe.

The history of Christianity contains periods of persecution by and of comfortability with society—the latter often an effect of failed watchfulness. (How do you, walker of the stations, experience the culture in which you live, hostile or friendly?) Some historians see the after-effects of the conversion of the emperor Constantine early in the fourth century as a sell-out of the demands to be *resident aliens* (1 Peter 2:11) to everyday life in a now mostly friendly empire in which Christianity is becoming the state religion. But a more hopeful view is that the church was filling out its role in the empire as a creative response to the spiritual crisis of "late paganism" and declining empire, and as the political attempt of Christianity to hold things together and, with Augustine's help, create a new social vision of history that lasted more than a millennium.

But by the sixteenth century some new Protestant traditions were rejecting infant baptism because it too closely correlates with mere "citizenship" in the community and was too accommodated to the world. Modern appropriations of this stage of Jesus' life might vary from lives of radical resistance to purpose-driven forays through a post-Christian society. Whatever the meaning, baptism grasps some of the appropriate symbolism when it is accompanied by prodigious amounts of water so that its symbolism of drowning and resurrection is not lost. The threat of drowning wonderfully concentrates the mind. And St. Paul liked to assure new Christians that they were baptized into, and buried with Christ, so that they could rise up in his company by the power of the waiting Father.

Jesus' baptism, and ours, is followed by engagements in the wilderness, where the contrast between the reign of God and the appeal of God's rivals is seen more clearly. One way to describe this is to say Jesus was tempted; another way is to say Jesus immediately *engaged the powers* of evil; still another is to say that Jesus faced the world as it is. Jesus' "errand into the wilderness" (a lovely phrase describing the mission of the first Pilgrims to America) immediately after his baptism is usually called his temptations. Another way is to say *God's rivals are having it out with God's dreams.* This is Jesus' engagement with the powers of evil: Jesus names the powers. Jesus overcomes the powers, which is what is meant when the *resurrection is called the victory of God* and the Orthodox traditions call him *Christus Victor*.

Early Christian liturgies distilled this contest into a required *exorcism* in which the baptized—together with the watching Christian community—renounced the devil and all his empty promises. The devil is summoned to court and charged with staging false claims over humans. So historically, baptism echoes this struggle by beginning with an exorcism in which the community and the person to be baptized renounce "the devil and all his empty promises." Long ago, in the rite of exorcism that often accompanied baptism, the devil was summoned to court and convicted of entertaining false claims over humans. The candidate first turned west to reject the devil and then east to enter the realm of the church and profess God's reign. The devil's "pomps," once an allusion to idols paraded through the Roman arena, today might be seen as the "gods of this age" summoned to the stage, *named, unmasked, and engaged* during the ceremony.

An exorcism means that all the power of God and of the gathered community is brought to bear on the rescue from and renunciation of the domination systems that are the prevailing reality of life in the world. They constitute the state into which everyone is born and that implicitly requires allegiance to its larger purposes. For example, American babies are soon enough drafted into a vast army of consumerism, and it is devoutly hoped that the acquisition of goods will define their entire life and the winner will be the one who dies with the most toys!

Way Station 2

While the baptism of the status quo is only too well known and too readily practiced, baptism could exemplify a coming of age in which the community, fully implicated in this crisis of decision that gospel proclamation always involves, decides against the status quo and for God. For such a self-understanding, baptism signals a *change of jurisdiction* from the world system to the commonwealth of God. In announcing the reign of God, as we will see in the next station, *Jesus had the chutzpah to issue his own passports*. In Jesus' teaching, baptism as initiation would signal a new life that comes from above, which is to say that the believer begins drawing power from the heavenward side of earth, from transcendent hope. This is the origin of the phrase that all fundamentalists and evangelicals use to define themselves—born again. Abandoning this sometimes cloying phrase may mean losing the resolve to break with the status quo and construct more of a life than the one that passes for everyday existence.

So radical is the break, that baptism then and now is accompanied by the arrival of the Holy Spirit. Coincidental with the Gospel accounts of Jesus' baptism, Paul was claiming it as a powerful metaphor for burial with Christ into death, only to rise again to a new life. Commentators religious and secular sometimes consider the differences between those who see themselves fundamentally as *once-born* and those who consider themselves *twice-born*. Which are you—at ease in the world or striving to overcome it? I write all this to stimulate your religious imagination and resolve and to suggest that those who walk this station have much religious and moral work to do.

Interestingly, then, this baptismal station in Jesus' life can appeal to a wide cross section of Christian theology and practice, ranging from Catholic-Lutheran-Anglican to evangelical. The Catholic-Lutheran-Anglican axis wants to claim that baptism symbolizes *God's choosing us*, anointing us, showering us with grace, and sending us on a mission. This is the vision of the heavens opening above Jesus in the River Jordan and divine approval and election coming down. But the current trend in Jesus studies is to see Jesus "from below," not from the standpoint of a high Christology above. This view is more like that of the evangelical tradition, which sees *baptism as our choice* to open our life to God and live for God. It correlates well not only with modern Jesus scholarship but also with the *calls to decision* that everywhere accompany Jesus' proclamation of the reign of God. This is *baptism as altar call, going forward*—often called believer's baptism and not reduced to an overwhelming doctrine of grace that sucks all the oxygen off the human stage. In such a case of abundant grace, God happens, but humans do not happen! This was Wesley's critique of Luther. He thought Luther's magnification of justification ended up minimizing the sanctified life.

JESUS' BAPTISM WAS A COMMISSIONING FOR HIS PUBLIC MINISTRY. AND YOURS?

The Christian community was seen in New Testament times as a colony of heaven, the body of Christ on earth, the extension of the incarnation of God's Word into the world. *So step into the exodus waters God is stirring up. And start walking.* Don't lose heart or nerve on the bank's edge. Once your feet are wet, pause to listen to the whole community, including the heavenly one, cheering you on. Start determining what you need to renounce and what you now are ready to affirm. I'm making this sound very dramatic, so you may need to do this in groups, each cheering the other's baby steps on.

And if you'll excuse me for this heresy, it might imply, or require, a second baptism.

As a Lutheran, I hesitate to make my next point. Is *one* baptism going to be enough? I am hesitant because second baptisms (practiced by the Anabaptists in Reformation times) once merited capital punishment. Protestants and Catholics were equally aghast at baptizing a second time and almost gleefully participated in pronouncing the death penalty on those who practiced a second baptism. Why did the Anabaptists do it? They thought sixteenth-century baptisms of babies was little more than a birth certificate into European society. Many of today's evangelicals do not practice second baptism, they just decline infant baptism and wait for a dramatic *age of consent* when young teenagers, newly claiming Christ and *coming forward*, are baptized and commissioned. It's quite impressive. And compelling!

As I write this, a remarkable story is in the news. A Catholic priest has resigned in disgrace and all the baptisms he ever performed were declared invalid—because he always said *We* baptize you in the name of the Father, and of the Son, and of the Holy Spirit. Instead of *I baptize you . . .* As if the whole point were getting the formula right! The Catholic Church is trying to track down all these invalid baptisms and do it over. But does *we* better evoke the entire community and does *I* maintain the exclusive clericalism of the priesthood?

Way Station 2

At the end of my book *After Trump: Achieving a New Social Gospel*, I called for a recovery of the old practice of renouncing the devil and all his empty ways and for a new counterculture commissioning of Christians returning expectantly to the public square and playing their legitimate role in witnessing to the reign of God evoked by Jesus. Will Christians see that the times call for a move from national and cultural allegiance to affirmations of the kingdom of God?

Can confirmation classes, these days reframed as baptismal reaffirmations, compete with all this—sprinkled as they are between soccer practice and TikTok and school dances? In fact, the state and the culture are common defaults. Churches attempting to re-establish their own identity and function as a resistance movement are considered quaint or denounced as Islamic theocracy aspiring to sharia law.

In the face of this, Christians with baptisms newly reaffirmed are commissioned to play their roles. Yes, the way station of Jesus' baptism and commissioning by the Father must reappear, in the course of our discipleship and imitation of Christ, as our own way station. Baptism, and a life of its recollections and reaffirmations, is vital and indispensable to the Christian pilgrimage. We are already regularly praying "Thy kingdom come," are we not? Just to test whether you get the point, try saying occasionally, *Thy empire come.*

The fancy phrase for all this is "collaborative eschatology": we join together with God in moving the universe forward. Augustine said: "God without us will not; we without God cannot." William James, the psychologist of religious experience, famously asked: "What experiences will be different from those which would obtain if the belief were false?" If Christ was baptized, and crucified, and risen from the dead, and we are in on this way station, then everything about *our* baptized lives will be different. Across the ages, Christian baptism—Christ's and ours—is the liturgical performance of how we together with God in Christ can die and rise again. This is our commission.

As I come to the end of this way station I have exhausted myself. And I recognize that I myself do not remotely resemble what I am calling for. Martin Luther, who knew spiritual exhaustion and failure, followed it with grace. He called for periodic or even everyday renewals of the grace of baptism. He called for a return to the sources of our redemption and sanctification. He suggested that every day Christians should meet God around the memory of their baptism and say, "You promised."

Lutheran countercultural pastor Nadia Bolz-Weber describes a baptismal ceremony taking place amidst notorious sinners in her congregation. "Stand over him, God," she says. "Recognize him. Name him." And pronounce in the hearing of an inquisitive audience: "This is my beloved child in whom I am well pleased." Affirming the identity of a child of God is God's first move. Before we do anything wrong or right, God's first move is to name and claim us as his own, granting us a new identity.

To calm down a bit, and perhaps at the beginning of this way station observance, ask your family if there are any souvenirs or pictures of your own baptism. Any water from the River Jordan by chance? What was the location? A near by lake or creek? How about your children's? If you, or they, had a "believer's baptism," what were the circumstances in which you "came forward"?

At Jesus' baptism, he walked into an alternative reality. This is true for us as well. So remembering our baptism, as Luther so often recommended as our foundation in God's grace, really means going over and over again the life we have lived since we first walked (or were carried) through that door.

Oh, and just to complexify things: It's not necessarily the state that must first be renounced. It's probably the culture. And the economic system that carefully distributes poverty everywhere. And what about this: Look for opportunities to join together with the state to produce structures for a just social system. Now there's a baptismal miracle.

Way Station 3

Jesus Inaugurates His Vocation by Proclaiming the Arrival of the Kingdo of God with a Jubilee Message—Will We Recognize God's Reign When We See It? Will We Proclaim Jubilee?

JUBILEE IS THE YEAR at the end of seven cycles of Sabbath years, the fiftieth, in which land was returned to the original owners. This idea, set forth in the Old Testament book of Leviticus, chapter 25, proclaimed prisoners freed, debts forgiven, and land returned. A trumpet blast would announce the beginning of such a year. According to Leviticus 25, "You shall make the fiftieth year, and proclaim liberty throughout the land to all its inhabitants. It shall be a jubilee to you; and each of you shall return to his own property, and each of you shall return to his family." Rather than waiting for the fiftieth year, the Deuteronomic Code requires that Hebrew slaves be liberated during their seventh year of service, a kind of sabbath of sabbaths.

In recent years theologians and ethicists have acknowledged Jubilee probably didn't ever happen and tried to imagine how the radical Jubilee concept could be proclaimed and operationalized today, for example in world debt relief to poor countries. There has been an appeal to the very beginning of Jesus' ministry as a Jubilee announcement. When Jesus preached his inaugural sermon in Luke 4, lately called the Nazareth Manifesto, he announced: "The Spirit of the Lord is upon Me, Because He anointed Me to reach the gospel to the poor. He has sent Me to proclaim release to the captives, And recovery of sight to the blind, To set free those who are oppressed, To proclaim the favorable year of the Lord." This was almost a direct quotation of Isaiah 61, which Jesus presumably had opened before him.

Jubilee adds substance to the reign of God, which otherwise seems invisible. The kingdom of God takes up earthly space, and Jesus means to fill it. Will the church take its place at Jesus' side in the world? In a famous story in Matthew 25 Jesus suggests there is an eschatological setting in which the church conducts its mission, always aware the reign of God clothes reality. So Jesus mentions the hungry, the homeless, the sick, the imprisoned, and asks whether the church sees the presence of Christ in "the least of these." In case all this is not sufficiently clear in Jesus' inaugural sermon in Luke, read from the during the Common Lectionary in the Epiphany season of year C in a three-year lectionary, year B features the same proclamation in Mark 1, and year A repeats it from Matthew 4. *The message is being drummed into the church's worship that something big is afoot.* So in Luke Jesus closes his sermon: "Today this has been fulfilled in your hearing."

When Jesus uncovers the presence of God in the world, it means a new age dawning, creation restored, covenant renewed, people liberated, a return from exile. This is good news that can set people free. Yes, Jesus evokes Israel's destiny to be a light to the nations, but he subverts old plots and opens up new ways of being the people of God. *Jesus' announcement clears the air at this station.* All those who come together at station #3 are invited to see that a change in climate is being proclaimed, that brings both judgment and vindication.

Historic religious ideas appear in new light and require different responses. The gospel Jesus preaches is good news for all the people, and it authorizes unexpected ways of thinking. The *reign of God is less a place than a plot*, a modality that requires new language, new rhetorical strategies, new ways of hearing and following God. This will be a play in search of new actors who will live "as if" God's plot were the truth on stage. And outside the theater, Christians departing from worship inside the church discover a social gospel out in the world.

Jesus arrives like a new mutation in God's sequencing with the human race. Would you be willing to audition for new roles in the guerilla theater that is the reign of God on earth? In Catholic piety the baptism of Jesus is the first luminous mystery in the rosary and the proclamation of the kingdom of God and call to repentance is the third. These way stations are thus kept alive as the rosary beads are fingered.

Way Station 3

It is important that pilgrims at this way station see that Jesus' announcement is not only good news but *subversive news*. Christians gathering at this station are not merely to experience a quiet reverie. Jesus calls his disciples to be *nonconforming*, an identity badge the Puritans once adopted. Or a *spiritual resistance*, a posture Anabaptists adopted. New wine calls for new wineskins, new context, new world, new people, new discipleship. What will all this mean? Does God now come unbrokered and unmediated by a religious establishment? Will the church be something more than a franchise in a salvation system? Is God's formula too explosive to be bottled in social or political systems? To be sure, Paul will see the collections of Jesus' followers as colonies of heaven, but unending reform movements across Christian ages will have to keep questioning comfortable compromises and permanent accommodations and settlements. Radical discipleship destabilizes the longing for old comforts. Subversive repenting means no drifting back.

We have recently learned to be cautious about naming Jesus' legacy the "kingdom of God" because *kingdom* seems male gendered. And it keeps suggesting a fixed place where we can settle down and decorate. And there's a temptation to reduce God to a political party. Or to one hallowed space (white supremacy?) over all others. Unwary believers get themselves in trouble when the unwieldy divine initiatives become political calculations. So we have come to call it the *reign of God*, rather than the kingdom of God. Reign seems more dynamic, less predictable, more in motion. But the advantage to the word *kingdom* is that it suggests that God's reign on earth *takes up space*, occupies territory, is not invisible or more an intention than a reality. Calvinists used to say that there is not a single square foot that God does not claim. It's much more than a space in the believer's heart.

As we pilgrims walk on from this way station, we see that we cannot continue without changing. Jesus' announcement at this station provokes a crisis of decision, as "parables of the kingdom" yet to be considered in Way Station #10 will make clear. If God is moving in new directions, will we sign on? Leave everything behind and follow? There are many way stations to come. Will we persevere? Will *pilgrim-talk start to become pilgrim-walk*, as life-changing as Jesus' early preaching was? Does God's revolution begin with pilgrims on their way? Chaucer's *Canterbury Tales* chronicled the emergence of an unexpected community in the discourses on the way. People who reflect together come together.

What should we who walk the stations be thinking about this one? Pause and consider the provocative presence of Jesus when he meets us at these stations. New Testament scholars in the last fifty years have emphasized that the inescapable dimension of Jesus' proclamation of the arriving reign of God is that it provokes a "crisis of decision," and so-called "parables of the kingdom" demonstrate this. This station requires a decision about persevering, about casting your lot, about embracing the stations that lie ahead. Consider the sermons you hear or the Bible study you engage in. Are they life-challenging, as Jesus' early sermons were? Is the company of the church permanently transforming?

When Jesus began his public ministry proclaiming the arrival of the reign of God, he was playing the role of the prophet. And he was fulfilling the role Old Testament prophets had practiced and foreseen. And we today who gather at this station are to go away as prophets. The reign of God is staffed by prophets whose mission is to "fashion a people for me." Will such prophets be preceding us to this station, waiting on tables, teaching the menu, welcoming us? Is the church good at spotting prophets these days?

What does the reign of God have to do with *prophets?* We say in this way station that Jesus began a prophetic ministry. What would it mean for us to imitate it, or to call pastors to be prophets, to expect them to act and preach like prophets, or to become prophets ourselves, to help our church become prophetic, to practice prophecy in small groups walking the stations, to expect prophecy to blossom on pilgrimage? Is our age longing for prophets or are they mostly unwelcome? Abraham Heschel, in his important writing on prophets, wryly notices that *prophets always sing an octave too high.*

There are different kinds of prophets. Some are ecstatic prophets with shaman-like experiences in mystical isolation. Another kind is a "leadership prophet," who calls disciples to model God's will and become an intentional community with a distinctive vision. Jesus is a radical prophet. His call is preemptory—beyond and sometimes against the claims of family, custom, and established religion. Leave everything else behind, Jesus admonishes. Jesus' call is the beginning of the disciples' (and our) experience of their own fourteen stations in God's design.

How does all this get started? Ordinary people—unlikely and unexpected "prophet material"—find themselves perplexed by all the things that have gone wrong in life and look earnestly for the promised handwriting of God in history. What could be happening at the stations? A call from God, almost always unwelcome or at least unexpected, turns pilgrims into God's emissaries. They are deputized to move forward with God's ambitions for earth and humanity. They slowly find their way as actors in a society and perhaps a church that has lost its moorings. They are determined to believe that history has a meaning and that the religious agenda is to name it. In acts of guerilla theater they *play God's dreams on public stages*. They mean to disturb and captivate new audiences. Our mission derives from the ministry of Jesus, which is why we walk the stations. Compassionate for the world, we walk forward into death and resurrection.

Sometimes prophets discover lost (or discarded) texts and retrieve their significance. When Solomon's temple was being refurbished during the reign of King Josiah, a neglected back room was discovered. And in it was found what seems to have been the book of Deuteronomy. The exodus from bondage in Egypt and its implication for a covenanted life had become over time, like social justice and good news to the poor, *discarded images*. Today social justice is often dismissed as a tired leftist slogan with nothing to say to the contemporary economy and society. Few today, it seems, see *justice* as "the social form of the New Testament love commandment." When Deuteronomy was rediscovered, the king immediately ordered national repentance and renewal. That was then. Is anyone *today* connecting the reign of God and baptismal commissioning to a just society? To a rediscovery among ruins?

If prophets *escaped from ancient pages and appeared on the streets today*, or preached political sermons in churches, or became unwelcome uncles at Thanksgiving tables, would their messages be self-validating or disturbingly off the wall? If people who felt commissioned by their baptism to appear in city council chambers, would the mayor ask who let them off the reservation? In the sixties, protesting Berkeley students with a new vision were asked, by California's Governor Reagan, "Who let you off campus?" True prophets move resolutely "from page to stage" and appear where they're not invited. Keepers of ancient writings try to lock them in the Old Testament canon and throw the key away.

A similar attempt was made to lock up the apostle Paul when he came to town preaching on his missionary journeys. "Lock her up, lock her up" has a certain ring at recent political rallies. To those who feel commissioned to ask difficult questions comes the taunt, "Go back where you came from." In a presidential debate, Ronald Reagan said to Jimmy Carter trying to be a prophet, "There you go again." Still, prophets refuse to ask for official authorization and disdain required passports. The Chinese say: "Better than the assent of the crowd is the dissent of one brave man." Pascal admonished: "Trust witnesses willing to sacrifice their lives." Martin Luther King Jr. and Mahatma Gandhi sealed their legacies with martyrdom.

This is how prophets arise. *Seekers and seers* with good eyes and ears find themselves perplexed by all the things that have gone wrong in this world and look for the handwriting of God in history. In the face of *troubling contexts*, they begin to recall great *historic texts*. They put them together and go out into the streets. A call from God, unexpected and possibly unwelcome (remember Jonah), turns them into converts and witnesses and social critics. They are deputized as voices for God's ambitions. Not long ago the comedian Jon Stewart prophesied to Congress on behalf of healthcare for the 9/11 first responders, and even broke into tears while doing so. You can't always guess where a prophet might come from. Prophets seem to believe that *history has a plot and they are called to name it and claim it.*

Playing God's dreams on public stages is guerilla theater meant to disturb audiences and enlist them to take it outside. Like Marx, commonly called a secular prophet, they offer an analysis meant to change the world. The *freedom of God to do something new* becomes the prophet's calling card. God told Moses to tell Pharaoh, in case he should ask who's calling, that God's name is *"I will be who I will be."* American blacks decoded the liberating God of the exodus who stood in the face of the status quo. Black Christianity is not merely a derivative from the slave-master but a new discovery when no one was watching. God is not content to be a household idol kept at the Smithsonian, but an iconoclast on behalf of a new age. Like the well-known garden gnome, he keeps appearing everywhere, from kitchen tables, to church entrances, to public squares.

True religion echoes the pain of God and transforms the numbness of history. Prophets sound alarms, concentrate the mind, escape sentimentality, face evil, expose our hiding behaviors. They do not stick to the sentiments of Hallmark cards. We see again that baptism implies an *altar call*, coming forward in response to a call to commitment. To stay close to your baptism spend your life practicing *"Thy kingdom come."* Try to actually think about it when you're saying it. (Someone called the Lord's Prayer one of the great martyrs of the Christian religion. You can say it over and over without thinking.)

Prophets insist the reign of God is liberating news, and salvation is on the market. Salvation means light in darkness, sight to the blind, enlightenment, liberation for captives, return from exile, healing of infirmities, food and drink for the hungry, resurrection from the land of the dead, being born again, knowing God, becoming clothed with Christ, made right with God. It's a constant hint of what the world could be like if Christ were king and the reign of God descending.

In Francis Ford Coppola's first *Godfather* film, life and death are juxtaposed in a famous scene. As we see Michael's baby son being baptized in church and Michael listening to the liturgy "renounce the devil and all his works and all his ways," simultaneously there is being carried out, at Michael's orders, the assassination of all the heads of the rival mafia families. It is a chilling scene. What do you make of it? Is everything in the news life and death being acted out?

Baptism has become a common metaphor in public culture. The phrase "baptism by fire" originated in the nineteenth century, referring to a new soldier's initiation into battle. Do you ever hear people referring to a baptism of fire in their own lives? In literature baptism is a common sign of character development where immersion in water marks a turning point in a character's life—letting go of the past and initiation into a new future. Baptism can also refer to spiritual cleansing, from the death of the old character to rebirth and new identity. Baptism is the response to the proclamation of the reign of God.

Way Station 4

Jesus Is Calling and Making Disciples—
How Do We Answer? Do We Consent to Be Made New?

THE NEW TESTAMENT GOSPELS are a whirlwind of discipleship—Jesus calling them: Leave all and follow me; Jesus making them; the disciples repeatedly not getting it; Jesus' patient tutoring, Jesus' final commissioning of them: Go and make disciples of all nations.

You'd think that's all Christian denominations can talk about whenever they open their mouth, whether it's Catholic or Lutheran or Baptist, is making disciples. But only one denomination, founded in the mid-nineteenth century on the American frontier, names "disciple" in its subtitle: "Christian Church: Disciples of Christ." The Gospels, however, make it clear: whenever preaching or teaching on authentic Christianity, make discipleship the proper measure of action and authenticity.

Dietrich Bonhoeffer, the Lutheran martyr to Nazi Germany, famously wrote about "the Cost of Discipleship"—identifying "cheap grace" as its slippery negation. Discipleship in his view was a calling, a vocation, an identity. Try it out on yourself: Does it feel right calling yourself a disciple of Christ when introducing yourself? Or would that be pretentious? Or something only evangelicals would say? Or even cultish? If someone asked you to name the characteristics of a disciple, what would you list? If discipleship is a pilgrimage road, how far have you come? Do you tend to hang out with other disciples?

Christian sculptural art lends itself to metaphors for discipleship. If Michelangelo were in Florence making famous discipleship sculptures, would you sit for him? Does it help imagining him hammering and chipping away? Does he (or you) have an image of an inner sculpture that he is doing his best to bring out of the marble until it addresses and speaks to every onlooker? How raw is your marble self? Or is the project mostly done and ready to show? Think of the young David ready for his confrontation with Goliath, one of the most famous sculptures in the world. Interestingly, Michelangelo's contemporaries thought his marble to be unworkable. Think of Mother Mary, holding in her lap the dead body of her son, Jesus. And I will be mentioning several times in this book my favorite book title: *Fashion Me a People*. That's God speaking, and God wants the church to respond with a total life curriculum that would do the job.

The readings for Sunday from the Common Lectionary reverberate with Jesus' constant calling to follow him. The first four readings in the Epiphany season (Matthew 4:18–22; Mark 1:16–20; Luke 5:1–11; John 1:35–51) record Jesus' calling of disciples as the first thing he did at the beginning of his public ministry. In Matthew he calls Peter and Andrew, both fishermen, and famously says, "Follow me, and I will make you fish for people." Holding up their example for all future Christians, Matthew says they immediately left their nets and their home and followed him. Mark tells the same story in the same way. Luke has Jesus first preaching his inaugural sermon in Nazareth, which doesn't go well. After a healing miracle he then preaches to people gathered near the fishermen and preaches to the crowd, arranges for a spectacular catch of fish, elicits a response from Peter, and then calls his first four disciples "to catch people" and they immediately "leave everything and follow him."

Calling disciples is so important that the Gospel writers tell several additional stories about it. Mark 2:13–14 has Jesus calling a tax-collector to follow him. When this elicits criticism from the crowds Jesus replies, "I have come to call not the righteous but sinners." Mark 3:13–19 also reports that Jesus called twelve apostles "to be with him" and "to be sent out to proclaim the message" and names them. Luke 6:12–16 also reports Jesus, after a night of prayer, calling the disciples and he also names them. Luke 10:1–16 has Jesus appointing seventy others and sending them out two by two. Matthew 10:1–4 also reports Jesus choosing the Twelve. In Matthew 9 Jesus sees that the harvest is great but the laborers few. In Matthew 10:7–16 Jesus gives the disciples directions for what they are to do as they proclaim the good news. Perhaps to bolster the disciples' confidence, Jesus says in John 13:20: "Whoever receives one whom I send receives me."

Part Two: Walking 14 Stations along the Christian Way

If one goes only by the frequency of its reporting, *calling disciples would seem to be the most important thing Jesus did.* And answering Jesus' call may be the most important thing we do. Not to be too cute about it, imagine that life gives you frequent moments of "Jesus is on the line: Can you take his call?" At this way station, we practice saying yes. Which we must do again and again, not just once. Have you answered a call from God on your iPhone? Might you catalog types and frequencies of calls on your phone? Does Jesus show up on the TikTok review every night before you turn out the lights? Are you on God's algorithm?

If you are at this station with other pilgrims, why not take turns telling your stories and sharing how you're doing? What are some conspicuous developments in your own discipleship after Jesus knocked on your door? What's been the hardest for you about Christian discipleship?

The cost of discipleship is of course a common theme as well. Jesus cautions that he "has nowhere to lay his head." To someone who says he must first bury his father Jesus says, "Follow me, let the dead bury their own dead." Think about what this could mean—no excuses, no hesitation, nothing allowed to hold you back? Don't let anything get in the way of responding to Jesus' call. Luke tells the same story, underlining the point. Matthew cautions about putting family ahead of him and urges the disciples that if you do not "take up your cross and follow me" you are not worthy of him. He sums up: "Those who find their life will lose it, and those who lose their life for my sake will find it."

What can this mean?! Mark 9:49–50 warns that disciples must be salt that has not lost its savor. Luke 9:23–27 and again 14:25–35 has Jesus cautioning his disciples to leave everything and follow him, carrying the cross and giving up all their possessions. Matthew 16:24–28 requires denying yourself, taking up the cross, and following. Mark 8:34–49 says the same thing, reiterating the theme of taking up the cross. And Luke 9:23–27 also says the same thing. In John 12:25–26 Jesus says those who love their life will lose it, and those who hate their life in this world will keep it for eternal life. "Whoever serves me must follow me, and where I am there will my servant be also." It is clear that across all four Gospels discipleship is in. Is this getting tiresome?

In a touching story in Matthew 19:16–30 and Mark 10:17–31, a young man comes to Jesus and asks what good deed he must do to have eternal life. Jesus says keep the commandments, and then enumerates them. The young man says, I have kept all these. Is there anything else? Jesus says, If you wish to be perfect, go, sell your possessions, and give the money to the poor, and you will have treasure in heaven, then come, follow me. The young man goes away with a heavy heart, for he had many possessions. This raises a discussion among the disciples whether no rich person can inherit eternal life. Ched Myers shrewdly wonders whether the real command the young man refuses is the injunction to repatriate land acquired from the poor defaulting on debts. We will return to this point when examining whether "Forgive us our trespasses" in the Lord's Prayer may in fact imply the responsibility of debt relief for the poor.

And yet all ends with joyful and confident expectancy. The *great commission* comes at the end of Matthew (28:18–20): Go and make disciples of all nations. And Luke (24:44–53) ends with Jesus' last words to his disciples: Repentance and forgiveness of sins is to be proclaimed to all nations: *You are witnesses.*

If we are to take seriously the very prominent place that Jesus' call of disciples is given in the Gospels, it may still be a surprise to consider an ancillary theme: *the consistent failure of disciples to "get it."* Is that a crowd we're part of? Of course the most conspicuous failure is Peter's denial just before the crucifixion that he even knows Jesus, a story repeated in each of the four Gospels: John 18:25–27; Matthew 26:69–75; Mark 14:66–72; and Luke 22:56–62. But it doesn't end there. Matthew's Gospel has been called a *discipleship manual* for early Christianity towards the end of the first century. Consider how carefully Matthew chronicles the disciples' failures. Meditation at this way station might include enumerating one's failures, all the times we missed the point in our lives. We've been busy writing the book of our lives, but the chapter that reveals the point of it all has gone missing. Is discipleship a "discarded image" in the modern church?

In Matthew 4 Jesus laments a light that is put away under a bushel basket instead of on a lampstand—which inspired the Sunday school ditty "This little light of mine/I'm going to let it shine." In Matthew 6 Jesus cautions about a discipleship that lets wealth trump serving God. Matthew 19 offers the story of how the disciples responded when little children were brought to Jesus: *Get these kids out of here.* In Matthew 20 comes the lame request that James and John be given the two places of honor in Jesus' kingdom. Jesus rebukes them. Could he have been foreseeing that it would be the two criminals at the crucifixion who would be at Jesus' left and right hands? In chapter after chapter of Matthew, we hear Jesus continuously teaching—certainly to everyone hearing and not just the twelve disciples—what discipleship should look like. We could practice hearing and digesting this entire manual of discipleship as we walk this station. What is hardest for you about being a disciple? What was hardest for the early church at the end of the first century to whom Matthew was writing? Is the New Testament, in the Gospels, and in the letters of Paul, in fact a story about church forming, which is to say, and let us not forget, disciple-forming?

Think of your relationship to the Jesus Christ of the New Testament. Do you prefer to call yourself a Christian or a disciple? Today, if you're an evangelical you may be accustomed to saying that you've invited Jesus into your heart—and that's all that needs to be said. Many Christians mutter "Thank you Jesus" many times a day when things happen they've prayed for or things come upon us that just seem like blessings from God. (A couple years ago I deliberately began saying it a few times every day and in my evening prayers. It grew on me.) Thank-you-Jesus may be a bit hokey, or country and western, or, as with me, a little saying you've picked up from unsophisticated Christians. In liturgical worship, whether Catholic or Protestant, one does not typically say "Thank you Jesus," although there may be more elaborate ways of bringing our praise and thanksgiving.

Christians typically praise Christ and formally elaborate on who he is in the plan of God and in the universe, as when they confess the creeds of the ancient church. In liturgical churches an elaborate eucharistic prayer precedes the actual eucharistic words of institution and then functions to contextualize Jesus' life and death in the total plan of God over the ages and particularly in this sacrament.

The Lord's Prayer is addressed to "Our Father," but most Christians are aware that it was Jesus who taught his followers to pray it. As we will see in the way station on prayer, the Lord's Prayer functions as a model prayer across Christian history. Do "thy kingdom come" and "thy will be done" allude to the Christian walk of discipleship?

But all this leaves one dangling question: Where in public and private worship, or in small group Bible study, do we say the words about Jesus calling us to follow him and become his disciples? Where, every week, are words in liturgy or private prayer that caution us about the cost of discipleship? How often do we beg help in our discipled lives to "take up the cross and follow"? Should every church service conclude with a prayer that a discipleship agenda would carry us out the door back into the world? Where acting out a social gospel becomes our agenda?

Way Station 4

Spend some time in private meditation or on a spiritual retreat asking yourselves these questions: Am I conscious on a daily or weekly or lifelong basis of listening for Jesus' call to follow him and become disciples? Is *disciple* one of the words that quickly comes to mind when contemplating my Christian walk? Could you learn the discipline of regularly examining yourself and asking, How am I following Jesus at this point in my life, or in these challenging times? Could you reframe difficulties and obstacles as opportunities to "take up your cross"—or avoid doing so?

This may be the time to retrieve the fourteen stations of the cross so crucial to Catholic piety and which are certainly prayed and followed throughout the year. In Jerusalem there have been since time immemorial fourteen stations of the cross that purport to follow Jesus' original *via dolorosa* as it runs through his last days and up to the site of the cross itself. Indeed, today this way runs right through the market, so that shoppers occasionally will notice groups of Christians crossing themselves, kneeling, and praying as they look up to the artistic depiction of one of the stations. Could we "set up" in our own lives the imagination of taking up the cross and answering the call to do so—while at the market?

Marcus Borg and John Dominic Crossan are two "historical Jesus" scholars who emphasize that we are called to a *relationship* and a *life of following and imitating Christ* more than we are called to believe things. Pete Scazzero has written a book *Emotionally Healthy Discipleship: Moving from Shallow Christianity to Deep Transformation*. He thinks there is a discipleship crisis in modern Christianity. Traditional discipleship strategies fail to:

Slow down people's lives so they can cultivate a deep, personal relationship with Jesus.

Challenge the values of Western culture that have compromised the radical call to follow the crucified Jesus.

Measure our spiritual maturity by how we are growing in our ability to love others.

Scazzero calls for a discipleship practice that would create an emotionally healthy culture and multiply deeply changed people in every aspect of church life—including leadership and team development, marriage and single ministry, small groups, preaching, worship, youth and children's ministry, administration, and outreach.

In *We Make the Road by Walking: A Year-Long Quest for Spiritual Formation, Reorientation, and Activation*, Brian McLaren lays out a plan for exploring what a difference an honest, living, growing faith can make in our world today. He puts tools in your hands to create a life-changing learning community in any home, restaurant, or other welcoming space. The fifty-two (plus a few) weekly readings can each be read aloud in ten to twelve minutes and offer a simple curriculum of insightful reflections and transformative practices. Organized around the traditional church year, these readings give an overview of the whole Bible and guide an individual or a group of friends through a year of rich study, interactive learning, and personal growth.

Could the arts help, as they do in the historic stations of the cross? *Discovering God through the Arts* evokes the arts as tools for faith-building and life-changing spiritual formation for all Christians. Author Terry Glaspey, who also wrote *75 Masterpieces Every Christian Should Know*, examines:

How the arts assist us in prayer and contemplation.

How the arts help us rediscover a sense of wonder.

How the arts help us deal with emotions.

How the arts aid theological reflection and so much more.

In the Gospel of John, just before inaugurating the sacrament of the Eucharist, Jesus washes his disciples' feet—as we will see again in way station 12. At first they protest. But they may in fact be protesting the *servanthood* this act implies. In fact, Jesus is imaging the posture of the servant, something that will be required of all disciples. Think of footwashing as a habitual practice, a Christian yoga, which trains you for the posture you are called to adopt for your whole life—the way you keep yourself in the shape of servanthood.

Can you resist this lovely story from a Christian magazine? It happened in an Episcopal parish that practiced an annual foot washing on Maundy Thursday. It was time for the foot washing ritual to commence. A homeless man, a stranger to the parish, happened to be sitting in the front row. A pause. What next? The rector's five-year-old daughter happened to be sitting next to him. With no hesitation the little girl picked up a pan, an urn of water, and a towel and approached this man. As she untied his shoes and took off his socks and pushed his pants up, he began to sob. And then, as they caught on to this scene, the entire congregation began to cry. Only the little girl thought what she was doing to be perfectly natural.

If it would help to sing yourself into following Jesus, try this one: "Jesus Calls Us O'er the Tumult." It was written by a devout evangelical-Anglican woman dedicated to raising children in the faith, and it became the most popular of all discipleship hymns. It is sung to the tune of "Galilee."

Way Station 4

Jesus calls us o'er the tumult
of our life's wild restless sea;
day by day his voice still calls us
saying, "Christian, follow me."

As of old Saint Andrew heard it
by the Galilean lake,
turned from home and work and kindred,
leaving all for Jesus' sake.

Jesus calls us from the worship
of the vain world's golden store,
from each idol that would keep us,
saying, "Christian, love me more."

In our joys and in our sorrows,
days of toil and hours of ease,
Jesus calls, in cares and pleasures,
"Christian, love me more than these."

Jesus calls us: by your mercies,
Saviour, may we hear your call,
give our hearts in glad obedience,
serve and love you best of all.

Way Station 5

Jesus Teaches Us to Pray, with the Lord's Prayer as a Model— Could We Learn to Pray? Are We Paying Attention to the World Around Us When We Pray?

SOMETIMES WHEN IT'S TIME to pray the Lord's Prayer in church I quietly say it along in German, to make me think meticulously about each word I'm saying. *Vater unser im Himmel, geheiligt werde dein Nahme....* Another way to think about the Lord's Prayer is occasionally to consider a modern paraphrase, such as this startling one from the Anglican New Zealand prayerbook:

> *Eternal Spirit, Earth-maker, Pain-bearer, Life-giver,*
> *Source of all that is and that shall be,*
> *Father and Mother of us all,*
> *Loving God, in whom is heaven:*
> *The hallowing of your name echo through the universe!*
> *The way of your justice be followed by the peoples of the world!*
> *Your heavenly will be done by all created beings!*
> *Your commonwealth of peace and freedom sustain our hope and*
>   *come on earth.*
> *With the bread we need for today, feed us.*
> *In the hurts we absorb from one another, forgive us.*
> *In times of temptation and test, strengthen us.*
> *From trials too great to endure, spare us.*
> *From the grip of all that is evil, free us.*
> *For you reign in the glory of the power that is love, now and forever.*
> *Amen.*

Way Station 5

Would it be useful if you and a group of fellow Christians wrote your own paraphrase? How many different meanings could you imagine? Could your church try it out the following Sunday?

In his book *Abba,* John Cobb argues that we must see God through the eyes of Jesus. Seeing God as Father is Jesus' ultimate statement on the nature of God. This is a clue to the whole of Jesus' life and ministry, death, and resurrection. And what does *our* mean—the surrounding crowd, all people, all creation? In Matthew's account of Jesus' teaching the Lord's Prayer, evildoers and oppressors of the poor are standing nearby. Does this specifically imply including one's enemies when praying? Could "trespassers" point towards those who gain wealth by foreclosing on the property of the poor—and of the poor seeking repatriation? There is so much to consider if you take the time to meditate through the Lord's Prayer—or any biblical admonition.

What prayer practices do you follow? When? How often? Before meals? Even in restaurants? Every night at your bedside? Kneeling? Before a major venture in your life? Preceding a family trip? At the beginning of every day?

It has been said that when we immerse ourselves in a life of prayer we stay in communion and communication with God. In Sunday readings from the Common Lectionary, the Lord's Prayer is found in Luke 11:1–4, and a slightly longer form is in Matthew 6:9–13. The Gospels introduce the Lord's Prayer with these instructions: *Pray then in this way,* or *When you pray, say.* The first three of the seven petitions in Matthew address God; the other four are related to human needs and concerns. The Matthew account alone includes the "Your will be done" and the "Rescue us from the evil one" (or "Deliver us from evil") petitions—a stark realism about our life in the world. Only Protestants conclude with a doxology mentioned in some manuscript traditions: "For thine is the kingdom and the power and the glory, forever and ever, Amen."

In the fourth century of early Christianity St. Augustine offered *instructions and reflection on praying the Lord's Prayer:*

> We need to use words (when we pray) so that we may remind ourselves to consider carefully what we are asking, not so that we may think we can instruct the Lord or prevail on him. When we say: "Hallowed be your name," we are reminding ourselves to desire that his name, which in fact is always holy, should also be considered holy among all people. And as for our saying: "Your kingdom come," it will surely come whether we will it or not. But

we are stirring up our desires for the kingdom so that it can come to us and we can deserve to reign there. When we say: "Deliver us from evil," we are reminding ourselves to reflect on the fact that we do not yet enjoy the state of blessedness in which we shall suffer no evil. It was very appropriate that all these truths should be entrusted to us to remember in these very words. Whatever be the other words we may prefer to say, let them be words which those praying choose so that their disposition may become clearer to themselves.

It may seem surprising, given the central place of the Lord's Prayer in Christian piety at home and in church and specifically as part of the eucharistic liturgy, that the Lord's Prayer occurs only in Matthew and Luke and only the Lucan account appears in the Common Lectionary. However, the Lord's Prayer is also a part of the Catholic "daily offices" of matins, vespers, and compline, and is also a prayer in many marriage and funeral services, and as a common closure to many small group meetings—which gives a special mark to the event.

When I was a boy, and still awake in late evening, I would hear from the adjacent bedroom my parents praying the Lord's Prayer together every night before they went to sleep. It is often said that music and liturgy become *sedimented* into the consciousness, even into the body itself, of churchgoers for whom it has been a lifelong practice. Every Lutheran pastor, for example, knows a story of visiting a sick, barely conscious person in the hospital and hearing them lapse into praying the Lord's Prayer in German or a Scandinavian language—from their childhood. It emerges out of nowhere to comfort them towards the end of their lives.

One chief part of Luther's Small Catechism is devoted, after the Ten Commandments and the Creed, and before baptism and Communion, to the Lord's Prayer. It begins: "Our Father in heaven." What does this mean? "With these words God wants to attract us, so that we come to believe he is truly our Father and we are truly his children, in order that we may ask him boldly and with complete confidence, just as loving children ask their loving father." Luther also set the Our Father to music and it became a common Reformation hymn with eight stanzas. It was very important for Luther to emphasize, so that no prayer becomes rote, that we are petitioning that this come true among us also.

The Lord's Prayer has been called the greatest martyr in the Christian religion. Because anyone can pray it without a thought, simply going through the motions and coming to the end without noticing. Protestant

Way Station 5

theologian Jürgen Moltmann suggests that *watching and praying are like synonyms.* Praying is good, watching is better, he says. *Praying is to live attentively. Those who watch have a world in common.* Imagine the Lord's Prayer spread through prayer stations, as in the stations of the cross. Or in these fourteen stations we are walking in this book.

Just what all is in the Lord's Prayer that we may have been missing all these years? Prepare yourself for a shock. One thing to do is examine individual petitions and translate them in a slightly different way. For example, instead of "Thy kingdom come," say "Thy empire come." It could be that *kingdom* has become a fuzzy word, maybe referring to some spiritual realm of the believer's heart but having no existence in the world outside, taking up no public space. But doesn't the "reign of God" (another, even preferred way, of saying kingdom these days) imply God reaching out to every corner of the earth, even every square foot of the public square? What is it like to imply that just as God rules over all the angels in heaven, God also intends to rule over all the earth? His claim over the earth began with creation and climaxed with the incarnation. Let this come true for us!

When one gets to bread and debt—perennial concerns of the poor—what kind of alertness, watchfulness, is called for? What kind of images from material culture will be set out? It is rightly said by some commentators that hunger and debt relief are two of the greatest concerns of the poor—and here they appear in this prayer Jesus taught! A challenging suggestion from some contemporary scholars is to question the meaning of the petitions, "Give us this day our daily bread. Forgive us our sins (trespasses) as we forgive those who sin (trespass) against us." This raises the question of how the Lord's Prayer should be translated. Its presence in Luke and Matthew may be rooted in the heritage of the Old Testament known as the "seven-year debt forgiveness" laws of Deuteronomy. Is the Old Testament fifty-year Jubilee also in the imaginal background of the Lord's Prayer as well? The Bible's general concern for the poor and the context of Old Testament covenant prescriptions make it impossible to spiritualize the Lord's Prayer into sin-forgiveness and avoid any connection to debt forgiveness or trespassing as land reappropriation by displaced peasants. After all, *debt and bread are primary survival issues in peasant life.* Are we praying for bread for all, or just for ourselves? If one does not spiritualize bread, perhaps neither should one spiritualize debt. Prominent Old Testament scholar Walter Brueggemann has called debt forgiveness *the most radical idea in the Old Testament.* Imagine such a consciousness permeating every prayer station among disciples seeking to walk with Jesus. Subversive!

To avoid such reality and implications that would challenge our whole way of thinking and acting in a capitalist system, it is common to make debt about sin (and hence spiritualizable) and not money owed or forgiven. There's the rub. Social science analyses of the American underclass allude to the *permanent hand-cuffs of debt*. What does debt mean, anyway? Is it a fixed concept or one subject to cultural evolution and changing definitions? Economics is a social science, not a law like gravity, but debt is typically seen as, like gravity, a natural and objective fact. But societies may mythologize debt, in the interests of the debt-holder class vs. the debt-ridden class, so that it is accepted as an unchangeable given, not part of a system that could be changed. Do debt forgiveness and social justice go together?

Early and medieval Christianity probably understood this petition of the Lord's Prayer in terms of real-life debt or land-trespassing—if also the moral dimension of sin forgiveness. Bible translations by the time of the Reformation also understood the Lord's Prayer in such an earthly context. Many might assume that the King James Bible translation "forgive us our trespasses" alludes to the forgiveness of sins and deliberately avoids actual debt, but this is almost certainly false. In the sixteenth century trespassing is set in the context of the upper classes gradually appropriating most land, while peasants were trying to reappropriate their ancient property rights. The early Reformed traditions, typically associated with the trading and poor classes, also maintained the financial dimensions of debt forgiveness in the Lord's Prayer. For Calvin the poorer classes needed to rely on some kind of debt forgiveness, and he refused Communion to those who practiced usury! Imagine today priests who engage in "wafer watching" to guard the integrity of Holy Communion denying it to bankers and lenders! We've come a long way since then with the triumph of capitalism! Debt is no longer considered a moral issue (except for the debtor who can't pay up), usury is indispensable, and the vision of the Lord's Prayer is high off the ground, up in the sky somewhere. No banker or debt collector sitting in church when the Lord's Prayer is said gets nervous. It is probably the case that the great majority of English speakers who pray the Lord's Prayer today imagine they are dealing with sin forgiveness, but *not* a debt or trespassing that has both monetary and nonmonetary, or ownership of land, overtones. How did this sanitizing and spiritualizing of the Lord's Prayer come to be in the modern world! And especially in the United States, which has the greatest economic inequality of any developed nation? *In whose interest have the poor been removed from the social imaginary?* (For an analysis of these issues, Google various statements on debt/trespass/sin in the Lord's Prayer, especially the statement "Forgive us our debts: The economics of the Lord's Prayer," written by Marcia Pally.)

As I write, there are debates about whether President Biden and the Democrats in general and certainly independent thinkers like Bernie Sanders or Elizabeth Warren, should propose the forgiveness of education loan debt—or whether such an idea is simply too utopian. (Never mind that all of northern Europe funds all college debt with taxes on the wealthy.) The reason this is even thinkable in Europe is that college loans are most often thought of as owed to the government, rather than to private lenders. So government becomes a benefactor for public education. Recent studies in the United States lay the dilemma of soul-crushing student loan debt at the feet of money lenders, who have greatly profited from making student loans while the government mostly keeps its hands off. Some students several decades after college owe more in college debt than when they first financed it—due to interest compounding.

At the time of the 2008 Great Recession and the banking crisis and its rootedness in home mortgages, President Obama and his treasury secretary, Timothy Geithner, "just knew" that they must bail out the banking industry. But they did not "just know" that homeowners required debt relief—even as they were making it possible to preserve handsome bonuses for bankers. *This came to be called generous socialism for corporate America and ruthless capitalism for homeowners.* If big government politicians were praying the Lord's Prayer, they knew it had to mean actual debt forgiveness for banks but only sin forgiveness for the middle class who had allowed themselves to be talked into loans they couldn't afford. When a relative of my wife filed for bankruptcy, with its generous debt relief provisions, another (evangelical) relative was scandalized at her poor money ethics.

Of course prayer is not limited to the Lord's Prayer, even if it has over the centuries become the model prayer for Christians. The Psalms have been called the prayer book of the Old Testament, and in churches which use a Common Lectionary a stirring antiphonal reading or singing of the Psalms occurs every Sunday between the Old Testament lesson and the New Testament lesson. The Psalms are also indispensable to monastic prayer life, as some monks pray through the Psalter each week.

The Gospel of Luke has the most attestations of Jesus' own prayer life, private and public. The models of Jesus himself praying far outnumber the Lord's Prayer itself. Perhaps the model of prayer, of Jesus praying, is in the garden of Gethsemane where he wrestles with God over the destiny that awaits him. Do we ever experience such high stakes prayer?

The Lord's Prayer, like the Ave Maria, has famously been set to music and many soloists have sung them at weddings, funerals, and at regular Sunday services. It is no surprise that music would be a significant carrier of prayer. Before reading on, pause to see if any sung prayers come to mind. Or whether you have a soloist setting of the Lord's Prayer in your childhood memories, as I do. To this day, I can sing the whole thing, even though I haven't heard it since I was a teenager.

What kind of prayers are you accustomed to before meals? Even in restaurants? How would you compare memorized prayers to made-up on the spot prayers? My mother-in-law, a devout evangelical, was always surprised and somewhat disapproving when I led a memorized prayer before meals that I had learned in my Lutheran childhood. Are there any other petitions in the Lord's Prayer that may have meanings you haven't thought of? Try to dream some up. See if God's dreams for you are more expansive than your own for each other.

Do you use short prayers with your children at bedtime? Do you know any good ones? Are you familiar with: "Now I lay me down to sleep/I pray the Lord my soul to keep/If I should die before I wake/I pray the Lord my soul to take"? These and other prayers before meals and at bedtime will only be learned by children if they have godly parents who teach them. For a period of time in my childhood we even practiced the now unheard of practice of a prayer *after* meals as well as before. It went: "We thank thee Lord for meat and drink, Through Jesus Christ our Lord, Amen."

Prayer, of course, is a two-way street, God calling and we answering. It is sometimes said that any Christian prayer to God should include *confession, adoration, petition, and thanksgiving*. Probably you have not been thinking of that entire catalog when you make up your prayers at bedtime. A famous hymn-prayer is "Softly and Tenderly Jesus Is Calling":

> *Softly and tenderly Jesus is calling,*
> *Calling for you and for me.*
> *See, on the portals he's waiting and watching,*
> *Watching for you and for me.*
> *Come home, come home, You who are weary, come home.*
> *Earnestly tenderly Jesus is calling, calling O sinner, come home.*

Way Station 5

A famous and beloved prayer sung in worship and at revivals is "What a Friend We Have In Jesus."

> *What a friend we have in Jesus, all our sins and griefs to bear!*
> *What a privilege to carry everything to God in prayer!*
> *Oh, what peace we often forfeit, oh, what needless pain we bear—*
> *All because we do not carry everything to God in prayer.*

A very famous and emotionally stirring evening song is "Abide with Me."

> *Abide with me, fast falls the eventide.*
> *The darkness deepens, Lord, with me abide.*
> *When other helpers fail and comforts flee,*
> *Help of the helpless, Oh, abide with me.*

In the Taizé monastic community, a common petition, chanted over and over and over, is: "Jesus, remember me, When you come into your kingdom." If you learn saying this on many different occasions, over and over and over, you may find yourself fashioned anew—expectantly waiting for God your Father to appear in your midst. This was the petition to Jesus from a thief on the cross. From the Iona Community in Scotland comes this sung petition: "Take, Oh, Take me as I am, summon out what I shall be; Set your seal upon my ear and live in me." And the *Kyrie eleison* (Lord have mercy) became the first of five parts of the historic Sunday liturgy. Our lives are surrounded with the practice and the opportunity for prayer!

A hymn I have always known will be sung at my funeral some day is the Reformation hymn "Lord, Thee I Love with All My Heart," the third stanza of which Bach used to close his Magdalenion:

> *Lord, let at last thine angels come, to Abrahm's bosom bear me home*
> *That I may die unfearing; and in its narrow chamber keep*
> *My body safe in peaceful sleep until thy reappearing.*
> *And then from death awaken me, that these mine eyes with joy may see,*
> *O Son of God thy glorious face, my Savior and my fount of grace.*
> *Lord Jesus Christ, my prayer attend, my prayer attend,*
> *and I will praise Thee without end.*

This book is about way stations in the Christian life, that mimic these same stations in Jesus' life. Prayer, along with meditation and perhaps pious conversation and dialogue, seems the perfect accompaniment to walking the stations—just as it is in the historic stations of the cross.

Part Two: Walking 14 Stations along the Christian Way

Prayer stations! It has a nice ring to it. We have seen earlier the writer Anne Lamott's famous summary of prayer: Help, Thanks, Wow!

In the Introduction to this book I called attention to the work of anthropologist T. M. Luhrman, who spent a couple years in participant-observation of American Pentecostal Christians. Although she seems to be an agnostic, she shows a remarkable ability to listen in on and grasp the piety of such Christians and titled her book *When God Talks Back*. She sees Christian piety, as in one's prayer life, as a two-way conversation. She named a more recent book *How God Becomes Real: Kindling the Presence of Invisible Others*, claiming that prayer is "paying attention" in its purest form. It requires a "faith frame" as its mode of thinking. You have to believe someone is on the other end of the line of your religious conversation. To practice prayer is to kindle the realness of God. Over time, prayer changes people. It becomes evidence of the reciprocity of religion: we speak/God responds. Or vice versa. To pray, she witnesses in her subjects, is to express a sense of how things should be. The practice of prayer becomes its own outcome. It changes the person who prays. In prayer one imagines a better world and how one would live within it. Asking in prayer becomes an assertion of hope. It makes a religiously defined world real by putting it out there, in public space. Every day in prayer, she sees, Christians address all of God's presence within themselves.

Consider the New Zealand prayerbook's version of the Lord's Prayer, with which I began this way station. Challenge yourself to write your own version of the Lord's Prayer. Let it become a persistent prayer that defines you.

Prayer can become a consistent marker of your piety and your religious reflection. And the easiest thing to reduce to rote practice, like giving your spouse a quick kiss before leaving the house. If you hang a picture of Jesus praying on your wall, it may help to mark a "home altar" that both stages a place to go to pray and reminds you to do it.

Way Station 6

Jesus Eats and Drinks with Outsiders and the Excluded—
Could We Learn Christian Table Manners?

JESUS' EATING AND DRINKING practices are reflected in several readings from the church's Common Lectionary. Famously, Jesus miraculously fed five thousand people out of five loaves and two fishes and there were considerable leftovers. In Matthew 14:13–22 Jesus saw a great crowd of followers, and he had compassion for them. The Greek word suggests he felt so sorry for them it made his stomach hurt. Towards evening, the disciples suggested sending the crowds away—as we too might do? Not our problem, the disciples implied. "You feed them," Jesus says. Out of five loaves and two fishes Jesus makes enough food for five thousand, with leftovers! Mark 6:30–44 tells the same story, but notes the crowds looked to Jesus like sheep without a shepherd. John 6:1–15 also tells this story and has the crowd responding: "This is the prophet who is to come into the world." Luke also has an account of this story. So all four Gospels found this noteworthy.

Eating and drinking together at table (or campfire) can be noteworthy markers of human relationships, what is going on socially, what is the relationship among people. Given that eating and drinking are extremely common human practices, except perhaps among the poor and desperately hungry, the social aspects of meals can be very telling if people are paying attention. Consider Paul's severe reprimanding of the Corinthian congregation for preceding their eucharistic celebrations with high-end eating and drinking among the more well-to-do members of the community. Once their extravagance is over, the poorer members would have arrived and the regular worship begun. This was a gross sin against the community. The observation of "table manners" is so common to anthropologists that they have developed the concept of *commensality* as a key to social customs and orders. How people come together around food is widely observed as equally important as the eating and drinking itself. Sharing a meal with others is a distinctive and much valued social activity. Relationships are built and communities developed around food. The Bible sometimes denounces the gluttony of the rich whose lavish eating comes from robbing the tables of the poor. The opposite would be a potluck, a well-known practice in religious communities. How meaningful it is, then, when Christians heed Jesus' example and extend the ministry of potlucks throughout the community—a form of sharing and preaching a social gospel.

Since all four Gospels tell the same story of feeding the five thousand, differing only in some of the details, we must ask ourselves what it all means, what conclusions we are to draw from such complete and repetitious reporting of Jesus' public ministry expressing itself through the distinctive table manners of eating and drinking. Remember also that the conclusion of Matthew 25 spells out that a judgment day inquiry asks whether believers have fed the hungry, attended the sick, housed the homeless, as if in "the least of these" Christians are seeing Jesus himself. This story of ministering to all kinds of desperate people occurs against the backdrop of Jesus' ministry coming to a fulfillment in which the church is called to see him elevated as a messianic king. It is this very king of heaven and earth whose presence is to be recognized among the sick and the unhoused and the imprisoned and the hungry. My book *Matthew 25 Christianity: Redeeming Church and Society* unpacks all this.

To drive home the new commensality that Jesus inaugurates, Mark 2:15–17 and Matthew 9:10–13 tell the story of Jesus sitting at table with tax collectors and sinners, which is to say social and moral outcasts. Of course this produces criticism from the guardians of table fellowship, who can't believe a real prophet would break bread with such people. To which Jesus replies: "Those who are well have no need of a physician; I desire mercy, not tradition-keeping; I have come to call not the righteous but sinners." In Mark 7:1–9 and Luke 11:37–54 the keepers of traditions accuse Jesus of lacking proper table manners of washing. Jesus here and elsewhere admonishes that what is inside coming out is much more to worry about than what is outside coming in.

Way Station 6

Through much of my life I assumed Jesus' famous feeding of the five thousand was just a miracle story: Jesus can turn a meager amount of food into an amazing abundance. Nothing for us to do here except marvel at the miracle. Now I have come to see that this is an anticipation of an eschatological banquet in which all the world is invited to eat with Jesus. So this is a story about Jesus vastly expanding the idea of *table fellowship*. "Table manners" have common conventions. One is not to break the rules. They are hierarchical by definition, determining who is worthy and who is to be excluded. They make visible and concrete what exactly is going on in social systems, who is included and who is excluded. The table, after all, is the original example of social networking—or not. And of course the gospel is, among other things, the good news that the strict and socially exclusive rules of eating and drinking have been abrogated. Imagine a church which every Sunday produced a lavish potluck, with the good news that the poor are excused from bringing anything—except themselves.

A recent addition to the study of table manners is "digital commensality"—what effect cell phones at the table have, or the possibilities of eye-opening Zooming. Following this lead, I have allowed myself to imagine using digital technology (the latest version of an apple strap-on headset that uniquely enhances what can be seen) to *see, while we are eating, all the world's people who are in hunger distress* and what call they have on my table. Imagine regularly using in church services the latest digital toy, the Oculus Rift, which is a set of telescoping glasses one puts on and which alter what is seen into disturbingly lifelike visions. Could one use an Oculus Rift, whose images would be projected on a large screen while the sermon goes on, to imagine the world's hungry before an entire congregation? (Another use for the Oculus Rift would be to put it on and look at the hungry or unhoused and simultaneously see Jesus sitting there among them, a required ability Jesus depicts in his last-judgment story in Matthew 25.) In monastic communities sometimes the refectory (dining hall) has the monks eating in the presence of a great wall painting, often of Jesus' Last Supper. The most famous example of hallowing a meal by eating it in the presence of an artistic depiction of Jesus' Last Supper is DaVinci's famous painting of that scene on a wall in a monastic refectory in Milan, Italy. Go see it. Try it out in your dining room.

Lately a saying among New Testament commentators is that "Jesus broke bread and boundaries." Think about that, about what boundaries your community would be willing to break in order to welcome the poor and hungry and unhoused and sick. Minimally, what would it mean to invite the poor to share the Eucharist with you, and the passing of the peace that precedes it. Or a ceremonial foot washing, with the underprivileged getting their feet washed and the more comfortable practicing the yoga of servant ministry. But more, it could mean your church reaching out to the community to feed the hungry. The Lutheran church I go to in Chico, California, recently adopted a strategic plan statement which calls for "a place at the table for everyone."

Could this become a stage in social evolution, mastering an open-ended etiquette of the table, opening religious commensality to strangers? Turning outsiders into guests is precisely what God was doing in the ministry of Jesus. And what we are called to imitate. This could become the meaning of copying this way station in Jesus' life onto ours. *Or inviting outcasts to meet you at this way station for mutual discussions of good news in the religious community.* To make sure we get the point, Luke 14:12–14 has Jesus saying: "When you host a dinner, don't just invite friends and rich neighbors, so they can reciprocate. No, when you host a banquet, invite the poor, the lame, and the blind, and you will truly be blessed."

As we try to follow and mimic Jesus in this way station we can be thinking about how all societies replicate social, economic, and cultural norms through their eating and drinking practices. Local tables symbolize what is going on in the larger society. Table fellowship establishes and replicates bonds of fellowship not to be violated. The table becomes the social site where ritual distinctions are made—between clean and unclean, rich and poor, Jews and gentiles, religious and irreligious, black and white (as required practices in the South so sternly demanded), sometimes men and women (as at some country clubs). Uncleanness is contagious and so we tell ourselves that eating and drinking must be socially patrolled. *Uncleanness may be defined by ethnicity, occupation, class, wealth, or gender.* The poor are never invited to the president's inaugural banquet, or even to the Rotary's annual Christmas party.

But what if one ate and drank promiscuously, what if the table became the site where the paradigm-breaking reign of God touched down on earth, what if the compassion of God overflowed into everyday eating and drinking? What if assumed continuities in social systems were challenged, if discontinuities were overcome? Jesus provides food prodigiously as a pointer to a new age banquet to which everyone will be invited and no one excluded. At a wedding reported in the Gospel of John, a foretaste of divine-human celebration and abundance, Jesus responds to his mother's gesture and turns 180 gallons of water into wine! In the divine commonwealth Jesus is previewing, all the world are welcomed as table companions, and no one is to be excluded.

Imagine eating and drinking as *religious acts*, for example the celebration of the Eucharist. "All baptized Christians are welcome," many churches say, while others stipulate that no one but their own in-group is welcome. There passwords are required to get through the firewall surrounding the table. *But Jesus seems to reverse the normal order of repentance first and fellowship second, conversion first and then communion.* Just think about that! Surely you first have to prove you're worthy, then the invitation comes! Jesus reverses that order. So in Jesus' ministry it goes like this: *initial contact, shared communion, life-changing conversion.* Imitating this, St. Francis once advised his brother monks overly worried about thievery by those outside the monastery gate: Offer these threatening outsiders food for several nights; then move up to wine; only after that is it time to discuss inquiries about the Franciscan order.

The point is to win sinners and outsiders back to their lost but rightful place in the family. Of course, this may seem to undermine the position of the righteous, as we see in the case of the prodigal son's elder brother who resented his father's generous spirit. The pious and the learned and the pure are easily provoked when their accomplishments and entitlements do not seem rewarded. (Today, people who can afford their food are preoccupied with imagining that poor people might be using their food stamps to buy crab legs or lobster.) Of course, Jesus always has his eyes on a great heavenly (or earthly?) banquet to which outsiders are particularly welcomed. Hence liturgies of the Eucharist today sing of, even if they do not practice, "a foretaste of the feast to come." Nondiscrimination is not a nicety but a fundamental, a conspicuous sign of outreach and ingathering. The table is a miniature map of the wide dimensions of God's reign.

The *inclusiveness* that Jesus evidenced throughout his life, and especially at table, is not only a marker for contemporary Christians to follow, but also a check on the oppressive and self-righteous certainty of too much religious faith. Inclusiveness tempers our proclivity to make God fit into our constricting doctrinal sentences. We have a tendency to want God to color within our lines. *How odd that Jesus allowed himself to be defined by his low concern for social definitions.* Women, foreigners, public sinners, tax collectors, soldiers—all were welcomed into the feast. Was Peter remembering his early life with Jesus when he had a vision, in the book of Acts account of the early church, in which he sees that all ritual boundary markers must be left behind as Christianity opens itself, and its table, to the world? The entire missionary activity of the apostle Paul, who was called, like us, to be a disciple, took God's inclusive reign public and made it available to all comers across the Mediterranean world. *The divine guest list is always larger than the disciples' imaginations.*

Today, against the encroachments of a secular age, the religious impulse is often to choose *exclusion* as the mark of religious fervor. We think it shows how seriously religious we are. When Catholic bishops practice their "wafer watch" (against Pope Francis's catch-up instructions), they mean to single out potential guests at the table who do not practice the orthodoxy of the table—the opposite of Jesus' practice. Protestant fundamentalists exclude from the community of true Christians all who do not use the same words for religious experience as they do. Orthodox rabbis, especially in Israel, closely guard the definitions of who is a true Jew. Other religions have their own problems with inclusiveness. Many Shiite Muslims object to Sufis for being too mystical and not cognitive enough, while other Muslims are condemned for insufficient commitment to jihad or sharia law. In the current enthusiasm for exclusion as a mark of serious religion in a wishy-washy age, the radical inclusiveness of Jesus' own ministry goes unrecognized. *Jesus' ministry is an undiscovered country.* Just imagine if LGBTQ people were found to be living there. Or if women were to be discovered dressed in liturgical vestments.

Jesus loved to tell stories that feature *replacement guests*—someone other than those who dither about their invitations. If the customary heirs can't make it, God will fill the empty seats with outsiders. Of course Jesus always has his eyes on a great eschatological banquet to which all the world is welcomed, particularly those who have never been invited to a party before. Public schools are sometimes ahead of the churches in commensality. If Johnny is going to bring an invitation to his birthday party to his class at school, the whole class must be invited. Nondiscrimination is not a nicety but a fundamental and conspicuous sign of outreach and ingathering. If even public schools can get this, surely the Christian table can become a miniature map of the wide dimensions of God's reign. Imagine the mayor in a town enforcing the churches' commensality practice!

Think how the righteous father of the prodigal son threw away his dignity when he spied his errant son coming home and ran through the street, his robes flying, to welcome him. He ordered a banquet to celebrate the son's return from exile, a real reason for a party. Jesus' stories like this were meant to set off explosive charges in people's hearts and worlds. Does compassion trump holiness-keeping? The good Samaritan did not trouble himself worrying about the contamination of his purity by the man in the ditch. Everything in this station subverts normal assumptions. *It is Jesus who becomes contagious.* Meanwhile, the ritually tidy just waft "thoughts and prayers" to those in desperate situations. They couldn't imagine God might be found on the road to Jericho!

In John 6, Jesus enters a discussion connected to the feeding of the five thousand but surely evoking the Eucharist as well. Astonishingly, Jesus calls himself "the bread of life." Indeed, the bread that came down from heaven no doubt evoked the Old Testament manna with which God fed his hungry people in the midst of their exodus from Egypt. Christians who insist on an unearthly, spiritual meaning to their religion should contemplate what it could mean that Christ calls himself bread, food for the hungry.

To draw a distinct conclusion: take seriously Jesus' pattern of ministerial eating and drinking, then draw an expansive map of how this way station could be expanded throughout your world. Beginning with the unkempt who wander by this station just when you're getting serious.

Can we not but sing about all this? And Google how much Christian art has come from these Jesus' commensality stories? A particular favorite among all who have been on a summer retreat around a campfire is the African American spiritual (often sung by Joan Baez) "Let Us Break Bread Together."

> *Let us break bread together on our knees;*
> *let us break bread together on our knees;*
> *when I fall down on my knees*
> *with my face to the rising sun,*
> *O Lord, have mercy on me.*
>
> *Let us drink wine together on our knees;*
> *let us drink wine together on our knees;*
> *when I fall down on my knees*
> *with my face to the rising sun,*
> *O Lord, have mercy on me.*

Part Two: Walking 14 Stations along the Christian Way

Let us praise God together on our knees;
let us praise God together on our knees;
when I fall down on my knees
with my face to the rising sun,
O Lord, have mercy on me.

A hymn evoking a larger vision is "We Come to the Hungry Feast" (Google it!). The text avoids the spiritualization of hunger and connects religion, and Christ himself, directly to earthly need, as also in the Lord's Prayer's "Give us this day our daily bread." Oh, and forgive us our debts as well. To keep our religious lives in shape and lively hallowing memory, we sing a hymn like this. And we find ways to welcome those who are always hungry. Ask yourself: How can we who pause at this way station in Jesus' and our own lives welcome those who are missing?

Perhaps we have come to the rightful conclusion of our meditation on and practice of this way station. Jesus has made a way for us, and now we are wayfarers. But wait! Everything we have considered so far assumes that Jesus set an example for us, that we try hard to follow it but often fall short. What if assumed continuities in social systems were challenged, if discontinuities were overcome? Jesus provides food prodigiously as a pointer to a new age banquet to which everyone will be invited and no one excluded.

What if Christian reality is much worse than trying but sometimes failing to practice Jesus' commensality? What if, in fact, we have set the rules of the table to prevent Jesus' practice from coming true? What if we have specifically set up boundaries to *prevent* a holy commensality. As our tax codes do! Or at least not removed those that have existed? You may see where this is going.

What if white supremacy or patriarchy were deliberately practiced social and cultural markers that keep Jesus' own practice from coming true? We could scarcely move on to the next station without acknowledging, and naming, the most egregious by far of the church's sin against Jesus' inclusiveness: the very long history of the *wedding of the church and white supremacy*. The great tragedy of racism is not primarily that we have declined to invite people of color into our Christian community, but, worse, that *we have deliberately set up a social system to exclude them,* that this system has been in place for a very long time, that it is only ever so slowly being questioned, that many people are outraged when told to confront their racism, and so teaching our dark history is beginning to be excluded from public schools. To look around, scrutinize social systems, and ask what they have come to mean.

It's not that there are no witnesses to and champions of Jesus' deliberate inclusiveness. In *Jesus and the Disinherited,* Howard Thurman was already in 1949 crying out on behalf of the excluded people of color and denouncing a system deliberately constructed to shut them out. In 1970 James Cone wrote *A Black Theology of Liberation* and then in 2011 he forced white Christians to confront the astonishing claims of *The Cross and the Lynching Tree,* which we will consider in way station #13 on the crucifixion of Jesus. Meanwhile, a so-called *whitemanism* continues to exert its counter-story to Jesus' inclusiveness.

But astonishingly, the evangelical publisher Zondervan in 2020 sold 100,000 copies of Jemar Tisby's compelling book *The Color of Compromise: The Truth about the American Church's Complicity in Racism.* It not only claims that white Christians have been missing in action (they didn't take the lead in following Jesus' revolutionary commensality), but they have often specifically worked *against* racial justice. They manned the system Jesus set out to disrupt. Tisby called for a vigorous Christian activism by white Christians. His book is a stunning and unrelenting denunciation of white supremacy from the colonial period to the present. He writes: "When faced with the choice between racism and equality, the American church has tended to practice a complicit Christianity rather than a courageous Christianity. They chose comfort over constructive conflict and in so doing created and maintained a status quo of injustice."

Don't dig in now against a "critical race theory" that makes people feel bad. The blurb for Tisby's book says: "*The Color of Compromise* is *not* a call to shame or a platform to blame white evangelical Christians. It *is* a call from a place of love and desire to fight for a more racially unified church that no longer compromises what the Bible teaches about human dignity and equality. A call that challenges black and white Christians alike to stand up *now* and begin implementing the concrete ways Tisby outlines, all for a more equitable and inclusive environment among God's people."

So this way station is not only a call for thoughtful Christians to follow Jesus' example, but a challenge to form Christian communities that analyze these issues and then set out to change things to match Jesus' vision. Christian social ethicists make the point that actually creating space in which to do good is an act of moral imagination. It opens up space for God, as we will see Jesus' parables also doing. Room for action toward the good is

Part Two: Walking 14 Stations along the Christian Way

cleared. Questions about what sorts of persons we should be and how we should live return to public discussion. Consider this book, too, to get you started: Eric Mason's *The Woke Church: An Urgent Call for Christians in America to Confront Racism and Injustice.*

Way Station 7

Jesus Offers Healing Amidst Human Brokenness— *Could the Church Become a Field Hospital and We Its Chaplains?*

THE COMMON LECTIONARY KEEPS church members alert to healing ministries by featuring many readings from the Gospels in which Jesus heals disease both physical and social. He heals a man with an unclean spirit, a leper, a paralytic, the daughter of Jairus, the daughter of a foreign woman (but only after testing her faith), a deaf man, a blind man and another blind man named Bartimaeus, on the Sabbath a man with a withered hand, Simon's mother-in-law, and then many more that evening. The Gospel of John tells a remarkable story about healing a man born blind, which leads to an argument with the Pharisees who refuse to accept this over who is really blind—them!

It is worth mentioning here that when Jesus tells a story about the last judgment when the world is lined up and questioned whether they were able to see Jesus in "the least of these," they are enumerated and their needs come to be known in the Middle Ages as the "corporal works of mercy"— feed the hungry, give water to the thirsty, clothe the naked, shelter the unhoused, visit the sick, visit the imprisoned, and ransom the captive. Later, Catholicism added, bury the dead.

Now start imagining how you might practice imitating this way station in Jesus' ministry. Is the church responsible for universal health care? Or lobbying politicians to make health care a government responsibility (as in most European countries)? Whether the church does health care itself or lobbies government to do it, or cooperates in a just society, it is an example of the social gospel—seeing that the good news proclaimed in churches makes it out to the streets and neighborhoods. What if you were a hospital chaplain, or just a volunteer visitor at your local hospital? You would be given the names of new patients and any religious "preference" they state. Would you just visit those with the same designation as your own (Lutheran, Catholic, Methodist, Presbyterian, evangelical) or would you try out visiting everyone on the list? What would you do—pray with them, try to heal them (!), anoint them with oil, offer them some kind of "last rites" if they are dying?

When I returned to Concordia Seminary for my fifth-year reunion, one of our classmates told us a gripping story of how he, who had been a lifelong Lutheran, was becoming a Pentecostal! His change began when, newly intrigued by Pentecostal traditions, he attempted to heal a member of his Lutheran congregation while on a hospital visit. It caused a stir. The elders of the congregation met and cautioned him that "you can't heal Lutherans." This was when he moved to a new denomination. He assumed that you could heal Pentecostals, and he intended to do so.

Most pastors-to-be undergo Clinical Pastoral Education (CPE) before they leave seminary. One of the functions is to test the psychological as well as spiritual state of the pastor. I once knew a seminarian who was not certified for a call into the ministry when too many red flags went up during his CPE. How might you succeed or fail at CPE? What does it take to visit and minister to the sick? Of course, if you do not "pass by on the other side" on the road to Jericho, you can find the sick in many places other than in hospitals—in their homes, on the streets, in prisons, in homeless shelters or halfway houses, in drug treatment centers, in hospices for the terminally ill. You could seek to qualify for some of these ministries, whether or not you are a pastor or priest! When the hospice movement came to Chico, I volunteered to help set it up and plan for its ministries.

What do you think about anointing the sick with oil? Catholic priests regularly do this but it is much less common among Protestants. It is not that the oil is magical, but that it is a means to register a deeply human response, one that connects the healer and the healer's community and the sick. What about last rites, a famous and well-known practice among Catholics, almost indispensable, but scarcely practiced among Protestants? When someone is clearly dying, and is a Catholic, a priest is immediately called to their bedside. Also known as the Commendation of the Dying, last

Way Station 7

rites are the last prayers and ministrations given shortly before death—to those terminally ill, or mortally injured, or awaiting execution. As I write, two instances were attracting wide attention and criticism. When a British parliamentarian was mortally injured a Catholic priest was not allowed to offer last rites because it was a crime scene. An American awaiting capital punishment was denied the ministrations of clergy because of fussy rules surrounding the administration of capital punishment. Eventually the Supreme Court reversed the local ruling and granted him his wish to have his pastor present during his execution. How do we represent or insert Jesus' presence into people's greatest needs? Are we called to be Jesus' messengers, following his example, trained for this task at this way station?

Protestants, too, of course have institutionalized ministrations to the sick and the dying, while also encouraging spontaneous ones. A Lutheran corporate and communal order of healing, printed in its hymnal, introduces healing as a regular ministry in these words:

> The order for healing is an expression in worship of the church's ministry of healing. Here all who sense the need for God's healing in any aspect of their lives may join in prayer for others and themselves. Here each person may come to receive a word of blessing and prayer. Here each one may also receive a physical gesture of healing: the laying on of hands, which may be accompanied by anointing with oil. These signs, first given in baptism, tell us again that we are sealed by the Holy Spirit and marked forever with the cross of Christ, who is health and salvation for the whole world.

It is suggested that the minister introduce services of healing with these words: "Our Lord Jesus healed many as a sign of the reign of God come near and sent the disciples to continue this work of healing—with prayer, the laying on of hands, and anointing. In the name of Christ, the great healer and reconciler of the world, we now entrust to God all who are in need of healing." The service includes prayers of intercession and the laying on of hands, concluding with a blessing and sign of peace.

A subtle issue, easy to miss, is the fact that in many cases Jesus' healing is extended to *social illnesses*. Leprosy, which Jesus goes out of his way to heal, was in Bible days not only a terrible physical disease but also a socially isolating one. It marked the person as unclean and untouchable. Are there diseases in the modern world that we feel okay about avoiding and writing off as beyond the responsibility of worthy people? Drug addiction? AIDS? Alcoholism? Mental illness? Poverty? What are all the kinds of healing that people seek and how perceptive and open-minded are our responses? What responsibilities do the church—and the state!—have towards the sick, whether in hospitals, or healthcare systems available to all? Whether bodily illnesses or human degradation or social ostracism, Jesus, fulfilling the vision of Isaiah, means to come with good news for all in their captivities. Are Christians responsible for seeing to it that their state or country offers universal health care? Would this be an example of turning the gospel into the social gospel? Would such justice be the social form of love? Should Christians attempt to institutionalize communal values into their national life? Should gathered Christians who hear Scripture lessons about healing also carry this aspiration out the door, when they become "sent Christians"? At this way station do you feel commissioned as a sent Christian? Does care for the sick belong to the "natural law" or the sense of the sacred in our legal systems, that many, including the founders, see underlying our country?

At this station does Jesus the way-maker turn you into a wayfarer? We are called to imitate this way station. In the New Testament, healing stories are like *enacted parables,* in which what is happening is more than what meets the eye, in which space is being opened up for the presence and movement of God. Perhaps more than with any other way station, this one cries out from sick beds and death beds and healing places and prison cells, and invites you as a disciple imitating Jesus to stop by and exercise Jesus' ministry.

Contemporary Jewish tradition inherits from the Old Testament the precious idea of repairing the world *(tikkun olam).* Some say this idea of repairing is almost mystical—returning sparks of divine light to their source by means of ritual performance. A lovely image is grandma in her rocking chair, mending the blanket of the world.

Social and not just physical forces are challenged in the New Testament accounts, and a larger conflict comes into view. Unpreoccupied with his own purity, a typical religious obsession, Jesus touches an unclean woman, and makes her whole in body and soul. Jesus intervenes in the social world, refusing to accept diseases' ritual uncleanness and social ostracism, thereby impugning the claims of society's boundary-keepers. Social exclusion, for example, is one kind of illness begging for Christians' attention. When Jesus heals a blind man in John 9, he plays with religious definitions of who actually can see and who cannot. All who long for exodus come to see, and all who enslave them do not see—what God's intentions are, God who told

Moses to tell Pharaoh "I will be who I will be." What Jesus can see puts him on a collision course with religious authorities who claim to be the doorkeepers of God's presence and hold the monopoly on what can be seen. The true miracle of Jesus' healings is the picture that emerges of human wholeness in a liberated world.

While everyone knows that Jesus went about healing all sorts of people, the impact and meaning of his actions in the first century are likely to be lost in the twenty-first century. Some make a distinction between disease, which medical practitioners attempt to treat, and illness, which can be, or was, considered a larger problem. The physician offers a minimal response, Jesus a maximal. The human body is a microcosm for the macrocosm of social and political society, an organic symbol of a carefully bounded social system. Leprosy, for example, is more than a skin disease. Isolating the leper is an attempt at boundary segregation across the community. (Notice all the things we project onto the undocumented immigrants, which challenge their very humanity, and we treat homelessness as a possibly deserved affliction for which society bears no responsibility.) There is acute anxiety about bodily orifices being subject to contamination, and this leads to confusions about orifice and surface, what's outside and what's inside. And this leads to confusion about purity and holiness vs. shame and separation. Lately we have come to call the homeless the *unhoused,* to make the point that homelessness is not a disease they have somehow caught. They are unhoused because a social system has unhoused them.

Jesus' agenda is much larger than the surface symptoms of leprosy; he means to reconstitute the entire community as the people of God. Jesus' "healing miracles" are meant to symbolize the larger shifts underway with the arrival of the reign of God. Amidst the "shame culture" that surrounded some kinds of disease, Jesus means to bring back to life those who have become dead to society. The two religious figures in the parable of the good Samaritan believe they cannot render aid to the man in the ditch because it would render them impure. The individual event and the larger symbolic process are brought together in Jesus' compassionate telling of a foreigner's ministrations. Radical changes in a social world, and in the covenant between God and humans, are underway. Do we fear that getting too close to alcoholics or the mentally ill might render us unclean? Or complicit?

Of course Jesus' healing has left a lasting legacy in the Christian tradition. Early Christianity became known for its ministry to the sick, medieval Christian hospices became the first hospitals of Europe, run by monks, and the present wide expanse of Catholic healthcare and its distinctive values is well known. But as highly scientific medicine has become one of the great accomplishments of the modern age, without a distinctive religious tone to it, it may be time for the church to follow Jesus in asking the larger questions about human illness and acting compassionately and imaginatively in their face. Where besides hospitals does the church need to be present?

Just as Jesus the good shepherd or Jesus who feeds the hungry, Jesus the healer should be a central icon through which we see, understand, and embrace Jesus. And the world, through his eyes. Are Christians contributing to the widespread literature on achieving a good death? I have myself written a book called *The Last Passage: Recovering a Death of Our Own*.

Way Station 8

Jesus Preaches Sermons That Reveal a Gospel from God for All Peoples—Do We Hear a Gospel That Sounds Like This Every Sunday and Preach It in the Midst of a World Longing for Good News?

CAN YOU SPOT GOOD news when you hear it? Do you define the Christian community as the place where good news is regularly proclaimed? Imagine that at the end of each worship service, on their way out the door, parishioners were asked to fill out a short form asking: Did you hear any good news today? How did it reach you? These note cards would become a vehicle for the church council and the pastor to review how their services are being experienced.

Some Lutheran theologians and preachers are heavily invested in a movement called the Crossings Community. It is dedicated to (obsessed with) preserving the distinction between law and gospel: because/therefore, no/yes. The law curbs sin in the world and accuses us so we see the need for Christ. The gospel is the good news that Christ is there for us, rooting for us, offering his own righteousness for us to wear. Slightly more complicated is that some insist on a "third use" of the law, for example the availability of the Ten Commandments to map out how we should be loving our neighbor. Another issue is Luther's insistence that all Christians are *simul iustus et peccator,* simultaneously saint and sinner.

Of the many way stations, perhaps the clergy, preachers, and evangelists should spend quiet time here. To say that preaching itself, imitating Christ bringing good news, belongs at this station is to insist it must be done well and belongs as a station in churchly life. Apparently successful preaching is a matter of tone; hence the complaint, "Don't preach to me." Or does this complaint indicate a defect in the hearer? But preachers themselves must demonstrate careful preparation and delivery, and reflect training and theory.

Preaching should be considered an inaugural constitution of the church, as we see clearly in the New Testament witness to the early days of the church. Where all should preaching be heard? Certainly in churches and on campuses. To say also in soup kitchens may suggest, as some suspect, it is the price of admission. When Jesus came to Nazareth at the beginning of his ministry, he opened the scroll before him to read from Isaiah, and concluded saying, Today this is fulfilled in your ears. This was Jesus in Luke 4, quoting Isaiah from 61: "*The Spirit of the Lord is upon me, because he has anointed me to bring good news to the poor. He has sent me to proclaim release to the captives, and recovery of sight to the blind, to let the oppressed go free, to proclaim the year of the Lord's favor.*"

This lately has come to be called the Nazareth Manifesto. What if sermons, at least on special occasions, would come to be known as "manifestos"? Or inaugurals. Or for the braver, what if every Sunday's bulletin, or a dramatic slide on the wall, would label "manifesto," where the sermon usually comes!

If you mostly relate to Jesus, and follow him, as the incarnate Son of God, the Word made flesh dwelling among us, the one who broke bread with his disciples (and the world), the promised Messiah of Israel and the prophets, the one who took the enmity of the world up into the very life of God on a cross which became his unlikely enthronement, the one whom God raised from the dead and made triumphant news to the world, and who ended his earthly time by sending his disciples to preach the gospel to all nations, and especially good news to the poor—if all that *resume* is preoccupying you, you may not actually have noticed that he was a convincing preacher. One that all preachers wish they could emulate (but often don't).

Very many of the Gospel verses that attest to Jesus' preaching have made their way into the Common Lectionary, which means that pastors who take as sermon texts witnesses to Jesus-as-preacher will themselves be engaged in imitating Jesus on certain Sundays. Preaching seems to be the essence of Jesus' ministry, especially if his acts loudly speak for him and undergird his words.

Way Station 8

Mark 1:14 registers the beginning of Jesus' preaching. "Now after John was put in prison, Jesus came into Galilee, preaching the good news of God, and saying, 'The time is fulfilled, and the kingdom of God has come near; repent, and believe in the good news.'"

Luke 4:14–22, as we saw above, reports Jesus' inaugural sermon in Nazareth. "All spoke well of him and were amazed at the gracious words that came from his mouth." In case your pastors come to expect what congratulation is coming to them, fresh from seminary, after every sermon, consider how this story ends. As they began debating whether this was just Joseph's boy, they were filled with rage, drove him out of town, and tried to throw him off a cliff! Oh that some sermons would produce this effect.

Matthew is packed with Jesus' preaching. Right after enduring his temptations, Jesus begins his public preaching. Matthew 4:17 announces: "From that time Jesus began to proclaim, 'Repent, for the kingdom of heaven has come near.'" From then on, it's unrelenting! Many scholars divide the entire Gospel of Matthew into five discourses, or sermons, from Jesus, each one concluding with "when Jesus had finished speaking": 7:28; 11:1; 13:53; 19:1; and 26:1.

The Sermon on the Mount at Matthew 5–7 is probably Jesus' most well-known and quoted sermon. It is the longest continuous discourse of Jesus found in the New Testament and has been one of the most widely quoted elements of the Gospels, holding forth the central tenets and the radical vision of Christian discipleship and community. The Sermon on the Mount includes the Beatitudes and the Lord's Prayer. To many Christians, the Sermon on the Mount contains the central tenets of Jesus' mission. (Luther was perhaps less taken with Matthew because he does not sound enough like Paul.)

The Beatitudes are a list of those Jesus considered "blessed," or "fortunate," due to his coming and their subsequent inclusion in the kingdom of heaven. They are a welcoming statement to this group of people, and as an introduction to the sermon. One may say they constitute *an imagined utopian community*, a community unlike most found on earth, a community Jesus will go out of his way to evoke and welcome, a community made whole by the gospel, by good news. If Jesus' sermon is intended for the instruction of all Christians, then this community of the downtrodden and rejected is identified as those the larger community of Christians are called to welcome, *to constitute them as the chosen community who otherwise will never be blessed*. The Beatitudes name and constitute those who are blessed

Part Two: Walking 14 Stations along the Christian Way

to be welcomed into the kingdom of heaven. The Greek word translated as "blessed" can also be rendered as "happy." Matthew names eight blessings, while in Luke there are four, followed by four woes. The Beatitudes represent a new set of ideals that focus on love and humility rather than force and mastery. They echo the highest ideals of Jesus' teachings on spirituality and compassion. They name the new community Jesus calls. As you walk this station with fellow pilgrims, be on the lookout for "the blessed" whom you should be welcoming. (Are they over there sitting on a curb?)

It occurs to me that if a community of middle-class or wealthy Christians were to hear the Beatitudes aright, they might assume that it must certainly describe them (!) and they might not pause to consider that the people the Beatitudes go out of their way to name are the poor and neglected of the earth who are being selected for good news—waiting for comfortable Christians to recognize and constitute them as the lost sheep now found, a new utopian community constituted by the gospel.

A second discourse, sometimes called the Missionary Discourse, is in Matthew 10. These instructions to the named twelve apostles are sometimes called the Little Commission (in view of the Great Commission at the end of Matthew). The point seems to be that the apostles, and then the Matthean church, are now designated as the stand-ins for Jesus. Think of your pastor's preaching as occurring in the name of Christ, and as appointed by Christ. Martin Luther insisted that preaching the gospel was an indispensable mark of the church. This is a heavy agenda for pastors to get right and to shine through all the cute stories they love to tell.

The third discourse, in Matthew 13, is often called the Parabolic Discourse. Sitting outside by a lake, Jesus tells the parables of the tares, the mustard seed, and the leaven. Going inside then he tells the parables of the hidden treasure, the pearl of great price, and drawing in the net. Does your pastor like to tell stories? Do they unlock new worlds for you, invite you to see things in a different (or disturbing) way? We will look at how parables work at a later way station. Suffice here to say that they are considered genuine works of art that invite the curious into a familiar world, close the door, and surprise everyone with a convicting point. They cannot be reduced to the latest episodes from the pastors' family.

The fourth discourse is called the Discourse on the Church, Matthew 18. Including the parables of the lost sheep and the unforgiving servant, they anticipate the future community of Jesus' followers, the church, and the role of his apostles in leading it. *Are you open to considering your Christian*

Way Station 8

community as the successor to Jesus' own ministry? Could you think of your pastor as the *substitute preacher for Jesus?* (It could be good for both of you.) Does your pastor share liturgical space with you and open worship up to multiple voices? My pastor in Chico began an adult instruction class on preaching, and then appointed each participant to take a turn actually preaching a sermon. They were quite wonderful, even if (or because) they were so autobiographical. Up close and personal.

The fifth discourse, in Matthew 25, is sometimes called the Discourse on End Times, with parables of the ten bridesmaids and the talents, and the story about the last judgment. The coming destruction of the Jerusalem temple and an eschatological mood surrounding the coming of the reign of God are the setting. The stage is being set for a final exam, waiting to test all Christians: Did you always look for and find me among "the least of these"?

To call Christians disciples of Christ, to recognize that Jesus moves through his ministry calling disciples, is obvious. Have you thought *that Jesus the preacher may be calling you to be effective preachers—using him as your model?* Does effective preaching saturate the church's worship life and launch it into the world outside? Is walking this station a constant practice that keeps you and your church in good fit? Can you imagine yourself preaching a sermon on campus? Or in the public square?

Way Station 9

Jesus Welcomes Women and Outsiders, and Calls Us to Do the Same—*How Do Women and Outsiders Fare in Our Congregations?*

IN THE SUMMER OF 2023 the Southern Baptist Convention, the largest Protestant denomination, voted to exclude from its fellowship any congregation that called a woman pastor. And, of course, the Roman Catholic Church has for a very long time forbidden the ordination of any women into the priesthood, on the grounds that Jesus and his twelve disciples were all male. They appear to assume that the meaning of the incarnation was not God's embrace of *humanity* but his embrace of *maleness*.

Patriarchy is a system in which men hold the power and women are excluded from it. In the Catholic tradition, this primarily establishes a male order of priesthood in the structure of the church. But many of the evangelical Christian traditions believe the Bible teaches that God created a hierarchy in the human condition in which the husband-father, as well, is the head of the household, a family leader, provider, and protector. Male authority in the home typically carries over into the structure of the church. Critics, of course, see this as a social and cultural traditionalism, but not instituted by the Bible. But it is also said that patriarchy is the attempt to adhere as much as possible to Old Testament structures of family and society.

During the second half of the twentieth century a vibrant Christian feminism arose to oppose the subordination of women and to establish the equality of women with men. An example of these efforts appears in exemplary book titles: *Theology of the Womb: Knowing God through the Body of*

Way Station 9

a Woman; The Ordination of Women: An Essay on the Office of Christian Ministry; How God Sees Women: The End of Patriarchy; Mary, Mother of God: In Search of the Woman Who Changed History; Jesus through the Eyes of Women: How the First Female Disciples Help Us Know and Love the Lord; Ten Lies the Church Tells Women; In Memory of Her: Feminist Theological Reconstruction of Christian Origins. Imagine groups of women (perhaps together with men) gathering at this way station to discuss such books. Might there be a women's library on the grounds of this station?

As we begin to study Jesus' own example, we might consider whether woman is a good symbol of the outsider—then and now. If we begin to reflect on how women are treated in local parishes we would find vast differences—increasing percentages of women in seminaries and then as pastors and bishops of the church, women leaders in local churches, including serving as presidents of parish councils. These are not merely secular encroachments of modern feminism, though that undoubtedly plays a major role—including reading the Bible with disencumbered presuppositions.

The Gospels are full of stories about the socially transgressive Jesus. Meditate on this at this way station. Lutheran countercultural preacher Nadia Bolz-Weber likes to insist that Jesus, standing in for God, always takes the first step by announcing that you are his child, confirming your new identity and status and grounding—and working out from there. Consider the evidence, and how it plays out in the Gospels.

In John 4:4–42 Jesus meets a Samaritan woman at a well, where Jesus has gone to rest on his way through Samaria. He says to her, Give me a drink. She wonders how Jesus, a Jew, is even talking to her, a despised Samaritan. Jesus says that if she even had a clue about the gift of God waiting for her, she would have asked for *living water*. But you have no bucket, she says, and where would you get such water that our ancestor Jacob provided when he gave us this well. *Jesus says that when he gives water, she will never thirst again. Give me such water, she responds.* The question of her husband comes up, or rather her fifth or sixth husband. Undaunted, Jesus says he knows all about her husbands. Since he seems to be a prophet, she asks a (diverting) religious question of the day, whether one can worship at this mountain or must go to Jerusalem. Jesus says there are much bigger questions whose resolution now awaits. (It is becoming clear that Jesus was seeking a meeting, not water.) He tells her that ethnicity or gender are beside the point, because the time has come when all are invited to worship the Father in spirit and in truth. God is much bigger than social divisions and prejudices.

She says, aghast, I've heard a Messiah is coming. Jesus says, I'm the one. The woman runs back to town to announce her discovery. The disciples return, curious that Jesus has been talking to a Samaritan woman. You must be hungry, they say, but Jesus answers he has food they do not know about. Clueless, they wonder who's been bringing him food. Jesus says his food is to do the will of him who sent him—to welcome such a woman as this. Look around, there are many such, the fields are ripe for harvesting. The woman turned into an evangelist in her village, and they all came to meet Jesus, and he stayed among them for two more days. Of course the men of the village decline to give the woman credit, for they have come to see Jesus with their own eyes. Consider all that is going on in this story, and what you might learn from practicing it.

Now on a roll, John tells a follow-up story about Jesus healing invalids on the Sabbath. The religious critics respond: This prophet seems to know no boundaries! You just don't do the work of healing on a holy day. But religious rules do not fence in the movement of God. The righteous persecute Jesus for breaking the rules, but Jesus says his Father is still working and he is too.

Mark 5:21 and following tells a story about how Jesus, on the way to perform a perfectly acceptable healing of the daughter of a synagogue leader, pauses to notice a strange sorrowful woman who has suffered bleeding for many years and is thus ritually impure as well. She thinks she might be healed if she can just touch this famous prophet. She is immediately healed, and Jesus says, Who touched me? The disciples, always clueless, say, Man, it's a big crowd. The woman, found out, presents herself. Jesus says, Daughter, your faith has made you well, go in peace, and be healed of your disease. Then people arrive to tell Jesus that while he was messing with this unclean woman the daughter of the synagogue leader died. Jesus takes care of her too.

Matthew 26, Luke 7, and John 12 (great coverage) tell the story about a woman with ointment who, seeming to grasp the path toward death Jesus is on, anoints him in advance. In Matthew's version, the disciples criticize her for wasting so much money on expensive ointment, but Jesus famously says that people everywhere will come to tell this story, "in memory of her"—a phrase fully embraced these days by feminist scholars. In Luke, it is a notoriously sinful woman who comes to Jesus, at table with the rich and powerful, to anoint him with ointment and with her unceasing tears. The Pharisees sniff that if Jesus were a true prophet he would have recognized

Way Station 9

this woman's unworthiness and not been so clueless. But Jesus accuses them for being obtuse about how those with large debts learn to love deeply those who offer forgiveness. Jesus then holds up this "unworthy" woman as an example to the haughty and self-righteous. In John, it is Mary, sister of Martha and Lazarus, who lavishly anoints Jesus, anticipating his imminent death. Judas takes offense at the waste, when the money could have been given to the poor—or to the purse he was in charge of.

In Luke 8, several women in Jesus' entourage had been cured of evil spirits and infirmities, including Mary Magdalene healed of seven demons. Jesus welcomes their ministrations. In a story in Luke 13, Jesus heals a long-crippled woman and sets her free, and she stands up straight praising God. While the leader of the synagogue calls it sacrilege to heal on the Sabbath, the crowd rejoices!

John 8 depicts a scene in which a woman caught in adultery is thrust in Jesus' face by religious patrols to see if he will condone the mandated penalty of stoning her. Very famously Jesus responds, Let him who is without sin be the first to throw a stone. As they all slink away, Jesus compassionately responds to the woman, Has no one condemned you then? And then: Neither do I condemn you; go and sin no more. In a contemporary work of religious art, the woman is portrayed cowering up against a wall on a city street, Jesus reaching out to her, and placing himself between her and a policeman with a billy club standing nearby in a threatening posture. This brings the stakes to contemporary observation in a startling way. Whose regime is the policeman enforcing? Whose side is Jesus on?

What would Jesus do? is a popular question among evangelical Christians to stir them to do the right thing. But in many cases, we don't have to ask this conveniently hypothetical question. In this station we can see what Jesus *did* do. When Christians are in doubt about biblical interpretation or struggling to tell the difference between deeply held prejudices and God's intentions, they can view and contemplate the unmistakable actions of Jesus that disclose what the reign of God would actually look like if it appeared among us, as Jesus declared it did in the opening of his ministry.

No doubt Jewish and Christian Scriptures were born in the midst of deeply patriarchal societies. And shame cultures obsessed with ritual purity and with what goes into the mouth rather than what comes out. It may be hard to get back to a time when women out of the control of men could practically be thought of as whores. Jesus' itinerant ministry consisted in a freewheeling dislodging of such a social order. But still today the veneer remains, so that some modern Christian women decide to leave the institutional church in order to set themselves free. Or stay in, but not buy in. Or, most hopefully, commit to radical reform from the inside.

It is one thing to have difficulty trying to walk Jesus' walk into new and uncharted territory, like haltingly welcoming women and outsiders into the full fellowship of the Christian community. But it is quite another to refuse to imitate Jesus' example by appealing to the Bible itself! Recent scholarship in American religion argues that the doctrine of biblical inerrancy, which emerged with special force in the South during the nineteenth century, has been put to use precisely to support arguments against integration and in favor of white supremacy. And to establish patriarchy as God's plan for humanity by appealing to a view called *complementarianism*, which claims to fully honor women but as always subordinate to their husbands, including, of course, forbidding of women's ordination.

Operationally, a function of the inerrancy doctrine has been to keep the clock turned back and support arguments against gender equality and social justice, and in favor of establishment racism. Not only has biblical inerrancy been made to support positions like white or male supremacy, but also to condemn "liberal" views on these issues as departures from the faith and betrayals of Christianity. Inerrancy became a sword for discrediting evangelical competitors and to establish a deeply held conservatism on race and gender. Inerrancy became the way to establish a Bible that serves white masculine authority. Inerrancy undergirded old-time religion in the South especially. To rub it in, the opposite of the social conservatism legitimated by an inerrant Bible was labeled secularism. In contrast to this "secularism" was the reproduction of hierarchies with white *men* on top. They eschew the more accurate terminology of sexism, misogyny, and patriarchy, holding that God ordained separate hierarchical roles in church and the home for men over women even if he created men and women "equal before God."

Kristin Kobes Du Mez's *Jesus and John Wayne: How White Evangelicals Corrupted a Faith and Fractured a Nation* is a recent bestseller that sees evangelical Christianity replacing the Jesus of the Gospels with an idol of rugged masculinity and Christian nationalism. She sees that the key to understanding this kind of Christianity is to recognize the centrality of popular culture in contemporary American evangelicalism. Evangelical books, films, music, clothing, and merchandise shape the beliefs of millions. So too does it on the indispensable problem of guns. And evangelical culture is teeming with muscular heroes who assert white masculine power in defense of "Christian America." Chief among these evangelical legends is John Wayne, an icon of a lost time when men were uncowed by political correctness, unafraid to tell it like it was, and did what needed to be done. Challenging the commonly held assumption that the "moral majority" backed Donald Trump in 2016 and 2020 for purely pragmatic reasons, Du Mez sees that Trump in fact represented the fulfillment, rather than the betrayal, of white evangelicals' most deeply held values: patriarchy, authoritarian rule, aggressive foreign policy, fear of Islam, ambivalence toward #MeToo, and opposition to Black Lives Matter and the LGBTQ community. A much-needed reexamination of perhaps the most influential subculture in this country, *Jesus and John Wayne* shows that, far from adhering to biblical principles, modern white evangelicals have remade their faith, with enduring consequences for all Americans. She argues that the reproduction of white masculine authority and the erasure of its abuses is a core characteristic of evangelicalism's history, not a Trumpian aberration. She sees toxic masculinity as a particularly lamentable by-product of this movement. In *The Making of Biblical Womanhood: How the Subjugation of Women Became Gospel Truth*, Beth Allison Barr has written a devastating historical analysis that sees "biblical womanhood" is a white, patriarchal construct that betrays a biblical position that had set women free. She demonstrates that opening the future requires controlling the past. This book aims to set us free from the historic (false) trajectory of patriarchy and complementarianism. She unsettles existing certainties and demonstrates what comes from *culture* and what comes from *Christ*. She sees that the time when racial or patriarchal presuppositions were expressed in the language of biblical idiom and evangelical theology may now be coming to an end.

To return to the question whether biblical inerrancy necessarily mandates these views, it must be asserted that Martin Luther, or the Protestant Reformation, did not develop an inerrancy doctrine. Luther in particular insisted the absolute authority of the Bible lay in its proclamation of the gospel of God's reconciling humanity, by grace, through faith. He did not appeal to an abstract theoretical doctrine of Scripture's inerrancy, but the centrality of Scripture coupled to grace and faith.

No doubt God has been evoked, induced, and commandeered to bless the power and privilege of men. Said better yet, patriarchy was seen as God's own plan, God's order for human relations, God's vision for the church. Jesus was a man and so were his leading first-century disciples, so all Catholic priests have to be men, if they are to imitate Jesus' ministry and role in God's plan. Instead of what we actually can see in the fourteen stations of Jesus' life, in this patriarchal view *Jesus' maleness is what most counts*. And never mind that the historical and game-changing doctrine of the incarnation is about God, in Jesus, becoming *human (not male)*.

The history of theology, no doubt including careful reflections on the stations of Jesus' life and attempts to turn discipleship into imitation of Jesus, is the record of *how people with new questions arising from new circumstances find new answers by following God's lead*. To those who have eyes to see, Jesus' ministry, in which women and the socially marginalized or unclean are singled out for divine favor and special treatment and specific inclusion, is already clear enough, but still always waiting rediscovery and reclaiming.

Chaucer imagined the "accidental community" that pilgrims, hitherto unknown to each other, gradually become as they make the journey. Will the contributions of women who walk the way be unique and will their male neighbors, walking together with them, learn from them? Will a new discourse evolve? Will it be discovered that women sometimes seem to speak a different language, or, if that is too essentialist, constitute *an alternative discourse community* waiting to be heard? If language arises from and is processed through experience, have women's experiences gone missing in the development of religious language?

Even though Jesus and some of the Hebrew prophets were comfortable with and sometimes appealed to feminine metaphors for God, why is the *earth as mother* still mostly missing from Western ways of thinking? Has our inability to name and to *mourn the lost mother* played a role in our ecological crisis? Religious feminists may have to dismantle oppressive idols and recreate new life-giving images. When Job closely interrogated God face to face, the entire cosmos opened up for him. When women meet in radical forums to practice new forms of worship and find new words for God and learn to do theology in their own voices, male hierarchies are loud in condemnation because the walls of tradition have been breached. Might women teach men to discover, and expect, the motherly dimensions of God?

There is Jesus and there are those women he shamelessly welcomes and interacts with. Are the Jewish and Christian stories of sin and salvation mostly framed in terms of male experience and male suspicion? Why wasn't Jesus preoccupied with women's "dangerous sexuality"? In John's Gospel, the esteemed teacher Nicodemus doesn't get it, and the Samaritan woman at the well does. Maybe Jesus' own style was, in some ways, more like that of first-century women than men. *He feeds, he washes feet, he identifies with the process of labor and delivery.* And turns the religious world upside down.

It has lately become popular to name women the "first apostles," because, having gone early to the tomb, they became the first witnesses to the resurrection on Easter morning, a story told in all four Gospels. They were the first disciples the risen Christ appears to, most famously Mary Magdalene. And they became the first witnesses to the male disciples who were mostly in hiding.

A common contemporary practice in biblical interpretation is to practice a "hermeneutic of suspicion" in which one closely engages biblical texts in order to discover women hiding, or hidden, or suppressed. Sometimes translators, through history, have turned Greek female names into male names—because of course the text could not possibly be referring to women. The English Bible translators were particularly good at disguising women's names as men's. Down through church history, in such figures as Hildegard of Bingen, people who are looking can find women who, in effect, got themselves "ordained" and were authorized to preach and do theology. It could be said of such women, as was recently said of some women in Congress, "Nevertheless, she persisted."

A "hermeneutics of hunger" or "of women" or of "the poor" has recently been practiced in order to discover intentionally what is beneath one's nose. For example, if a church is planning a class on justice for the hungry, one first goes out to find a sample of such people and invite them to participate in the class. Just imagine a painfully hungry person sitting in a comfortably middle class study group trying to get a grasp on hunger and what to do about it. She could perhaps share a thing or two.

I have used women as the chief example of a way station to be imitated because the Gospels are full of surprising stories about Jesus unexpectedly bumping up against women. But I also invite readers to consider these women as stand-ins for people of color, or lower class people, or LGBTQ people unaccustomed to being welcomed by a church—or any of the many who are not the kind of people church evangelism committees are looking for.

Finally, what about the arts, visual images, hymns? I have already alluded to a modern picture of a slightly unsavory woman against an urban wall as the police close in. We know what's going to happen. But wait, isn't that person standing between the woman and the law Jesus himself? The picture is stunning in its effect. It's enough for an entire discussion in a study class.

Consider too these provocative hymns by Carolyn Winfrey Gillette, the most prolific of contemporary hymn writers—on topics neglected or ignored. Better yet, sing along if you know the tune.

God Of the Women
(tune of "Be Thou My Vision")

God of the women who answered your call,
Trusting your promises, giving their all,
Women like Sarah and Hannah and Ruth—
Give us their courage to live in your truth.

God of the women who walked Jesus' Way,
Giving their resources, learning to pray,
Mary, Joanna, Susanna, and more—
May we now give freely as they did before.

God of the women long put to the test,
Left out of stories, forgotten, oppressed,
Quietly asking: "Who smiled at my birth?"—
In Jesus' dying you show us our worth.

God of the women who ran from the tomb,
Prayed with the others in that upper room,
Then felt your Spirit on Pentecost Day—
May we so gladly proclaim you today.

O God of Phoebe and ministers all,
May we be joyful in answering your call.
us the strength of your Spirit so near
That we may share in your ministry here.

That Woman in the Crowd
(tune of "The God of Abraham Praise")

That woman in the crowd—she could not stand up tall;
Her back was bent, her head was bowed—and Jesus saw!
That Sabbath day of rest, he saw her misery;
He told her, "Woman, from your ailment you are free!"

He saw another thing, when others thought her odd;
He saw a child of Abraham, a child of God!
And soon she saw it, too! She must have been amazed!
She stood up tall and offered God her thanks and praise.

A leader said, "You're wrong!" for sin was what he saw.
He could not understand this One who broke the law.
The Sabbath rules were strict and work was not allowed—
Not even when it healed a woman bent and bowed.

Christ said, "What matters most? What rules will you obey?
You care for ox and donkey on the Sabbath day!"
For Jesus knew the truth—that people matter more,
And God loves things that heal, encourage and restore.

What barriers do we build to God's abundant grace?
Do we want church to be a perfect, law-filled place?
Or will we dare to love—to see what Jesus saw—
That God's great welcome matters more than rule and law.

Christ Would Not Cast the Judgment Stone
(tune of "Where Cross the Crowded Ways of Life")

Christ would not cast the judgment stone
At one who stood afraid, alone;
He stopped the violence in that place
By speaking truth and showing grace.

To one the world would not protect,
Christ offered care and showed respect;
In one whom others cast away,
He saw a child of God that day.

May we show Christ's compassion here
To girls and women bound by fear,
To those who live in silent pain,
To those who can't go home again.

We pray for those who from their birth
Are never shown their human worth;
We pray for women hurt this day
While others turn their eyes away.

Part Two: Walking 14 Stations along the Christian Way

O God, may we who call you Lord
Now labor for a world restored,
Where, in your image, all will be
Protected, valued, safe and free.

She Suffered Twelve Long Years
(tune of "The God of Abraham Praise")

She'd suffered twelve long years! She longed to be made whole.
The pain to body, mind, and spirit tore her soul.
She felt the weight of shame, the lonely days of doubt.
Till one day she heard Jesus' name and she reached out.

As Jesus walked along, a crowd was gathering fast.
The people jostled close to him as he walked past.
She would not call his name; perhaps a touch would do.
She brushed against his clothing's hem as he passed through.

As soon as she reached out, she felt her body healed.
She knew the kingdom blessing of God's love revealed.
And Jesus sensed it, too. "Who touched me?" Jesus said.
The woman came and told the truth with fear and dread.

Yet Jesus' words were kind: "Now daughter, go in peace.
Your faith has made you well and healed you from disease."
He sent her on her way, her health and hope restored.
Her life was changed from her encounter with the Lord.

We've suffered many years from things that should not be;
We're ill in our own lives and in society.
Lord Jesus, now we pray that you will heal us, too.
Give us the faith to reach out, fully trusting you.

So how, then, to walk this station? Imagine groups of women walking this station as an act of self-empowerment, achieved through Jesus' acceptance. Imagine groups of women and men achieving true community in one body of the church while walking this station together. Imagine church leaders conducting retreats (perhaps led by women) at this station, where they will come to see that if Jesus could "ordain" women as worthy of God's special attention, so can the church. Imagine husbands and wives walking this station where they will come to abandon patriarchy and achieve equality.

Way Station 9

Imagine arranging to meet the poor, the least of these, at this station where we will practice seeing Christ's presence among them.

But will it take Oculus glasses?

Way Station 10

Jesus Teaches Wisdom in Parables That Open up Alternative Worlds with Space for God—*Will We Walk Into That Space and Learn to Live In It?*

HAVE YOU BEEN TOLD that parables are more than quaint stories? Do people mostly not tell new parables today? Why would that be? Would it be pretentious if you decided to make some new parables to share with friends walking the stations with you? Do pastors try out new parables in their sermons?

Think for a moment to see if you have a bucket list of favorite parables. Why do you like them, or remember them? Doesn't it seem odd that only Jesus told parables, that they are unique to his teaching style? Are there analogous literary devices that other people have used?

By the way, are there parables that, at least at first hearing, you don't get? Are you inclined to think the parable was kind of dumb and so you're embarrassed that Jesus bombed? But here's the thing: parables are often not obvious. Because Jesus often told them to disclose the mysteries of the kingdom of God. Jesus became incarnate (God in human form—what a surprise!) to proclaim the arrival of the kingdom of God. But as Jesus repeatedly suggested, the ways of God are often mysterious. So you may not get them, at first. You may need tutoring. When you do get the point, you may not like it. Parables can produce discomfort. Or imply conclusions you have been determined to reject. Like many of Jesus' sermons, some of his parables may call for repentance, for changes in your life. If you're walking these stations in groups, you may discover that some parables arouse fierce disagreements. Differing possible meanings may contend with each other. If you say, Why didn't Jesus make the parables more transparent, more easy to grasp?, it may be because the kingdom of God is not immediately obvious. God's reign may run into human misunderstanding, or even rejection.

A common understanding of how parables work goes like this: Before a closely listening crowd pressing in, Jesus tells a parable. At first the parable may seem familiar territory, so the crowd relaxes into it. It's as if Jesus is saying, See that house over there? Notice its four walls and roof and windows and door. Let's walk over and check it out. When everyone is inside, Jesus closes the door, so people have to think within its comfortable confines. But then Jesus comes to the point, and it blows the roof off, or breaks the windows. What! people yell in response. Even the disciples mostly didn't get them on first hearing, or until they'd been hanging out with Jesus for a long time. Even then! They didn't get the crucifixion after all.

I like to say that parables open your imagination and understanding to *make room for God in the everyday world.* So the roof may need to come off or the windows be broken so God's presence can appear and be felt, and God's intentions and way of being can be understood. The point is that a secular society (or the capitalist economic system with its fundamentalist free market) may be constructed precisely so that God cannot appear, nor his presence be felt. Even on children's television, sometimes only Mr. Rogers can intuit the presence of God.

The Gospels are replete with the parables Jesus told, and the Gospel readings assigned for every Sunday by the Common Lectionary reflect that as well. Luke contains twenty-four parables, with eighteen unique to Luke. Matthew contains twenty-three parables, with eleven unique to Matthew. Mark contains eight parables, with two unique to Mark. Sometimes what some readers call parables would better be called "sayings" that are pithy and brief.

Here are twelve of the most famous parables, in ascending order of significance, selected by one scholar:

> The talents (Matthew 25:14–30)
>
> The marriage feast (Matthew 22:1–10)
>
> The sower (Mark 4:3–9 or with Jesus' explanation 4:3–20)
>
> The wheat and the weeds (Matthew 13:24–30 or with Jesus' explanation 13:36–43)
>
> The mustard seed (Mark 4:30–32)

The rich fool (Luke 12:13–21)

The lost sheep (Luke 15: 3–7)

The sheep and the goats (Matthew 25:31–46)

The dishonest manager (Luke 16:1–9)

The good Samaritan (Luke 10: 25–37)

The prodigal son (Luke 15: 11–32)

The unmerciful slave (Matthew 18:23–35)

Maybe you would choose differently for your bucket list. Or, maybe you'd like to name a few of the most famous parables. Or the most difficult ones. Or your favorites.

Here's a famous four list:

The ten virgins
The rich man and Lazarus
The prodigal son
The good Samaritan

Here's a famous thirteen list:

Good Samaritan
Prodigal son
Mustard seed
Lost sheep
Talents
Sower
Ten virgins
Workers in the vineyard
Rich fool
Wise and foolish builders
Unforgiving servant
Pearl of great price
Good shepherd

Now pick three or four parables and discuss their probable meanings. How do they make room for God, open up moral obligation (who's my neighbor), make you see what you are determined not to see? Watch how human life (even yours) is pried open in surprising spaces to make room for God. When God finally gains admission to your imagination, what does God say? Here, for your immediate reflection, are several famous parables and their probable meanings.

Good Samaritan: Be alert for who your neighbor might be, no matter how different from you or how unsympathetic, and offer your help, because love and service demand it.

Prodigal son: The hero of this parable is God, with the compassionate, ever-forgiving father as the stand-in for God. Consider too the elder brother who prides his own self-esteem over God's love.

Mustard seed: The kingdom of God may start out apparently insignificant, and easily ignored, but its trajectory will surprise you and you should train yourself to expect God's surprises.

Lost sheep: One of the surprises about Jesus' acting out the reign of God is his concern for the lost, even singling out those who most need finding. Jesus came seeking such people.

Sower: When the seeds that symbolize the work of God are scattered, they inevitably fall on a variety of ground, some on ground highly favorable to the reign of God quickly bearing a good crop, but others on a path where birds (who are they?) came and ate them up. Others fell on rocky soil without much depth and so they quickly withered in the heat of the day, yet others among thorns (who are they?) that quickly choked them. What kind of soil are you? What roles do shallowness, or worldly cares, or the heat of the day play as detriments to your Christian life? Get an inspection, consider a diagnosis, measure your weaknesses!

Ten virgins: If something big like the celebration of God's presence is heading your way, don't miss it because you're careless or not alert or missing the point of it all.

Rich fool: Accumulating wealth or success is the secret to prosperity or a good life. Isn't that so? How do I act out such foolishness in my own life?

Wise and foolish builders: When building the edifice that is your life, did you notice if you were situating it on sand? Or is there evidence you built it on solid rock that can sustain it?

Pearl of great price: If and when you come upon the evidence for the greatest treasure in life, don't blow it. Sell all, give up everything you have in order to claim it.

Good shepherd: Life has many hired hands who do not ultimately care for the duties they are charged with. When the dangers of life encroach, they take off. What the world needs is a good shepherd who will truly care for the sheep, even laying down his life for them. Jesus is that Good Shepherd.

Some commentators call *Jesus himself a parable of God.* Some healing miracles are seen as *enacted parables.* Jesus turned his own life into *teachable moments* meant to disarm his audience and open them to the reign of God. Parables offer us captivating and disarmingly familiar stories, the kind we all know. In the view of parables whose point is confrontation, consider again this Occupy Wall Street anecdote: A famous artist constructs an intimidating massive sculpture which comes to be called the "Wall Street Bull." (Guess why.) Years later, another artist comes along and creates an inspiring but delicate sculpture which comes to be called "Fearless Girl." Unintentionally, the Fearless Girl is situated face to face with the Wall Street bull. Wall Street mythology, with the giant bronze bull as its icon, is called into question by those seeking the meaning of life. Who is the "Fearless Girl" anyway? Jesus lures his hearers into situations reflecting their own assumptions, but then challenges them with surprising counter-stories. Wait, is Jesus the fearless girl? Is God acting out the answer to economic imperialism?

As in scenes from the musical *Godspell,* Jesus moves through scene after scene of common life blowing peoples' minds. With confounding paradox and liberating reversals, Jesus opens determined hearers to consider alternative worlds—worlds of good news to those whose circumstances oppress and confine them—if they can but see. Jesus proclaims the arrival of new forms of community that show off a new kingdom of God. Jesus grants little validity to commonly accepted truths, yet his new tellings seem uniquely convincing. New wines require fresh wineskins, he says. In our own times, old Reaganesque political and economic stories about welfare Cadillacs and the lazy poor, so loved by those in power, are turned upside down. Good news is diverted to the encampments of the poor, who typically have no address.

God's political campaign starts out small, with all those lacking the means to vote, but portends immense consequences. To tell his story, Jesus must first challenge the stories told by the religious establishment. Or the common culture. As did the Old Testament prophets, Jesus sees them as arrogant upstarts who have taken over God's vineyard and betrayed the intentions of the master winemaker. Jesus would have understood the viral Facebook posts that today decry the culture-bound Christianity that betrays his image. Jesus has the audacity—so bold is his God-story—to claim that those who come to hear him *have come into the presence of a life-changing reversal of the world's course.* No risk-averse preacher who fears political speech or politician who fears the implications of the poor has been running on this platform. Jesus tries to provoke his audience to respond, to join him on the new God-stage he has constructed. This new arrival of God to reclaim lost territory incites a crisis in human life. The stage set trembles, the curtains fall. Aroused audiences leap from their seats and rush the stage to become part of the plot. Might you and your friends do the same, joining the stage where the action is and where fresh actors are taken up into newly available parts? Crises turn to joy, the prophets had already said, when the poor get good news and everyone discovers new meaning to life.

Good news specially aimed at the poor would not be a Wall Street intuition. The Jesus story is countercultural, not assuring bedtime reading for the 1 percent, not for the fifty billionaires who own half of all national wealth. Telling stories is a way to construct a provocative (and alternative) social world, as myths do. After they have taken Jesus' teaching to heart, disciples are meant to go out and create new communities, new forms of society that mimic the God whose story is being suggestively told. At the turn of the Roman Empire, the Christian message became embedded in ways that would change the history of Europe by arising to carry Christian uniqueness into a perilous age. So parables as new paradigms deliberately subvert the world we take as a given and disestablish its truth claims. Followers of Jesus come to live in that new world. The sixteenth-century Puritans who thought they were on to something called themselves nonconformists. And so did their indignant enemies.

Jesus' pithy little mustard seed comparison occurs in Matthew 13:31–32, Mark 4:30–32, and Luke 13:18–19. He says that the coming of God to start the revolution might seem like a tiny mustard seed that surprises everyone with its growth. The arrival of the reign of God is not compared, as expected, to the proverbial cedar of Lebanon that offers shade to the beasts and lofty heights to the birds in its branches, but surprisingly to the little mustard bush. Never mind the pedantic comments that mustard plants never indeed achieve the size to attract birds: Jesus' point is that everything you know about things is far exceeded by what the arriving kingdom of God will be. Are trees shrubs and shrubs trees then? Or is it that mustard bushes attract birds that pick apart the cultivated fields of the comfortable? Do we have everything upside down?

In the parables of the lost coin and lost sheep, Jesus portrays a liberal God preoccupied with those missing out. God takes no delight in a banquet from which some are missing or deliberately turned away. In the parable of the good Samaritan, Jesus suggests that humans are obligated to anyone in need, but more than that—it's an undocumented alien, not a good citizen, who actually stops to help. Those who pass by on the other side are determined to protect their purity and so like many Americans they just waft thoughts and prayers at another gun death. In the parable of the king who gives a great feast and nobody comes, Jesus may be saying that if the officially religious, or perhaps Israel itself, do not show up for God's party, then God will go out of the way to seek the lost and neglected as *replacement guests*. Or, perhaps, the hearers are just to exclaim: How odd that a man is throwing a party with friends absent and untidy strangers present! In the parable of the prodigal son, the elder brother represents the self-congratulation of the pious and of every self-made man. God, in the form of the welcoming father, bewilders the hearers with unhesitating, prodigal love for the lost son. A proud man gives up his dignity to run through the streets to greet a loser—never an American electoral strategy, never a Horatio Alger story. In a story about building one's house on solid rock instead of shifting sand, Jesus suggests that all the reality commonly thought solid, the stuff of the Wall Street investor letters, is, in fact, insubstantial and undependable. Parables provide space for the unexpected. They *give God room* (an act of moral imagination), shattering the structures of the accepted world and puncturing holes in the stories by which most people live. Parables mean to remove human defenses and make their hearers vulnerable to God's action.

As we have seen, the early Christian communities came to see that *Jesus himself was a parable*, the parable of an unexpected God come to earth. If God intended to create a demonstration project on earth, if God wanted to portray what human life on earth would be like if it were fully open to mimicking God, what would it look like? It would be like the life of Jesus. *And like ours?* Do we who walk the stations of Jesus' life become God's parables to those who notice? Are way stations parable sites? In Jesus God both unmasks the world's pretensions and sets people free from the alienating constraints they themselves have trapped themselves in. The point is that God's new reign is construed as the true meaning of life on earth. So Jesus undermines the memorized lines, challenges assumptions that have turned into bad news for the 99 percent, and proclaims a new and free space where God and humanity could again join hands.

But the mindset of the crowds, not to mention the establishment, is very hard to penetrate. Parables are meant to unseat those who respond with a shrug, the fatuously unconcerned and untroubled, all those who pride themselves on ironic detachment or who have "settled" early. Is it going to be restoration or ruin? Clinging to Abraham, or comfortable orthodoxies, as unconditional security will not work. But by what authority is the challenge laid down? Jesus correlates questions about himself with descriptions of the new reign of God. He invites people to see in his actions the climactic and definitive restoration of the people of God. There is no reign of God that does not resonate with the life of Jesus. This is the challenge to those who walk (and talk) the stations.

As you prepare for this way station, consider for yourself and ask your friends, What are some of your favorite parables? What do you think they mean? For you? If they remain a puzzle, could you and your friends solve them? It is sometimes said that it took American blacks to decode the exodus narrative amidst racist religion. Of course, it has recently been discovered that plantation owners who wanted the enslaved to become Christian, first excised the exodus narrative from their carefully edited slave Bibles—so they wouldn't get any ideas. Try out some new thoughts, for example: Is the prodigal son parable really more about a prodigal father than a prodigal son? Who knew you could find God on the road to Jericho? Is every road a possible road to Damascus event, when Paul heard a voice, was thrown to the ground, and became a reborn apostle?

Schedule a parables retreat and ask yourselves these questions: What parable most convicts you? Or comforts you? Is there some important issue that faces you, or your congregation, that a preacher might find a parable for? New Testament parables are a long time coming. Or they can arrive in the nick of time when our eyes are opened and our will activated.

How about some art projects, for example, having an image in your church sanctuary of a mustard seed—growing larger each Sunday as everyone oohs and aahs? Consider its "watch us grow" effect. Look for hymns that unpack parables. If parables constitute about one-third of Jesus' teaching, ask your pastor to get with the program and start preaching on, or with, parables. No need for preachers to come up with corny parables of their own. Jesus' parables are unbeatable. For a group study, choose five parables and unpack them. Let them help you see something new. Can your congregation latch on to parables that move them out of lethargy, or stubbornness, or sloth?

There are about thirty different parables of Jesus in the four Gospels. *Only four* were regularly depicted in European medieval Christian art: the ten bridesmaids, the rich man and Lazarus, the prodigal son, and the good Samaritan. The prodigal son may be Jesus' most famous parable.

Consider the following if you would like to increase your parable repertoire: Luke 10 has the parable of the good Samaritan told to an overly confident young man inquiring what must he do to inherit eternal life with a follow-up on "Who is my neighbor?" Luke 15 features the parables of the lost sheep, the lost coin, and the prodigal son and his brother and father. Matthew 25 features the parable of the ten bridesmaids, the talents, and closes with Jesus' story of the last judgment when all the world will be examined on whether they were able to see Jesus in "the least of these." The various "parables of the kingdom" are stories that illustrate how Jesus' proclamation of the imminent reign of God throws his hearers into a crisis of decision. Will you come forward? (Evangelical Christianity is on to something.) Indeed, nearly all the parables pose the necessity of a response to Jesus, whose ministry is *less about information than transformation*. Matthew's very short parables (13:44) of the hidden treasure in a field, or the discovery of a pearl of great value, for example, depict someone who comes upon hidden treasure (the message of the kingdom of God) and immediately sells all he has to buy that field or sells all to obtain a pearl of great value.

Parables are meant to open your eyes and evoke a new vision. If you need help with this, you might study artistic depictions of the great parables. What do you now see, or think, that you haven't seen before? Or, might people in your church create their own art? Or banners to carry? Or occasional sculptures in worship space?

Parables can be assembled in groups that depict certain themes. Hearing, seeking, and growing with the *kingdom of heaven* are featured in the parables of the sower, the hidden treasure in the field, the pearl of great price, the seed growing, the mustard seed, and the leaven. *Loss and redemption* are depicted in the lost sheep, the lost coin, and the prodigal son. *Love and forgiveness* are displayed in the good Samaritan, the two debtors, and the unforgiving servant. *Prayer* is pictured in the friend at night, the unjust judge, and the Pharisee and publican. *Eschatology* is the theme of the ten virgins, the faithful servant, the great banquet, the rich fool, tares in the field, the wicked husbandman, the net, and the fig tree barren and budding.

Consider a couple of hymns inspired by parables.

Way Station 10

"The Ninety and Nine"
There were ninety and nine that safely lay
In the shelter of the fold.
But one was out on the hills away,
Far off from the gates of gold.
Away on the mountains wild and bare.
Away from the tender Shepherd's care.
Away from the tender Shepherd's care.
— Elizabeth Clephane, 1910

"My Hope Is Built" (Edward Mote, c. 1834) is inspired by the parable of the wise and the foolish builders:

> My hope is built on nothing less than Jesus' blood and righteousness
> No merit of my own I claim but wholly lean on Jesus' name
> On Christ the solid rock I stand, all other ground is sinking sand.

Way Station 11

Jesus Rides Into Jerusalem, Challenging the Religious and Political Establishment—*Do We Dare to Speak Nonconforming Truths as Communities of Resistance?*

WHAT IS IT ABOUT Jesus' ride into Jerusalem that excites our imagination? The donkey? A surprise parade? An uninvited celebrity? A religious challenge in the public square? A lived parable? This is one of those rare events (Christmas, Good Friday, and Easter are the big ones) that attract a special Sunday in the church year: namely Palm Sunday, which begins Holy Week. Is that auspicious? Have we thought of, or risked actions today that could imitate Jesus' ride into Jerusalem? Of course there is the sheer fun and joy of gathering early outside the church on Palm Sunday, happily chatting as palm branches are handed out by the ushers, and then beginning to march and wave the palms as the organ and choir invite the parade into church singing:

> *All glory laud and honor To you redeemer king,*
> *To whom the lips of children Made sweet hosannas ring.*
> *You are the king of Israel and David's royal Son,*
> *Now in the Lord's name coming, our King and Blessed One.*
>
> *The multitude of pilgrims with palms before you went*
> *Our praise and prayer and anthems before you we present.*
> *To you, before your passion, they sang their hymns of praise.*
> *To you, now high exalted, our melody we raise.*

Way Station 11

Their praises you accepted; accept the prayers we bring,
Great author of all goodness, O good and gracious King.

But there must be commemorations more risky than a Palm Sunday parade on a Sunday morning into our own church. Christians walking the stations may confront worldly power in the seats of power, or religious corruption at church headquarters. Will they decide, in response, to commit to *continuous reformations and challenges to authority?* The Common Lectionary recognizes Jesus' triumphal entry into Jerusalem in the Gospel readings for Palm Sunday: Matthew 21:1–11; Mark 11:1–11; or John 12:12–19, and Luke 19:28–38. So we can fortify ourselves every year.

Jesus' triumphal entry into Jerusalem is filled with irony, and we should grasp it while walking this station. Instead of a powerful warhorse, as a powerful general would have chosen, Jesus rides in with a donkey and colt, a poor man's farm animals. But his act is unmistakable in its evocation of the prophet Zechariah, at 9:9, who sees God reigning triumphantly over all his enemies—from the Mount of Olives. While walking the stations it is important to open our eyes to the overtones they evoke. Zechariah provides an eschatological backdrop to Jesus' entry on Palm Sunday. Those with no power celebrate Jesus' arrival, and the excluded come into the temple. Revolutionary celebration breaks out, as some challenge Jesus' authority—to cleanse the temple, cure the blind and lame, provide for the poor, and start a children's choir (!).

Jesus' enthroned death and resurrection will set all this in context. God was returning to Zion, but who knew it would be like this? The entry into Jerusalem and the challenge to the religious and political establishment constituted a single symbolic action. It had been part of a king's duties to maintain the official worship in Jerusalem, but what kind of king and what kind of worship? We are to see a messianic program in which *the present age is being overtaken* by *the age to come.* This is a time of fulfillment, occurring before our eyes as we strew our palm leaves to mark the path. Palm leaves are a nice example of using "material culture" to thicken and embody our experiences of a way station.

Imagine Christians today, riding in Jesus' name into the public square, a seriously contested space from which many would like to exclude religion by appealing to the hallowed separation of church and state. Maybe we could just ride nonchalantly on a donkey so no one would object and we could still be recreating an ancient drama. After all, pilgrims today "walk the Camino" road towards the tomb of St. James in Western Spain. Yes, and they understand that the "road is made by walking." Could a donkey substitute for the bike or bus sometimes used as the appropriate vehicle for pilgrimage? It does attract genuine attention (even a movie made out of it) and everyone even gets a special certificate they can wave back home and post above their home altar.

But what if your church, or at least your fellow way-walkers, decided to march into a city council meeting to stimulate your and their religious imagination? Actually it's not that unusual to picket Congress and then even walk inside, sit in the balcony, and hold up signs. Bread for the World, a Christian citizens' lobby, does its best to get the attention of representatives who are about to cut food stamps. It's even become common to engage in the not very strenuous or risk-taking *offering of letters* that bring Christian viewpoints to the attention of Washington, DC. Closer to home there are also the public sites of university events and political speakers. Public parades through town are always pregnant opportunities for Christians to join in and carry their banners. My daughter and I have carried signs into local parades in our university town to lift up the presence of women's rights. I have always loved the notion that comes out of theater analysis that eventful plays and the people who join them can produce "indrafts of meaning" around public events. And there's everyone's dream of a drama so poignant that the audience rushes the stage at the end to join the action. Or at least they can rise from their seats and clap. Or yell.

Or are reformers of Christianity and world systems destined always to take an ironic path, never one of worldly power but yet accomplishing great things in God's name? Think of the apostle Paul, after his conversion on the road to Damascus, taking Jesus' new dispensation public across the Roman world, by founding little churches across the empire as colonies of heaven. Consider St. Francis during the turn of the thirteenth century refocusing a wealthy church's vision by showing it where to look—the presence of Christ in village manger scenes. Across the twelfth century, Hildegard of Bingen preached, and did theology, and led women monastics, and prolifically composed music—altogether constituting herself as a visionary, self-ordaining woman leader. She did not wait for men to give her permission, or catch up with her. During a pre-Reformation period in the fourteenth century, John Wycliffe, and his community of rebels, taught his followers to read the Bible as a revolutionary act and a revolutionary document and evoked a holy poverty in the life of a comfortable church. Early in the sixteenth century Protestant Reformation Martin Luther began as a troubled monk, went into hiding to escape an emperor's edict, and translated the Bible into German just in time for Gutenberg's new printing press to engage a vernacular language, and through his voluminous writings opened north European Christianity into a new age. In the eighteenth century John Wesley, his heart "strangely warmed" during his conversion experience, took the world as his parish. In the mid-twentieth century, Pope John XXIII inaugurated the Second Vatican Council as a way to turn the church in new directions. At the same time, Dorothy Day in America led a Catholic Workers' movement by discovering and creating her own spiritual calling. Seen as disciples following Jesus, all these people were, over the centuries, walking the stations. Walking into seats of power riding on a donkey.

Today, an apparent attack on the religious establishment may resonate with all those on YouTube who love to contrast their love of Jesus with their disillusionment with the church. "Para-church" organizations have sometimes arisen to give Christians room to move, alongside and beyond the "established church." The contemporary "emergent church" movement wants to map a path different from that of the all too familiar church. The Protestant Reformation had argued that the church must aspire to permanent reformation (*semper reformanda*) as the people of God.

In Jesus' challenge to the establishment, we are watching a clash of symbols—holy Sabbath, ritual purity, established nation, land, ethnicity, tradition vs. whatever it is Jesus is suggesting. It does not seem to be purity and holiness, as typically understood, that Jesus is proposing. *Light of the world and salt of the earth are displacing the tried but no longer true boundary-markers.* Some kind of eschatological contest is underway. We are witnessing an enacted parable of destruction and restoration. Jerusalem was not big enough for both the old temple and the temple that is Jesus's presence. The so-called second temple in Jerusalem was the center of Israel's national and political life, with many royal overtones, just as the church became after the conversion of the Emperor Constantine, just as the church often was in colonialist endeavors, just as Christianity sometimes aspires to be in American Christian nationalism.

Jesus' critique was not simply against legalism, nor did it imply that you could instead find God on the golf course or at Yosemite, but an eschatological critique: God would be judging the entire religious edifice and inviting all its adherents to move beyond it. Jesus was more worried about national self-congratulation and God as a patriotic icon than sharp financial practices among the money changers. A symbol of God's universalism would be required, and that would turn out to be Jesus' own body. Jesus' messianic program imaged in the ride into Jerusalem would not be politics as we know it. In fact, the reign of God would be *undermining rather than underwriting* the revolutionary anti-pagan zeal afoot. God is on the way, but not as you were expecting.

To those who walk in Jesus' way, reformation and change and challenge are in the air, as they always must be. Will the community of those who walk the journey of discipleship today be discussing it with each other on the pilgrimage road? The exiles who toward the end of the Old Testament period had come back to reclaim their heritage thought that holiness (set-apartness) would be the central mark and proof of their election. But Jesus is being inclusive not exclusive, and proclaiming the universalism of the reign of God—against the instincts and proclivities of every narrow religious establishment. Mostly the disciples didn't get it, until sticking to it for awhile. *Getting it* is the task of the modern disciples who walk the "inner pilgrimage" of reflection and try to form their lives around the life of Jesus as they talk these things over in small groups.

Will we who walk in this way come to match the journey in literary stories told, art like El Greco's *Jesus Cleansing the Temple*, hymns and songs, poetry, drama? On Palm Sundays when this story is read out from the Common Lectionary, will we fill the sanctuary with drama and banners and music and stations of discipleship acted out? Is this what the public space of worship has been waiting for? Performative liturgy means movement and singing and waving palms and enjoying the joyous company of all those gathered together. In Jesus' time, Jerusalem was the center of that world. It was where you had to go. Where do we go today?

Maybe as you sing and process, you will carry a little palm handed out to you before the service began. Maybe you will take it home, as Catholics do, and nudge it behind one of the crucifixes that hang in your house. Maybe you will bring it back to church on Ash Wednesday the following year, burn it to ashes, and have it smeared on your forehead in the shape of a cross. Maybe you will deliberately go to such an Ash Wednesday service early in the morning so that you can bear that cross on your forehead the entire day—so that people you know can make inquiries. Even TV commentators sometimes appear with foreheads crossed with ashes. What's that? Why?

The point of this way station is not for you to ride triumphantly into Jerusalem in particular, but to recall that Jesus once did, and what it meant, and what Jesus' claims might mean for you. *And where you might ride into.* Of course, your church body might indeed ride into Congress occasionally, or participate in "Moral Mondays" that exist to remind Congress that a federal budget is always a moral document—and the poor are waiting to hear how it will turn out for them. Or maybe you will lobby local officials capable of handing out food, or creating small houses for the unhoused. Or maybe your congregation can find the opportunity, perhaps even on Palm Sunday, to parade to the public square in the name of social justice. From church to the commons! If so, will everybody get it?

Way Station 12

Jesus Washes the Disciples' Feet, Dispenses a New Love Commandment, and Offers His Own Body to the World in His Last Supper—*Can We Learn "Christian Yoga" as Our Servant Discipline, Justice as the Social Form of Love, and the Eucharist as Our Weekly Refreshment for Difficult Journey?*

HERE ARE SOME QUESTIONS to pass around the group of pilgrims walking this station: What is it about foot washing that troubles you? Too personal? Do we suspect the pastor of picking out the best looking women, and perhaps moving from their feet slightly up their legs? (I've seen it.) Must it be literal or can it have multiple manifestations? Could it be reimagined as a Christian yoga—training us for discipleship, servanthood? Whose feet need washing? Who should do the washing? In my home church in Chico, everyone needs washing and everyone assists with the washing—but not all applaud.

Has this ritual run its course? Too quaint for the modern age? The whole point is to make servants out of disciples, who may be haughty and lacking a servant sensibility. If you're still unconvinced can you imagine alternative ritual actions? Or is this one pregnant with meaning, even in the modern world, and therefore indispensable?

I like to conceive of foot washing as a kind of Christian yoga. But yoga enthusiasts repeat their rituals every week, or every afternoon! Yoga *bends the body* through regular practice. It could be the visual confirmation of the Christian's posture in the world—bending down to serve. And add obedient love, with justice as the "social form of love," to mark our pilgrimage. We could practice shaping our Christian selves in small groups.

The Eucharist is a much weightier ritual—grounded in Jesus' last act before his passion—and practiced in every Christian church, from every Sunday to once a month or more infrequently. In this format, ever since, Christ appears among us and the church is shaped into a godly community extending the incarnation in the world and giving thanks for the gift of Christ's presence.

The church is called to practice a holy ordinance and an obedient discipleship that reflects God's love with a place at the table for everyone, reflecting Jesus' "commensality" with the whole world. Jesus' "table manners" are universal. Many churches offer a eucharistic liturgy every Sunday, with the Maundy Thursday service in Holy Week the mother of them all. The Common Lectionary readings appointed for Maundy Thursday are Matthew 26:26–30; Mark 14:22–25; and Luke 22:14–23. In some liturgies the rather long passion narratives are read in their entirety as the text of the sacred drama of Holy Week. In John 13–17, Jesus' "Farewell Discourses" are unique and very extensive, but John 6:22–71, following the feeding of the five thousand, also offers an extensive discourse on Jesus as the very bread of life, the *bread from heaven*. Only in John 13:1–20 is there a story about Jesus washing the disciples' feet before the Last Supper. In 1 Corinthians 11 Paul offers a commentary on how Communion should be celebrated when the church gathers. And what misuse to avoid.

While the Eucharist is central to Christian worship, and not a public meal, foot washing can be a public image of servanthood that all the world can learn from. Imagine the president of the United States kneeling to wash the feet of the poor just before his inaugural banquet. It would not need to be a Christian ordinance, but an unmistakable model of servanthood as the essence of political office. (Everyone would get it.) The pope indeed annually washes feet, including of women and the poor and some non-Christians in particular, to model for the church throughout the world its servant-calling. This is a good place to make the point, much needed in a time when religious sentimentality fails to kneel before a gritty world, that in John's Gospel Jesus gives a new "love command" and that *the love commandment realized in society would be social justice*. Or do we prefer to slim it down to just our personal relationships—adopting the gospel as a personal gospel but not a *social* gospel?

The larger setting for the Last Supper, even across the history of religions, is the significance of community meals and their susceptibility to larger referents or metaphors, such as a *commensality* authorized and modeled by God. In this case, the interpretive anchor for the Last Supper is surely Jesus' own life (and death) and its accumulating way stations, including certainly Jesus' eating and drinking practices we saw in way station 6, with their implication of inclusion and forgiveness, that had gone before this last eating and drinking. The *fellowship of the table* carries heavy weight across entire social and religious systems. There's a clue to who you are in whom you invite to your table. Ultimately, this meal anticipates a great messianic banquet to which the world is invited and *no one excluded*. Jesus means to be performing an efficacious sign, a prophetic symbolic act with universal significance, foretelling an eschatological banquet.

To call the Last Supper *symbolic* does not mean that "This is my body" is not substantively real, but that this offering of Jesus' own self is now *the depth dimension of everything real and concrete, of every eating and drinking*. Every bread, already requested especially for the poor in the Lord's Prayer, partakes of the eucharistic body of Christ—though who remembers, who thinks of it!? Ultimately, Jesus' impending death does not end the fellowship of this meal but gives it a new basis and an ultimate authorization. Jesus' identification with the bread and wine is not merely parabolic, but a real and efficacious action in which he gives himself to humankind, inviting and bringing all those far from God into a living fellowship with God, celebrated at this table. In this fellowship the reign of God arrives and comes true. The motif of self-offering for many in early Christianity led to the *teaching* of early Christianity (*lex orandi lex credenda*—the law of worship becomes the law of belief and confession). *If we get this meal straight, with all Jesus' intentions and "commensality," then we will get our theology straight.*

But we might pause here to lament the "wafer watch" practiced by some Catholic bishops and pastors who want to use non-admission to the Eucharist to underline their favorite sins—or their favorite, often politically driven, enemies. Some church bodies, ranging from Anabaptists to some Lutherans, restrict their celebration to *closed communion—members only*. The Anabaptist tradition wants the meal to mimic their own, local, closely held community. Some believe they have the true and unique doctrine of the real presence of Christ and other doctrines and use closed Communion to exclude all who are not in strict doctrinal fellowship with them. They pride themselves on protecting outsiders from "eating and drinking to their

Way Station 12

own damnation" because they fail to discern the body, though Paul's language in 1 Corinthians 11 means the opposite. His point is that those who employ the meal in a divisive manner fail to "discern the body," which is to say the entire community for whom God set out a welcome mat. Pope Francis has recently reminded the politically conservative American bishops that the Eucharist is "a gift of grace not a reward for good morals, not a prize for the perfect."

Almost all who walk these stations of discipleship will have participated in this way station, from foot washing to eucharistic eating and drinking that the church has celebrated in obedience to Jesus' invitation and command. So the Last Supper as eucharistic celebration has evolved throughout the history of Christianity, even as it also shares dimensions of religious piety with other religions, and certainly including Judaism's Passover celebrations.

Of course one can file up the aisle, or wait for wafers to be passed around, while hardly meditating on what we are doing, just as one can thoughtlessly pray the Lord's Prayer. All those who pause to reflect at this station will have much to think and pray and talk about, especially if the presence of the poor and the hungry and the excluded lie close to mind. Eating and drinking have always been opportunities to bring together the spiritual and the material and to practice and enjoy life together.

In the modern secular world, eating and drinking are central to occasions of celebration and community. A surprising element of the ministry of Jesus, rarely practiced by his followers, was eating and drinking with "sinners" and outcasts. Imagine a new US president celebrating her inauguration as a feast for the homeless on the Capital Mall. Or those in debtors' prisons. Jesus' persistent flying in the face of religious opposition and tradition and custom were acts of resistance and simultaneously acts of inclusion. He was staging a different kind of earthly life, anticipating a banquet served to all. He was mixing the yeast of radical theater into the everyday life of the world. Do we?

He took everyday substances, bread and wine, identified with them fully, and made them signs of all things given by God and offered back to God and served up to humanity. He amazed everyone by commingling his death and resurrection with the bread and wine of the human condition. The meal we call the Eucharist was the beginning of the church's wager that Jesus's ministry was going to be the ultimate shape of human life, the venture that *earthly existence* could be offered up to God at the same time that it was celebrating human togetherness. Everything is redeemable, everything can be saturated with grace, everything can bring God and humans together as table companions, every meal can be a sign of hope and inclusion to the world, every Sunday an opportunity for shoppers at Bloomingdale's and Walmart to bump into each other. The Eucharist will be the meal that celebrates a liberating God.

During and after New Testament times, common meals became the sites of dramatic experimentation and innovation regarding social roles and relationships, challenging expectations regarding gender, class, and status. Are modern disciples staging revolutionary meals as they pilgrimage in the tracks of the New Testament? Jesus himself had profoundly disturbed the status quo in his own eating and drinking practice. *Christianity came into existence at table.* Early churches continued the meal traditions of Jesus. This swirl of experimentation surrounded the early Christian assemblies, with their "love feasts" and "suppers of the Lord." Christianity was not able to sustain this vision because it forgot the evocative setting on the ground of Jesus' earthly ministry and the experimental setting of early Christian worship. The church at first was good at practicing this meal in order to re-present the life and death of Christ. But liturgical practice eventually changed as theories of Christ's atonement changed, so that the *Eucharist shifted from a feast of life to a reenactment of the killing of Jesus.*

Over the ages, *the Eucharist was transformed from a celebration hosted by a self-giving God to a private dinner hosted by a conservative church.* The church lost sight of the very body of Christ constituted by Jesus' deliberate presence among the marginalized. The Eucharist was turned into a meal where the church fed itself spiritually and even aggrandized its own authority and priestly power (bouncers controlling who gets in), while forgetting the shape of Christ in the life of the world waiting to be fed. Eventually the open-ended form of Christ, permeating every earthly boundary, was carefully narrowed to the form of the church. In a sorry sequence, the Eucharist began as a soup supper, then became the sacramental presence of Christ, and then the soup itself was withdrawn. But when it is healthy, Christianity is a meal fellowship still. *To preach in Christian worship is to interpret the Word in light of the table.*

When thinking of the Eucharist while walking the stations of Jesus' life, try to keep remembering all those in this country and abroad who have never been invited to any banquet, on whose backs our feasts grow lavish, from whose tables we have snatched our food, in whose faces our banquet hall bespeaks its closed privileges. But the one thing clergy are explicitly licensed to do is be servants, serving the Word as food and the supper as food, in the name of a church which is a meal community. "To minister" is to set out food. The Son of Man came not to be served at table but to serve the table, something *only women seem to understand*. Their words and their service are edible. Eating and drinking are radical celebrations when they foretell the fall of all existing domination systems erected to exclude the poor. At table, the early communities came to understand the presence of the risen Lord, the greater one who serves the food.

The much-prayed and much-ignored petition of the Lord's Prayer, "Give us today our daily bread," perhaps really means "Give us today the bread of the new age." Or, give the poor the food God has promised. As we saw earlier in our reflections on the Lord's Prayer, the next petition, "Forgive us our trespasses," might once have spoken to *debt relief, debt forgiveness,* one of the most radical ideas in the Old Testament. To celebrate the Eucharist thoughtfully and with moral discernment is to draw an arc whose full degree touches down on a new earth, whither a heaven descends. If already a joyous meal, it's really an antipasto, leaving us hungry for the final repast. So, in every celebration, the early church cried out in anticipation, *Maranatha*, Come, Lord! Once I saw the California Jesus Movement in the 1970s doing the same thing.

So too, can the Old Testament roots, the Passover meal underlying the Christian Eucharist, be revelatory to all who look closely. The unmistakable context is Israel's exodus from Egypt, the new covenant, and the restoration of the people of God. Forgiveness of sins is another way of communicating the end of exile and a new exodus, since exile means distance from God and exodus means deliverance from captivity and return to the reign of God. Forgiveness can also be seen as a return to family status. Think of the excluded people Jesus had been willing to eat and drink with, and the church's contemporary assignments become clear.

Just before this last supper Jesus had challenged a Jerusalem temple life that disadvantaged the access of the poor to the designated place where God would be found. Now Jesus seems to be offering himself as a new temple where God meets his people. In Jesus' ministry, in his fresh appearance in Jerusalem, and now in this last supper, Jesus is redrawing the boundaries of true religion—not a hallowed building but within the body of Christ himself.

Jesus identifies the Passover elements with his own body and blood to be offered at the inauguration of a new covenant. Early Christianity's repetition of this meal, and the church's weekly practice ever since, recapitulates this momentous event in the ongoing life of the community. All of it is to be seen within the larger story of Yahweh's redemption of Israel, but now Christians are to keep rehearsing it, keep bringing it to life again, keep *returning this play to the stage—as a light to the entire world.* Celebrating this meal and all it means becomes the vocation of the new community that evidences the reign of God. In this meal is conveyed exile and return, lost humanity and a new covenant, the actual redeeming presence of Christ. Still today, Christ keeps touching down and God's intentions are displayed. Use your imagination when you celebrate this meal!

We pilgrims who gather at this station reflect on all the way stations that have gone before. And on the final two still to come. All fourteen stations together become the determinative site—which is to say a re-enchanted earth—where God comes among us. So this table, now named an altar, carries heavy weight. The root word for the descending glory of God is *heavy.*

I have said above that every bread is a eucharistic bread, every eating can be imagined as a eucharistic eating with thanksgiving, every table—waiting to be expanded—is a eucharistic table. In every moment of life Christ is giving himself to us. So the every-Sunday Eucharist becomes a practice for the continuing sacramentalizing, or consecrating, of the world. Everything is waiting to be made holy. All persons are waiting to have the image of God recognized in them. Maybe this really is *hocus pocus*! The ancient Greek word *anamnesis,* from the early Christian liturgies on, means much more than "remembrance." It means *re-presentation.* While Catholics practice the adoration of the host, they often err in the direction of the re-sacrificing of Christ rather than re-presenting the risen Lord. For Catholics adoring the host, the host is displayed in a monstrance, an artistic and stylized display container. But the host should be displayed as the church, an extension of the incarnation, comes together with the world. And what if the adoration of the host took place in homeless shelters?

Consider a few very reverent Communion hymns commonly sung in Christian liturgies.

> Let Us Break Bread Together (African American spiritual)
> *Let us break bread together on our knees;*
> *Let us break bread together on our knees.*

Way Station 12

Refrain:
When I fall on my knees, with my face to the rising sun,
O Lord, have mercy on me.

Let us drink wine together on our knees;
Let us drink wine together on our knees.
Refrain

Let us praise God together on our knees;
Let us praise God together on our knees.
Refrain

Victim Divine, Thy Grace We Claim (Charles Wesley, last verse)
We need not now go up to Heaven,
To bring the long sought Savior down;
Thou art to all already given,
Thou dost e'en now Thy banquet crown:
To every faithful soul appear,
And show Thy real presence here!

Feast your eyes on Christian eucharistic art. If you are making art, or making art out of your own community practice of the Last Supper, be sure you make it a diverse banquet, ranging from the classics of medieval Europe to contemporary art, including from the Third World. To ready yourself, gaze on the nineteenth-century pre-Raphaelite Ford Madox Brown's *Jesus Washing Peter's Feet*.

When you conclude your tour of great hymns and art, and consider your next liturgical celebration of the Eucharist, think of Augustine's evocative words, often repeated at Sunday services: "Behold what you are; Become what you receive."

Way Station 13

Jesus Dies the Most Famous Death in History— Can Christians See in It a Messianic Enthronement and Their Salvation with God?

THE *PIETÀ* IS FAMOUS as a major work in Michelangelo's career. Its phenomenal success ensured the worldwide fame that the sculptor has today. A major biblical scene, the *Pietà* depicts the sorrowful Virgin Mary holding the dead body of Jesus just after he was taken down from the cross. This representation of the Virgin is distinguished by her particularly youthful and placid features. A strong symbol of Catholic devotion, this one of Michelangelo's sculptures still attracts hundreds of admirers daily. Today, it holds a place of honor in St. Peter's Basilica in the Vatican.

Now consider a proposed political and moral setting for Christ's death by two famous New Testament scholars, Marcus Borg and John Dominic Crossan: "People like Jesus and Paul were not executed for saying, 'Love one another.' They were killed because their understanding of love meant standing against the domination systems that ruled their world and collaborating with the Spirit in the creation of a new way of life." Loving each other was bigger and more threatening than anyone had imagined.

Or maybe you grew up with this quite different understanding of Jesus' death, the so-called "substitutionary theory of atonement." Jesus died to appease the Father's wrath over our sins. Another way of saying this is that Jesus took on the legal penalty that should have been pronounced on us in a cosmic court. As you ponder this station, see what explanations for Jesus' crucifixion arise in your own mind and in your own piety. And discuss it with other Christians with whom you walk this station. Are Borg and Crossan in effect saying that in Jesus God was disrupting the order of the world and pioneering a new godly vision of earthly life? My favorite way of understanding "the atonement" is that in his own Son God took up the world's darkness and sin into himself, redeemed it, and poured onto it his own love. If you are stopping at this moving and powerful station in a group, why not ask how each of you, if at all, have understood this story since their childhood. Or how they mostly understand it now. Invite everyone, however haltingly, to say how they appropriate it in their own lives today. Or how they would "witness" to it to someone just now coming into Christianity.

Sometimes the long narrative of Christ's Passion in John is read in its entirety during Holy Week, or even dramatically reenacted, on Good Friday. But each Gospel offers its own individual account: Matthew 27; Mark 15; Luke 23; John 19. All four Gospels have been described as elaborate passion narratives with a long preface in the life of Christ.

Although the apostle Paul passes on very little regarding Jesus' earthly ministry, he is very much a theologian of the cross. He discusses the cross of Christ extensively in 1 Corinthians 1:13 (Christians belong to Christ because Christ was crucified for them); and in 1:18 (the message about the cross is foolishness to those who are perishing, but to us who are being saved it is the power of God); and in 1:23 (we proclaim Christ crucified, a stumbling block to Jews and foolishness to gentiles); and 2:2 (I decided to know nothing among you except Jesus Christ, and him crucified); and in 2:8 (none of the rulers of this age understood this; for if they had, they would not have crucified the Lord of glory.) In 1 Corinthians 15:3-4, Paul writes: "I handed on to you as of first importance what I in turn had received, that Christ died for our sins in accordance with the scriptures, and that he was buried, and that he was raised on the third day in accordance with the scriptures." When Paul refers in Galatians 6:12-14 to "the cross of our Lord Jesus Christ," it is shorthand for the Christian's entire means of salvation, the source of a theology of a new creation.

In Luke's account in Acts 2:22-24, Peter preaches in his Pentecost sermon: "You that are Israelites, listen to what I have to say: Jesus of Nazareth, a man attested to you by God with deeds of power, wonders, and signs that God did through him among you, as you yourselves know—this man, handed over to you according to the definite plan and foreknowledge of God, you crucified and killed by the hands of those outside the law. But

God raised him up, having freed him from death, because it was impossible for him to be held in its power." And further in Acts 2:36: "God has made him both Lord and Messiah, this Jesus whom you crucified."

Early Christians believed that Jesus' suffering was foretold, or prefigured, in the Old Testament, such as in Psalm 22 (which Jesus seems to be praying on the cross: My God why have you forsaken me?) and the suffering and humiliation of the Messiah in Isaiah 53.

All scholars agree that Jesus' crucifixion is one of the most attested facts of the ancient world. For example, writing in *The Annals* around 116 AD, the Roman historian Tacitus describes the persecution of Christians by Emperor Nero and states that Pilate ordered the execution of Jesus.

Christians believe that Jesus' death was instrumental in restoring humankind, and all creation, to a relationship with God. Through Jesus' death and resurrection, people are reunited with God and receive new joy and power in this life as well as eternal life. Thus the crucifixion of Jesus along with his resurrection restores access to a vibrant experience of God's presence, love, and grace, as well as the confidence of eternal life.

Everyone learns in Sunday school that "Jesus died for my sins." Christians think they know just what this means—until someone asks them, and they begin stumbling while trying to explain exactly. In the Middle Ages Catholic theology developed an explanation of what the cross means with a theory of *substitutionary atonement* through which Jesus appeases God's wrath by dying on the cross. While there are remnants of this view in contemporary Christianity, especially among evangelicals and perhaps some Catholics, most contemporary theology has moved beyond that early medieval theory, which perhaps borrows from medieval legal theory. Consider again an example of contesting views of the atonement in an argument between a Presbyterian hymnal committee and the author of a new and popular hymn. The author's line was "Till on that cross as Jesus died/the wrath of God was satisfied." The hymnal committee proposed "Till on that cross as Jesus died/the love of God was magnified." The hymn writer was not willing to accept the proposed change.

To many contemporary theologians, the old view of the atonement pictures *God as a divisive, guilt-giving, punishing being whose desire for justice is satisfied only by the torture and crucifixion of his own son*. Counter-views today see Christ's death as a *venture with divine self-giving on earth* as the lead story. The cross bespeaks human suffering and God's suffering on our behalf. The cross counters worldly wisdom and gospels of success.

(Hence Martin Luther insisting on a theology of the cross rather than a theology of glory.) This New Testament God-story is dramatic because it is set amidst the forces that still today threaten authentic human life on earth, that still interpose powerful political and economic forces between a giving God and an earth waiting to live in a covenanted community.

In the face of this, God through Jesus is seen as taking human intransigence up into the very life and being of God, absorbing all earthly evil up into God-ness, where it is overcome and transformed. And so the gaze at the cross discovers a loving God, a union of suffering and hope, both unjust suffering and the victory over injustice. Through the cross comes God's right-making and the repair of the earth. As Luther insisted, through the cross God justifies us and makes us wear Jesus' own righteousness—even if we are also simultaneously sinners. So Christian theology, which often enough has gotten the cross wrong, is called again to *get the cross right, but not to abandon the cross.*

Here is one way this can be done: The Mennonite theologian Denny Weaver, in his book *The Nonviolent Atonement*, moves beyond Anselm's twelfth-century "satisfaction theory" and Calvin's "penal theory," in which God required a penalty before human sin could be forgiven. Weaver imagines *a sacrifice by God, not to God*. This view also avoids the excesses of a Catholic view in which every Sunday the priest performs anew the sacrifice of Christ, and this as the center of the Mass. Indeed weekly eucharistic liturgies celebrate Jesus as the bread of life from heaven, the one whose presence touches the whole world and invites it to a vastly extended table—the ultimate commensality.

An alternative to Western Catholicism is the Eastern Orthodox view of *Christus Victor*. In this portrayal Jesus was sent by God to defeat death and Satan and recover earthly life for God's intentions. Instead of a preoccupation with Jesus writhing on the cross, there is a Christ the triumphant king, dressed in eucharistic vestments and wearing a crown and gazing serenely at the world. Jesus is victorious and even the journey to the cross is to become an enthronement ritual. There is evidence of this in the New Testament Gospels as well, perhaps especially John but even Matthew. From this readily flows the Orthodox view of the *resurrection as a corporate event* in which Jesus ascending from the empty tomb has all of humanity in his train, the whole company of the redeemed being pulled along.

Still, even with a revised view of the atonement and an exalted view of the cross as a measure of God's triumph over evil, there is the bare bones face of the cross, clearly the most famous icon of material culture in Christianity. When you walk with Jesus on and through this way station, perhaps you will give some meditation to what the crowds thought they were seeing as they followed up to the cross on Good Friday. This has been the meditative agenda for all these centuries as Christians walked all fourteen stations of the cross during Holy Week. Meanwhile, the presence of an empty cross is surely one of the most famous symbols in all of Christian art, adorning countless Christian bodies.

Before the cross became the preeminent Christian symbol it was a gruesome artifact of the Roman penal system. Consider the following: Roman execution grounds typically had the vertical member of the cross more or less permanently installed at a site just out of town. Then when a crucifixion was to take place, the horizontal beam, perhaps with a body already attached, was dragged to the crucifixion grounds and affixed to the vertical member already in place. A cross is first of all the empty instrument of capital punishment, especially for slaves, pirates, and enemies of the state. The word *crucifix* always refers to the cross with a body already affixed, almost always the body of Christ. Crucifix comes from the Latin *cruci fixus* meaning "(one) fixed to a cross"), as opposed to a distinct bare cross. In Latin the representation of Jesus himself on the cross is referred to as the *corpus*, the body.

Skull and crossbones are often shown below the body of Christ, referring to Golgotha (Calvary), the site at which Jesus was crucified, which the Gospels say means in Hebrew "the place of the skull." Medieval tradition held that it was the burial place of Adam and Eve, and that the cross of Christ was raised directly over Adam's skull, so many crucifixes manufactured in Catholic countries still show the skull and crossbones below the corpus. One theme in New Testament theology sees Christ as the "second Adam" who undid the fall of the "first Adam."

Christian art has preceded the cross with the pronouncement, *Ecce homo* (Behold the man), then proceeding with the raising of the cross, the descent from the cross, and the entombment of Christ's body. Christian art is famously replete with crucifixion scenes, spread all over the Christian world, from museums to churches. Luther retained the crucifix in the Lutheran Church and it remains a common image in Lutheran parishes across Europe. In the United States, however, Lutheranism came under the influence of Calvinism, and the plain cross without Jesus' body affixed came to be used in many churches. In contrast to the practice of the Moravian

Way Station 13

Church and Lutheran Churches, the early reformed churches rejected the use of the crucifix, and indeed even the unadorned cross, along with other traditional religious imagery, as idolatrous. Calvin, considered to be the father of the Reformed church, strongly opposed both cross and crucifix as material symbols. He reinvoked iconoclasm, the rejection of images as idolatrous and unfit for Christian adoration and devotion.

Eventually the cross underwent symbolic embellishment. Christians hung a cross on the eastern wall of their churches, and of their houses, in order to indicate the eastward direction of prayer—toward Jerusalem. Catholics especially, upon entering their church, bow the knee to the cross toward the eastern wall of the sanctuary before they are seated in their pew. Prayer in front of a crucifix, which is seen as "a sacramental," is often part of devotion for Christians, especially those worshipping privately in a church.

Of course, much folk literature has grown up around the cross symbol. Tradition claims that Peter, to be martyred in Rome, requested to be crucified upside down, so as not to appear a Christ-figure himself. Peter's brother Andrew was crucified on an X cross, a cross at a forty-five-degree angle. Crosses or crucifixes are common artifacts of religious visions.

The Oberammergau Passion Play is a famous example of dramatically staging Christ's last days, in a village of southern Bavaria in Germany. It arose during the seventeenth century when the village vowed to do so in gratitude for being spared the plague. It has been performed every year from 1634 to 1680 and every ten years since 1680, by the inhabitants of the village of Oberammergau. It was canceled in 2020, but rescheduled for 2022. (I made a pilgrimage to the passion play in Oberammergau in 1970, 1980, 1990, 2000, and 2010.)

A recent appeal to the power of the cross, paired to that of the lynching tree, has been James Cone's *The Cross and the Lynching Tree,* a highly influential example of Black Liberation Theology. From the back cover:

> The cross and the lynching tree are the two most emotionally charged symbols in the history of the African American community. In this powerful new work, theologian James H. Cone explores these symbols and their interconnection in the history and souls of black folk. Both the cross and the lynching tree represent the worst in human beings and at the same time a thirst for life that refuses to let the worst determine our final meaning. *While the lynching tree symbolized white power and black death, the cross symbolizes divine power and black life*—God overcoming the power of sin and death. For African Americans, the image of Jesus,

hung on a tree to die, powerfully grounded their faith that God was with them, even in the suffering of the lynching era. Cone argues that the lynching tree is a viable reality symbol for reflection on the cross of Christ. According to Cone, understandings of the cross and lynching tree can mutually inform one another and explain how events of trauma and injustice can still inspire hope for the African American community. The beauty of the gospel can still overcome the evil if we embrace fully the story and love of Jesus himself. A God mending creation through the cross cannot avert divine love from the lynching tree.

I would add that white Christians are not entitled to gaze at the cross thinking of their salvation while looking away from the lynching tree as having no connection to the cross and no implications for white supremacy. White salvation requires both looks, one of redemption and one of repentance. While decrying the injustice of the cross, white Christians long prevented efforts to make lynching a crime. White Christians must face the connections. Only now, as I write this, is lynching being identified by Congress, but not unanimously, as a federal hate crime.

Above the altar, Catholic churches are most likely to picture, whether in paintings or sculpture, Jesus on the cross. Protestant churches are much more likely to depict an empty cross. The crown of thorns is generally absent in Eastern Orthodox crucifixes, since the emphasis is not on Christ's suffering, but on his triumph over sin and death. Christians of all kinds often wear cross necklaces (I do), oftener an empty cross rather than an actual crucifixion sculpture.

Recent New Testament commentary often sees the crucifixion as an enthronement ceremony, in which Jesus steadily proceeds to a kingship achieved through cross, resurrection, and ascension. The emphasis is on Christ's road to victory as essential to God's plan of salvation. We are invited not to turn away from the cross as shameful but rather to claim it as a dimension of New Testament redemption. So the Christian vision expands beyond the defeat of the cross, beyond explaining an embarrassment away. And so one contemplates other great deaths, such as those of Dietrich Bonhoeffer, Martin Luther King Jr., and Mahatma Gandhi—not to mention the very many deaths of Christian martyrs, in early Christianity and still today. Their peers understood them and so had to kill them, but in their deaths they also triumphed. The long Gospel chapter that is Matthew 25 offers an eschatological overhang, or backdrop, as Jesus is heading towards the cross. Provocatively, Jesus calls on all who would follow him to see him enthroned among "the least of these" on earth, such as the unhoused, the sick, the hungry, the naked.

Some scholars, especially those who emphasize Jesus' self-understanding as an eschatological prophet, assert that Jesus went to Jerusalem to die, an inevitability also present in the Gospels. That is, he understood this last journey to be a part of, and to trigger, the "messianic woes" often associated with God's ultimate efforts to restore Israel from captivity and deliver it to a new covenant. Catastrophic or apocalyptic events might accompany the inauguration of a new age of God's reign, as Jesus had begun his ministry proclaiming, and bringing about, the consummation of human history.

But to simplify all this by saying that "Jesus came to die for our sins" *too readily misses the prophetic and eschatological context of Jesus' ministry, misses all the stations of his life as gospel proclamation,* and turns this epochal moment in God's covenant with humanity into a simple juridical transaction whereby humankind gets its debts paid by a God who would accept nothing less than the death of a son.

In the language of modern theology and in the experience of modern life, there are better ways to take in what happened to Jesus and what Jesus did. (You should try out for yourself ways to talk about the death of Christ. What did you experience and how would you offer an account of it to your children or friends?) We would not today, for example, say that Martin Luther King Jr. came to die for civil rights. We would say that his assassination was a predictable result, one that he himself contemplated and acceded to, of his lifelong struggle for justice amidst a society mostly determined to resist and cling to its old ways of living. If Jesus' intention to reinvoke God's rule, return Israel from exile, and restore it was regularly being met with resistance, and if taking on the temple establishment was going to be centered in Jerusalem, Jesus must have been anticipating how this might end. Jesus dies not as an accident, nor as a transaction between an angry God and a sacrificing son, but as the inevitable result of his kingdom-inaugurating vocation. Jesus' death is the outcome of risks taken to carry out God's intentions amidst an often hostile society. As the Gospel of John says, "He came to his own and his own did not receive him." Or according to the Gospel of John's view of the incarnation, *"he was the light and the darkness tried to extinguish it but could not."*

Jesus carries the world's rejection (the cross) up into the heart of God. Moreover, Christian theology is bold to say that in Jesus' suffering and death we see *A Crucified God,* the title of a very influential book by

German Protestant theologian Jürgen Moltmann. In the incarnation, but especially in the death and resurrection of Christ, Christianity sees a coming and going. God descends into humanity and in Jesus' death takes back into God's own being the power of the world's rejection, where it is negated and overcome. When God fully identifies with the crucified one, the negative power that put Jesus to death is absorbed into the life of God and overcome. Some "process theologians" would say that the very being of God changes when God-made-present and God-forsakenness are joined together, though that way of speaking will be too risky for many. But God-present and God-rejected and God-overcoming constitute shifts in God's relation to humankind, new stages in the historic journey between exile and restoration, a unique consummation of God's reign.

Jack Miles's *Christ: A Crisis in the Life of God* is a second volume in his attempt to write a biography of God. From a description on Amazon:

> Miles tells the story of a broken promise—God's ancient covenant with Israel—and of its strange, unlooked-for fulfillment. For, having abandoned his chosen people to an impending holocaust at the hands of their Roman conquerors, God, in the person of Jesus, chooses to die with them, in what is effectively an act of divine suicide. On the basis of this shocking argument, Miles compels us to reassess Christ's entire life and teaching: His proclivity for the powerless and disgraced. His refusal to discriminate between friends and enemies. His transformation of defeat into a victory that redeems not just Israel but the entire world.

As we will see in the final station of Jesus' life, that of the resurrection, *Jesus' death is the conclusion of a life of compassionate love. Jesus' death is a triumph over evil.* Jesus defeats evil by letting evil do its worst to him. Absorbing evil, turning the other cheek, committed to nonviolence, Jesus lets the world see a God who is full of compassion for the human condition. From this reconstruction of the symbolic world of exile and return, loss and revitalization, comes the new mission to be a light to the world.

Today as we keep pausing at the cross in long contemplation, as Christians have done throughout the ages, the right questions to ask are not what did the Jerusalem establishment do and what did the Romans do, are the Jews guilty of killing Jesus, and how much of the Gospel narratives are historical fact. (Jews have come to resent the bad press they particularly see in the Gospel of John, and, especially after the holocaust, resent concert performances of Bach's Magdalenion. Astute Christian defenders have argued in response that a careful perusal of Bach's libretto demonstrates profound accusation and required repentance precisely from those German Lutherans sitting in Bach's audience.)

The issue is *formation, not information. And self-examination and perhaps penance.* Indeed: How are we implicated in these events? What roles have we played? How do we find our own salvation there? What do they mean for our own journey of discipleship, our own "inner pilgrimage"? As you stand beneath the cross, ask yourself, What is the gospel for me here and "How am I living?" How are we implicated in these events? How do we find our own salvation there? While looking around, ask, "Where am I among the crowds passing by?" and "How am I living in response to this event?"

DEATH OF CHRIST AND THE ARTS

The cross has left a plethora of "deposits" across religion and the arts, including worship and liturgy, the visual arts, music and hymns, poetry and prose, and theater. All of these are varied enrichments to the reflection and enactment of the events preceding and following Good Friday.

Across all branches of Christianity, from Catholic, to Orthodox, to Protestantism, the cross and its centrality to Christian theology is present in the worship life of the church. Nearly every Christian denomination, except some nonliturgical Protestants, observes Good Friday worship, and often also the other services of Holy Week. And of course all of Christianity celebrates Easter, as its very grounding. These events belong to the category of *movable feast,* since Easter is not a fixed date like Christmas but falls on the first Sunday, after the first full moon, after the spring equinox (which falls on March 19–21).

The so-called liturgical churches (Orthodox, Catholic, Anglican, and Lutheran) have more elaborate services with fixed liturgies commemorating the events of Holy Week, including for Catholics frequent observation of stations of the cross. Holy Week begins with Palm Sunday and continues to Maundy Thursday, Good Friday, and of course Easter, also including an Easter Vigil. The Easter Vigil may begin as early as 3 AM on Easter, but often is observed closer to sunrise, and besides elaborate liturgies may feature the baptism of new Christians. In some places, especially Europe, Latin America, and in some ethnic enclaves in America, Holy Week may also occasion parades and floats marched through town. All these together work to construct, shape, and renew the Christian community and lie at its heart.

The material culture emanating from European Catholicism, but now spread across the world in indigenous ways, grows out of the annunciation to the Virgin Mary and the Christmas story with shepherds and wise men, celebrates the many dimensions of Jesus' life featured in the life stations mentioned in this book, and reaches its fulfillment in the events of Maundy Thursday, Good Friday, and Easter. A very good exercise in controlling for Eurocentrism is to review the vast amount of religious art from Europe, the Middles Ages, Reformation, and modernity and compare it to the startling portrayals of the same themes in world art today, including of course Latin America, Africa, and Asia. Together they provide a wide range of artistic response to holy events and inviting all of us to absorb it.

VISUAL ARTS

There is a great abundance of visual art depicting the events surrounding the crucifixion. They are widely available in museums that one can think of as religious pilgrimage sites. One can purchase books of art and page through them for devotional meditation and find them enriching and stimulating. There are facsimile editions of beautiful "books of hours." These are Christian devotional books popular in the Middle Ages and the most common type of surviving medieval *illuminated manuscript* in which sets of prayers intended for the hours of the day and night are illustrated by leading artists commissioned, originally by wealthy patrons, to illustrate them.

A recent *New York Times* report displayed a wide variety of "home altars" or sacred spaces constructed in private homes that focus daily worship. These are common across all religious traditions, including especially Hispanic Catholic piety. Pictures portraying Christian scenes and personages may also appear in the homes of people in liturgical traditions, though they are quite rare in evangelical homes—except for a few very famous portraits of Jesus. An evangelical university colleague visiting my (Lutheran) home was startled, and perhaps slightly disapproving, saying he had never seen Christian art on the walls of a private home. But artistic depictions are increasingly available for sale, as in this ad that a Google search turns up: "The story of the Crucifixion is an important part of the Christian religion, and decorating your home with artwork around this theme is a way of demonstrating your faith. Choose an abstract scene of the Crucifixion and hang it in your dining room or the place where you pray or meditate. Choose one of our paintings of the crowds around the Crucifixion and hang it in the living room of your home for religious expression." Indeed, the most accessible and least expensive encounter with Christian art is available through Google searches, which turn up a plethora of visual art, many of which can be ordered in facsimile editions at reasonable costs. Religious bookstores also feature such art. Churches, even evangelical Protestant ones, which may not have a history of adorning their walls with religious art have recently been including contemporary religious art in the images they project on their walls for congregational song and other purposes.

MUSIC AND HYMNS

It is gratifying to hear repeatedly that Bach's St. Matthew Passion may be the greatest work of choral music of any kind ever written. There is also Bach's Magdalenion and, of course, Handel's Messiah is the most well-known example of religious music, especially in the English-speaking world. Unfortunately, these works, especially Bach's, require a level of musical expertise, both instrumental and vocal, that very few congregations, except in Germany, can provide. And so these works are primarily available in concert settings, oftener in secular than religious venues. An odd happenstance that I have always appreciated is that the most likely occasion for students (and audiences) in secular higher education to run into religious texts is in university choral concerts. There is no escaping religion in high end choral works; indeed the majority of such works by far feature religious texts.

Of course the most widespread use of music to exhibit religious texts, by far, is the vast treasure of Christian hymns. All across Catholic and Protestant worship, and every Sunday, hymns are sung—ranging from high art widely treasured across the ages to the latest in popular art in evangelical style. I mention here only a tiny number of famous passion hymns. Note the centrality of the cross as image and carrier of meaning.

"In the Cross of Christ I Glory " (nineteenth century)

"Were You There When They Crucified My Lord?"
    (African American spiritual)

"The Old Rugged Cross" (traditional American hymn)

"Jesus, Remember Me" (Taizé community, 1984)

Part Two: Walking 14 Stations along the Christian Way

"Beneath the Cross of Jesus" (nineteenth century)

"O Sacred Head, Now Wounded" (seventeenth century)

"Lift High the Cross" (nineteenth century)

Stabat Mater (At the cross her station keeping, thirteenth century)

The *Christus Victor* theme, Christ in triumph as the proposed view of Christ's atonement, is well expressed in this hymn from the early sixth century by Venantius Honorius Clematianus Fortunatus:

> *Sing my tongue, the glorious battle*
> *Sing the ending of the fray*
> *Now above the cross the trophy*
> *Sound the loud triumphant lay*
> *Tell how Christ the world's redeemer*
> *As a victim won the day.*

Also in the sixth century, more than one fragment of the "true cross" had been discovered and was sent, as a precious relic, by the Byzantine emperor to the Frankish queen in the town of Poitiers. Imagine a relic of the true cross moving, in procession, from Byzantium to Western Europe. In preparation for its arrival, the great mystic hymn writer Venantius Honorius Clementianus Fortunatus wrote the hymn above to accompany its arrival. Along its journey the relic was being carried in a grand procession that passed through cities and villages, and throngs of believers gathered along the roadside to see this heartfelt symbol of the passion. Two hours outside Poitiers, the hymnwriter and an accompanying chorus went to meet the procession and sang its way into town! Oh, if we had been there, millions of Christians have thought.

Singing this hymn today could center and inspire the passion meditations of many a modern believer. Fortunatus's Latin poem has been turned into iambic pentameter English, and set to several different tunes in the modern age. I invite you to imagine singing it, while visualizing the procession of the cross across Europe and into your town. You could do it in your own church, or around the block and then in the door. Or all in pious reflection! To whet your appetite, go to YouTube on your TV and under Q, type in "The royal banners go" and choose from over fifty selections.

> *The royal banners forward go;*
> *The cross shines forth in mystic glow*
> *Where He, by whom our flesh was made,*
> *Our ransom in His flesh has paid:*

Where deep for us the spear was dyed,
Life's torrent rushing from His side,
To wash us in the precious flood
Where flowed the water and the blood.

Fulfilled is all that David told
In sure prophetic song of old.
That God the nations' king should be
And reign in triumph from the tree.

On whose hard arms, so widely flung,
The weight of this world's ransom hung,
The price of humankind to pay
And spoil the spoiler of his prey.

O Tree of beauty, tree most fair,
Ordained those holy limbs to bear
Gone is thy shame, each crimsoned bough
Proclaims the King of Glory now.

To Thee, eternal Three in One,
Let homage meet by all be done;
As by the cross Thou dost restore,
So guide and keep us evermore.

POETRY AND PROSE

There is much classical and contemporary literature set in the season of Lent or specifically addressing Good Friday. You can search for it on Google or in the Amazon catalog.

THEATER

A Google search will turn up a long list of short dramas that can be performed in churches during Holy Week. An obvious simple opportunity is a dramatic reading of the entire passion narrative from one of the Gospels, with each part read (performed?) by different members of a congregation. Such a reading, usually from John, can be a powerful portrayal on Good Friday.

In all these remembrances, it may be good to consider a difficult insight from contemporary theology, as admonished by Pastor Nadia Bolz-Weber, "God is not looking down at the cross, but is hanging from the cross."

But another concern has arisen in modern theology, that the cross has overwhelmed all of Jesus' "speaking parts." The Gospels are in fact packed with things Jesus had to say and do, and these are often glossed over by those who want to get out from under them. It is not good to leave Jesus with nothing to say, even given the cross as a powerful center of New Testament proclamation. In *Nickel and Dimed: On (Not) Getting By in America*, the veteran muckraker Barbara Ehrenreich has written that it would be nice if someone would also now and then read the Sermon on the Mount from Matthew to a sad-eyed crowd who need a hike in the minimum wage. Of course the whole point of the present book is to provide a multidimensional take on the life of Christ.

Way Station 14

Jesus Rises from the Dead, Signaling the Triumph of God's Love and the Reconciliation of the World—Do Christians Spend Their Lives Following in the Train of Their Risen Lord?

IN EASTERN ORTHODOX DEPICTIONS of Easter and the resurrection, Christ is never pictured rising alone; he has Adam and Eve in tow—and by implication millions of others freed from the bondage of the old world. In some Orthodox iconography, Jesus' rising up (the Greek word *anastasis*) may be portrayed as rising from sleep or rising up against all the forces that stand in the way of God's eschatological plan for the world. This activist view of the resurrection also comes to mean that Christians too (and all humanity?) are *commissioned in baptism to rise up from compromised pasts and follow God into new futures*. And eventually bring the neighborhood with them. Christians are called to live lives anticipating the final resurrection, drawing down into their own lives, their own neighborhoods, their own societies, the resurrecting power of God who meets us in the world and draws us in God's final direction—and now participating in Christ's enthronement. Today God is circling overhead. Prepare the landing strip! God is intending to arrive in the present, not merely the sweet by and by. Chasing the Holy Spirit, that whirlwind-maker, provides the power for the triumph of spirit over matter.

Just to get started, what's most exciting about the Orthodox celebration of Easter? In the New Testament, why do women get the news first? Is that telling? Would you and your friends be hiding out (and where) when the news comes? Just where were you (in hiding!) when the Easter proclamation came around? Why do many assured doubters, including lofty Christians, refuse to believe that Jesus rose from the dead? How important is it to insist on the New Testament's (and Christian history's) unanimous proclamation of Jesus' resurrection?

The resurrection of Jesus, or *anastasis*, is the Christian belief that God raised Jesus on the third day after his crucifixion, beginning or restoring or establishing his enthroned life as Christ and Lord. According to the New Testament writings, Jesus was firstborn from the dead, ushering in the kingdom of God. He appeared to several women and then to eleven disciples after his resurrection, soon enough calling them to the Great Commission of proclaiming the gospel of eternal salvation through his death and resurrection, and then ascended to heaven (a mostly forgotten Christian festival occurring on a Thursday forty days after Easter).

The early Christian missionary Paul, newly and dramatically called by Christ himself in a dramatic conversion experience on the road to Damascus, wrote to the Corinthians: "For I handed on to you as of first importance what I in turn had received: that Christ died for our sins in accordance with the scriptures, and that he was buried, and that he was raised on the third day in accordance with the scriptures. He appeared to the disciples and then to more than five hundred brothers and sisters at one time. Last of all, as to one untimely born, he appeared also to me."

The resurrection of Jesus Christ from the dead is central to and indispensable for the Gospel accounts, the theology of Paul, the inauguration of early Christianity, and the historic course of Christian theology. This final way station is the climax of Jesus' life, and Easter is central to Christian proclamation and celebration. Let's celebrate when you arrive at this final station on your pilgrimage!

Yet there emerged in the twentieth century much controversy among historical Jesus scholars and some other contemporary theologians regarding the nature and historicity of the resurrection, ranging from its objective fact, to the empty tomb, whether he appeared embodied, to the role of witnesses, to post-Easter appearances, to the evolution of the Gospel narratives. The resurrection somehow remains outside the historically accessible data about Jesus' life and ministry. In this sense, the fourteenth station of Jesus' life, like the first, is different from the rest. Yet I mostly pass over the contemporary disputes, not because they are unimportant or should be avoided, but because I have tried to concentrate on the central New Testament proclamation regarding these stations and the deposit it has left in the life of the church. I have no sympathy with contemporary Christian theologians who travel the country astounding paying audiences with how little of the New Testament they actually can believe while still calling themselves Christians. I seek a robust appraisal of the bodily resurrection, not a light-footed one, in vigorous continuity with historic orthodoxy.

If one begins with Jesus' setting as an eschatological prophet of Israel, then his resurrection constitutes the new exodus, Yahweh's return to Zion, and the culmination of the true Israel's history as the light of the world. It is the vindication of Jesus' life and death, and a symbol for any and every return from exile. As eschatological event, it is a foretaste of the resurrection of all the dead—our sure future. There is a great variety to the New Testament witnesses to the resurrection and its meanings, an unmistakable concert composed of many individual voices. Disparate traditions came to be woven into an unmistakable theological and foundational confession.

The testimony to a risen Christ is early, firm, various, and acknowledged in all known currents of early Christian tradition as the foundation of Christian faith and the life of the church. Among its dimensions are the following: the Easter experience is not primarily the discovery of an empty tomb but the experience of the appearances of Jesus; the disciples see this as an eschatologically loaded resurrection; they find in it a divine vindication of Jesus that leads to an explosion of christological speech; the early Christian community understands itself as a restored community; it leads to an experience of forgiveness and reconciliation and new life; and integral to the resurrection is a missionary mandate of the risen Christ; at some point Christ will return as the culmination of history.

The resurrection provides a *revelatory seal and conclusion to all the stations of Jesus' life*. It is the destiny of the pilgrim's walk, with everyone cheering on the other side as we approach in inexhaustible confession. It is easy to make Jesus a teacher, and to translate him into useful modes of knowledge and moral action—a wise prophet. It is possible to make him a social or political revolutionary, and to find in him a model for action. All this is true, but there is more: Jesus is an eschatological prophet announcing the kingdom of Israel's God, now embracing all the world. In an age where people inquire how little you can believe and still be a Christian, or spiritual but not religious, it is worth recalling that we know of no early Christian movement that did not proclaim Jesus' resurrection and indeed worship him in the light of it. The early church works out its faith and its destiny while pondering God's relation to history and the unfolding of God's reign.

In one sense the fourteenth way station reframes all the others; in another it is in ultimate continuity with them all, climaxing them. Above all, the resurrection is continuous with the incarnation; the last station bookends the first.

But there is still the matter of our own self-understanding post-Easter. The modern dilemma is not for most of us the "delay of Christ's Return," but the ongoing task of enacting the meaning of Jesus' life-to-death-to-life agenda. It is not a focus on when is Jesus coming back, but a focus on what we are doing now, we and the entire Christian community as the *extension of the incarnation*, we the heirs of the Easter proclamation. Have we who walk the stations experienced resurrection? Consider the earthy realism in Lutheran pastor Nadia Bolz-Weber's assertion: "God keeps reaching down into the dirt of humanity and resurrecting us from the graves we dig for ourselves." God keeps loving us back to life, over and over. Diversions and obsessions about "the second coming" typically lead to the neglect of Jesus' first coming—what he actually said and did, all confirmed at Easter—and shift the church's gaze from its earthly witness to its heavenly diversion. (Okay, I have always enjoyed the bumper sticker during the 1970s Jesus Movement in Berkeley: "Jesus is back and he's pissed.")

Altogether, these fourteen stations do not reduce to interesting items in the history of ideas or religious curiosities, but are a call to discipleship, an evocation of the imitation of Christ, a call to be the community that models its own life after the stations in Jesus' life, that wants to go down into the water and rise again. *The theological task is to keep rethinking God around the actual history of Jesus.* The portrait of God Jesus evidences is not a terrifying God, but one humanity would be glad to meet, one who has reconciled the world. We who do not fully know ourselves are invited to the knowing of Jesus, traversing the long journey home, and discovering our destiny in God's eyes. Jürgen Moltmann extends Christ's resurrection into our dying and rising, our own resurrection to eternal life. He wants to shift the well-known art of dying (*ars moriendi*) to an *ars resurgendi*, our preparation for a fullness of life, which is eternal. Christ pulls all humanity from a kingdom of death to the light of eternal life. His resurrection is a collective act, delivering us to a world of life without death. It is not individual resurrection, Moltmann thinks, that Christ delivers us to, but universal life in common. (About once a week, in my nightly prayers, I ask God to communicate to my long since departed parents how much I cherish their example and thank them for their support and guidance. And ask

Way Station 14

God, please, to pass on my thoughts. Surely this is one purpose of heaven? Connection!) All humanity is pulled from the kingdom of death to the light of eternal life. Christ's resurrection becomes a collective act delivering us to a world of life without death—comparable to new creation.

This is what Christianity's Orthodox traditions have always depicted and maintained. Orthodox Easter icons depict a corporate resurrection. Having descended to the realm of the dead, Christ unlocks the gates of hell and death, rises triumphantly, with Adam and Eve and all humankind in his train, into a new kingdom of life. Now all is filled with light and life, and the church, in solidarity, portrays and celebrates and believes this. The Orthodox Easter liturgy carries the weight of this ambitious proclamation. Christ's passion and resurrection demonstrate his unity with all of us. Christ's resurrection represents the beginning of God's new world. As you gather with fellow Christians at this station, keep assuring one another, witnessing to one another.

It could be said that our own resurrection begins at the hour of our death. The entirety of our lived life is raised, not just our corpse. As Paul taught, the grain of wheat (as metaphor) ceases being a grain and blooms. What was perishable has a future. Dietrich Bonhoeffer, the German Lutheran martyr, thought Christianity has, and must have, a profound this-worldliness because of the constant awareness of death and resurrection. Within us and among us is the path home. We can become self-transcending because of the immanence of God's spirit in the innermost center of our soul. Teresa of Avila called it the *Interior Castle*. In his *The Seven Storey Mountain*, Thomas Merton depicts humanity encountering God in the seventh level of the soul. For the German apostle of liberalism Friedrich Schleiermacher, Christianity develops a sense and taste for the infinite. Luther sang: "The brightness of the Light divine/Doth now into our darkness shine/It breaks upon sin's gloomy night/And makes us children of the light." All of this, in summary, we Christians are called to observe and emulate as we walk toward and pause at the fourteenth way station.

Finally, consider this feminist observation from the Catholic theologian James Martin: The discovery of the empty tomb is the work of women. Women *deliver* the news of the risen Christ. Just as one woman, Mary, once *delivered* the birth of Jesus.

What are the opportunities to walk this station, to meet each other in community? The Easter season is the most obvious call to walk this station, and this might include discovering how other Christian traditions, like the

Eastern Orthodox, celebrate. Every funeral, every intimation of mortality, every confrontation with mass death like the COVID crisis, every new awareness of war death as currently in Ukraine, becomes an opportunity to proclaim the gospel of resurrection. Could the power and the call of resurrection inspire us to become hospice volunteers or inquirers into death cultures of hospitals, nursing homes, or inner cities? Could we come as inspired and empowered witnesses?

THE RESURRECTION OF CHRIST AND THE ARTS

As one might expect, the fourteenth station with Christ is not only a matter of theological observation and proclamation, but becomes flesh in every material art. These are the "dress performances" of the fourteenth station and vastly enrich and contextualize it.

VISUAL ARTS

There are many books featuring Christian visual art in general, both historic European and contemporary indigenous takes on Christian themes. There are also books devoted to portrayals of Easter. The greatest plethora for most Christians walking this station can be found by Googling, which delivers images without end. Especially to Westerners, art which depicts Orthodox views of the resurrection with Christ thrusting upward from the tomb with Adam and Eve and all humanity pulled along in his train are particularly thrilling.

MUSIC AND HYMNS

Handel's *Messiah* has a section devoted to Easter themes, and the Hallelujah Chorus as its center piece is known and sung around the world. Bach of course has written cantata #4 and oratorio #249 for the Lutheran Easter liturgies and these are readily available on YouTube, but less so in concert—except in Germany.

Among the many hymns for Easter, these are among the most well-known. All these are available on Google and YouTube. And in the hymnals of most churches. If you long for live hymnody, go to church and let it wash over you.

"Jesus Christ Is Ris'n Today, Alleluia!" (Charles Wesley's setting of a medieval carol)

> *Our triumphant holy day, Alleluia!*
> *Who did once upon the cross, Alleluia!*
> *Suffer to redeem our loss. Alleluia!*
>
> *Hymns of praise then let us sing. Alleluia!*
> *Unto Christ our heavenly king, Alleluia!*
> *Who endured the cross and grave, Alleluia!*
> *Sinners to redeem and save. Alleluia!*
>
> "Christ The Lord Is Ris'n Today!" (Medieval carol)
> *All on earth with angels say; Raise your joys and triumphs high; Sing*
> *O heav'ns and earth reply (plus five more stanzas).*
>
> "This Joyful Eastertide"
> *Away with sin and sorrow!*
> *My love, the Crucified, has sprung to life this morrow.*
> *Refrain: Had Christ who once was slain, not burst his three-day prison, our faith had been in vain, But now has Christ arisen, arisen, arisen, arisen.*

"Thine Be The Glory, Risen Conquering Son" (Set to Handel's majestic music from "Judas Maccabaeus" and with a text by the turn of the twentieth-century Protestant pastor Edmond Budry)

> *Endless is the victory thou o'er death hast won.*
> *Angels in bright raiment rolled the stone away,*
> *Kept the folded grave-clothes, Where the body lay.*
> *Refrain: Thine is the glory, risen conquering Son;*
> *endless is the victory thou o'er death hast won!*
> *Two more stanzas*

"This Day Of Resurrection" reflects the theological sensibility of the Orthodox tradition and was written by one of the early Greek fathers, John of Damascus:

> *The day of resurrection.*
> *Earth tell it out abroad, the Passover of gladness, the Passover of God*
> *From death to life eternal, from sin's dominion free,*
> *Our Christ has brought us over with hymns of victory.*

PART TWO: WALKING 14 STATIONS ALONG THE CHRISTIAN WAY

"*Victimi Paschali*" is a plainsong chant dating from the eleventh century and is seminal to Gregorian chant. (Find a monastery where you will hear this.)

> *Christians to the paschal victim offer your thankful praises, A lamb the sheep redeeming, Christ, who only is sinless reconciling sinners to the Father.*
> *Death and life have contended in that combat stupendous; the prince of life who died reigns immortal.*
> *Speak Mary, declaring what you saw when wayfaring. The tomb of Christ who is living, the glory of Jesus' resurrection, bright angels attesting,*
> *The shroud and napkin resting, My Lord, my hope is arisen, to Galilee he goes before you.*
> *Christ indeed from death is risen, our new life obtaining, Have mercy victor King, ever reigning. Amen.*

DRAMA

Continuously developing across the Middle Ages, liturgical dramas evolved as religious theatrical performances such as passion plays. They developed from Latin into vernacular languages, especially German. Liturgy-centered drama eventually gave birth to larger uses of drama, including secular ones. The most famous operational phrase, at the root of the evolution of nearly all medieval drama, was *Quem quaeritis*—the angels at the tomb addressing the women who came: *Whom do you seek?* Jesus of Nazareth they answer. "He is not here, he is risen, as he had said." The question "Whom do you seek?" became a very famous Latin phrase anchoring the drama that evolved from the Easter liturgy and became the best known example of liturgy evolving into enacted drama. Think of this as the central inauguration of the Christian message. After the short dialogue between the visiting women and the angels, a sung chorus of Hallelujahs followed. The drama inherent in much of the church's liturgy snowballed into a huge body of medieval religious plays, lasting 650 years through the end of the Protestant Reformation.

Of course liturgy is that central only to the so-called liturgical churches, Orthodox, Roman Catholic, and also Anglican and Lutheran. But rather belatedly, even also among many Protestant denominations, the dramatic element involved in worship and biblical stories began to evoke dramatic enactments, in some rare cases even *liturgical dance*. Of course

Way Station 14

the popularity of theater continued to develop on its own, especially in the secular world. Ironically, the Puritan influence in British Anglicanism began to move toward the suppression of theater and drama.

LOCAL PERFORMANCES

Perhaps especially in evangelical churches without "high church" liturgical traditions, there is no end to inventiveness, ranging from children's performances to rousing contemporary music led by song leaders and bands.

In my own church, a high point of every Easter celebration involves men constructing homely crosses, women coming with abundant flowers, and children standing in line to adorn them. Early in the service, just before the reading of the Gospel, the children process carrying the much adorned Easter cross and planting it right in front of the altar. On signal, the entire congregation erupts in oohs and ahs as the cross is turned around to face the congregation, and everyone congratulates themselves on the production.

As this book comes to a close, it is well to remember that way stations 1 and 13 and 14 coincide with three great Christian festivals—Christmas, Holy Week, and Easter. But in between is the entire Christian pilgrimage and all the stations that enrich it. It is well to remind ourselves that the Christian walk, in the steps of Jesus, is anchored by the very Easter event that led to the founding of the early church.

APPENDIX

Walking the Common Lectionary

Liturgical Inculturation

Liturgical inculturation is a term of art in the Roman Catholic tradition reasserted during and after Vatican II. The default position for liturgy was that it had once been permanently fixed, by revelation, in the practice of worship—as if it had dropped from heaven. Similarly, conservative Christians see the icon of social justice as a new secular idolatry dropped into the church, where it does not belong, from the world outside. But this *fails to see the world, through all its material symbols, as waiting for God's redemption and destined for God's friending—as abundant cultural symbols are carried into the church and installed in the liturgy.*

Imagine how inculturation would come to work over the life of the church and society and in the history of the Bible's effects over time. Envision how liturgy, including its performative function, could launch out and take up the pain of the world and its weighty symbols, consecrate them, and return to embody them in the church's worship. Think of the stations of Holy Week or of the exodus *movement* out of Egypt and into the promised land. A common admonition to those considering the ancient pilgrimage route to Compostela in Western Spain was, "The way is made by walking." First steps must be taken for the pilgrimage to begin. New liturgies would be called to appear in the vicinities of the least of these, with a view to import the suffering of the poor and their cries for redemption back into the worship of the church. Liturgical renewal wants to insert the church's consecrating power and presence into the culture surrounding the life of the church in such a way that the liturgy absorbs that culture and is thus able to speak from within it and then carry it back into the midst of worshipping communities. Simultaneously, those cultures outside the church might absorb the church's performative presence and thus the Christian faith upon which it rests. The church and its liturgical worship would become deeply integrated into the social fabric of a troubled world—and vice versa. All this continuously occurs, there and back again, as liturgy performs us, and we it, in the church gathered and the church sent. But ultimately the long journey towards God, the Christian pilgrimage, happens through the world, where we also recognize along the way the presence of God among the least of these. Go out from church into the world, look and see, and return to worship inside with the Christ you also encountered outside—among the least of these, and perhaps among systems that oppress them.

No Christ Without a Kingdom

Mark Labberton's book on this theme has the sturdy and surprising title: *The Dangerous Act of Worship: Living God's Call to Justice*. Consider this summary:

> What's at stake in our worship? Everything. Worship is the dangerous act of waking up to God and God's purposes in the world. But something has gone wrong with our worship. Too often worship has become a place of safety and complacency, a narrowly private experience in which solitary individuals only express their personal adoration. Even when we gather corporately, we often close our eyes to those around us, focusing on God but ignoring our neighbor. But true biblical worship does not merely point us upward—it should turn us outward as well.

A reviewer praises him: "Pastor Labberton has become a prophet calling 'Wake up! Reconnect Christian worship with biblical justice. From beginning to end, worship must pursue justice and seek righteousness, translating into transformed lives that care for the poor and the oppressed.'" Ritual movement involves transcending safe worship and awakening to the needs of the world. Have we convincingly begun this movement? Can we say that it is demonstrably connecting every Sunday to every Monday? Do we return the following Sunday exhausted and badly in need of replenishment?

Consider this shrewd observation from German theologian Jürgen Moltmann:

An other-worldly piety, which wants God without his kingdom and the blessedness of the new soul without the new earth, is really just as atheistic as the this-worldliness which wants its kingdom without God, and the earth without the horizon of salvation. God without the world and the world without God, faith without hope and hope without faith are merely a mutual corroboration of one another.

To get started and acquaint yourself with lectionary resources for various Sundays, Google textweek.com. These are weekly worship materials.

Then consider these appointed readings from the Common Lectionary that happen to align with each of the fourteen stations. See how the stations you are practicing by yourself, or in groups, can also be underlined on various Sundays in the church year: A, B, and C refer to the three yearly cycles in the Common Lectionary, Year A, Year B, and Year C. Numbers (1, 2, etc) refer to the weeks in a cycle, for example the third Sunday in Advent, the various Sundays on and after Easter, or the long series of Sundays in "Ordinary time," that is all the Sundays in the second half of the church year, meaning after the festival half: Advent-Christmas-Epiphany-Lent-Easter-Pentecost.

1. Jesus is born into the human world/
Will we meet him there as we are born again?

Here are the instances of the biblical witness to Christ's birth that occur in the Common Lectionary, the appointed readings for liturgical services on every Sunday of the church year in Years A (Matthew), B (Mark), and C (Luke), with parts of John sprinkled in.

Year A Advent 1 Matthew 24:36–44
    Advent 2 Matthew 3:1–12
        Advent 3 Matthew 11:2–11
            Advent 4 Matthew 1:18–25
Year B Advent 1 Mark 13:24–37
    Advent 2 Mark 1:1–8
        Advent 3 John 1:6–8, 19–28
            Advent 4 Luke 1:26–38
Year C Advent 1 Luke 21:25–36
    Advent 2 Luke 3:1–6
        Advent 3 Luke 3:7–18
            Advent 4 Luke 1:26–38

APPENDIX

Year ABC Christmas Eve Luke 2:1–14; Christmas Day Luke 1:8–20 or John 1:1–14
Year A Christmas 1 Matthew 2:13–23
Year B Christmas 1 Luke 2:22–40
Year ABC Christmas 2 John 1:1–18

2. Jesus is baptized, opens his life to God, and engages a world of temptation and possibility/*Have we been mostly clueless about the implications of our own baptism?*

Year A Baptism of the Lord Mathew 3:13–17
Year B Baptism of the Lord Mark 1:9–11
Year C Baptism of the Lord Luke 3:15–22

3. Jesus inaugurates his prophetic vocation and proclaims the arrival of the kingdom of God/*Will we recognize God's reign when we see it? Will we proclaim Jubilee?*

Readings from the Common Lectionary for the Third Sunday in the Epiphany season all depict Jesus beginning his public ministry proclaiming the arrival of the reign of God and calling people to a decision on how to respond.

Year A Epiphany 3 Matthew 4:12–23 Jesus' inaugural ministry is fulfilling Isaiah's prophecy: "The people who sat in darkness have seen a great light."

Year B Epiphany 3 Mark 1:14 Jesus is calling for a response to the arrival of the reign of God: "Repent and believe in the good news."

Year C Epiphany 3 Luke 4:14–21 depicts Jesus preaching his *inaugural sermon*, lately dubbed the Nazareth Manifesto, reading from Isaiah: "The Spirit of the Lord is upon me, because he has anointed me to bring good news to the poor, release to the captives, recovery of sight to the blind, and letting the oppressed go free." Before an astonished synagogue audience Jesus then announces: "Today this has been fulfilled in your hearing."

Year A Ordinary Time 32 Matthew 25:1–13 The parable of the ten bridesmaids is about preparedness for the arrival of the kingdom.

Year A Ordinary Time 21 Matthew 13:44–46 The appearance of God's kingdom is like discovering treasure in a field or a pearl of great price.

4. Jesus is calling and making disciples/
How do we answer? Do we consent to be made new?

The readings from the Common Lectionary reverberate with Jesus' constant calling disciples to follow him, the first thing he does in his public ministry.

Year A Epiphany 3 Matthew 4:18–21 Jesus calls Peter and Andrew, who leave all to follow Jesus.

Year B Epiphany 3 Mark 1:16–20 Jesus calls the first disciples.

Year C Epiphany 5 John 1:35–51 Jesus calls Peter and Andrew, both fisherman, and famously says, "Follow me, and I will make you fish for people." Holding up their example for all future Christians, Matthew says they immediately left their nets and their father and followed him.

Note that Epiphany takes up Jesus' inaugural ministry, after the heavily-weighted season of Christmas. Jesus' grand *transfiguration* closes the Epiphany season, and then Lent begins with Ash Wednesday.

5A. Jesus teaches us to pray, with the Lord's Prayer as a model

It has been said that when we immerse ourselves in a life of prayer we stay in communion and communication with God. In Sunday readings from the common lectionary, the Lord's Prayer is found in Luke 11:1–4 (Proper 12C), and a slightly longer form is in Matthew 6:9–13. The Gospels introduce the Lord's Prayer with these instructions: *Pray then in this way,* or *When you pray, say*. The first three of the seven petitions in Matthew address God; the other four are related to human needs and concerns. The Matthew account alone includes the "Your will be done" and the "Rescue us from the evil one" (or "Deliver us from evil") petitions. Only Protestants conclude with a doxology mentioned in some manuscript traditions: "For thine is the kingdom and the power and the glory, forever and ever, Amen."

5B. Jesus teaches us to pray, with the Lord's Prayer as a model/
Could we learn to pray? Are we paying attention to the world around us when we pray?

It has been said that when we immerse ourselves in a life of prayer we stay in communion and communication with God.

Year C Ordinary Year: Luke 11:1–4

Appendix

Besides in a reading from the Common Lectionary, a slightly longer form of the Lord's Prayer is in Matthew 6:9–13. The Gospels introduce the Lord's Prayer with these instructions: *Pray then in this way,* or *When you pray, say.* The first three of the seven petitions in Matthew address God; the other four are related to human needs and concerns. The Matthew account alone includes the "Your will be done" and the "Rescue us from the evil one" (or "Deliver us from evil") petitions. Only Protestants conclude with a doxology mentioned in some manuscript traditions: "For thine is the kingdom and the power and the glory, forever and ever, Amen."

6A. Jesus eats and drinks with sinners and outsiders/*Could we learn Christian table manners?*

Jesus' eating and drinking practices, the demonstration of his *commensality* (the social interactions and rules associated with people eating together in a society), are reflected in several readings from the church's common lectionary. Famously, Jesus miraculously fed five thousand people out of five loaves and two fishes and there were considerable leftovers. In Matthew 14:13–21 (Proper 13A) Jesus saw a great crowd of followers, and he had compassion for them. The Greek word suggested he felt so sorry for them it made his stomach hurt. Towards evening, the disciples suggested sending the crowds away—as we too might do? Not our problem, the disciples implied. "You feed them," Jesus says. Out of five loaves and two fishes Jesus makes enough food for five thousand, with leftovers! Mark 6:30–44 (Proper 11B) tells the same story, but notes the crowds looked to Jesus like sheep without a shepherd. John 6:1–15 (Proper 12B) also tells this story and has the crowd responding: "This is the prophet who is to come into the world." Luke also has an account of this story.

6B. Jesus eats and drinks with outsiders and the excluded/ *Could we learn Christian table manners?*

Year A Ordinary Year 13 Matthew 14:13–22 Jesus famously fed five thousand people out of five loaves and two fishes and there were considerable leftovers. Jesus saw a great crowd of followers, and he had compassion for them. The Greek word suggested he felt so sorry for them it made his stomach hurt. Towards evening, the disciples suggested sending the crowds away—as we too might do? Not our problem, the disciples implied. "You feed them," Jesus says.

Year B Ordinary year 11 Mark 6:30–44 Mark tells the same story, but notes the crowds looked to Jesus like sheep without a shepherd.

Year B Ordinary Year 12 John 6:1–15 John also tells this story and has the crowd responding: "This is the prophet who is to come into the world."

Luke 9:10–17 also has an account of this story.

In Matthew 15:1 and Mark 7:1–9 and Luke 11:37–54 Jesus dines with a Pharisee.

7A. Jesus heals physical disease and social illness/*Could the church become a field hospital and we its chaplains?*

The Common Lectionary features many readings from the Gospels in which Jesus heals disease both physical and social. He heals a man with an unclean spirit (Mark 1:23–28 Epiphany 4B). He heals a leper (Mark 1:40–42 Epiphany 6B and Matthew 8:1–4 and Luke 5:12–16) and a paralytic (Mark 2:1–14 Epiphany 7B and Matthew 9:1–8 and Luke 5:17–26 and John 5:1–9 Easter 6C). He heals the daughter of Jairus (Mark 5:35–43 Proper 8B). Remarkably he heals the daughter of a foreign woman, but only after testing her faith (Mark 7:24–30 Proper 18B). He heals a deaf man (Mark 7:31–37 Proper 18B) and a blind man (Mark 8:22–26) and another blind man named Bartimaeus (Mark 10:46–52 Proper 25B). He heals a man with a withered hand (Matthew 12:9–14 and Mark 3:1–15 and Luke 6:6–11 which mentions it occurred on the Sabbath). He heals Simon's mother-in-law and then many more that evening (Luke 4:38–41). John 9:1–41 (Lent 4A) tells a remarkable story about healing a man born blind, which leads to an argument with the Pharisees who refuse to accept this over who is really blind—them!

7B. Jesus heals physical disease and social illness/ *Could the church become a field hospital and we its chaplains?*

The Common Lectionary features many readings from the Gospels in which Jesus heals disease both physical and social.

Appendix

Year A Lent 4 John 9:1–41 Jesus heals a man born blind and then gets into an argument with Pharisees who contest it. Who is it then who is actually blind!

Year B Epiphany 4 Mark 1:23–28 Jesus heals a man with an unclean spirit.

Year B Epiphany 6 Mark 1:40–42 Jesus heals a leper. Also in Matthew 8:1–4 and Luke 5:12–16.

Year B Epiphany 7 Jesus heals a paralytic. Also in Matthew 9:1–8 and Luke 5:17–26.

Year B Ordinary Year 8 Mark 5:35–43 Jesus heals the daughter of Jairus.

Year B Ordinary Year 18 Mark 7:24–30 Jesus heals the daughter of a foreign woman, but only after testing her faith.

Year B Ordinary Year 18 Mark 7:31–37 Jesus heals a deaf man. And a blind man (Mark 8:22–26).

Year B Ordinary Year 25 Mark 10:46–52 Jesus heals blind Bartimaeus.

Year C Easter 6 Jesus heals a paralytic.

Among the many healing stories that do not appear in the Common Lectionary are the following: In Matthew 8:18–22 and Luke 4:40–41 Jesus heals the sick who are brought to him in the evening. In Matthew 9:1–8, Mark 2:1–2, Luke 5:17–26, and John 5:1–9 Jesus heals a paralytic. Jesus heals a man with a withered hand (Matthew 12:9–14 and Mark 3:1–15 and Luke 6:6–11, which mentions it occurred on the Sabbath). He heals Simon's mother-in-law and then many more that evening (Luke 4:38–41). Mark 1:23–28 Jesus heals man with unclean spirit Mark 1:23–28. Jesus heals a leper (Mark 1:40–42) and a paralytic (Mark 2:1–14, Matthew 9:1–8 and Luke 5:17–26 and John 5:1–9). Mark 5:1–10 Jesus heals the Gerasene demoniac. In Mark 5:35–43 Jesus heals Jairus's daughter. In Mark 7:31–37 Jesus heals a deaf man. In Mark 8:22–26 Jesus heals a blind man at Bethsaida and in Mark 10:46–52 he heals blind Bartimaeus.

8. Jesus preaches sermons that reveal a gospel from God for all peoples/*Do we hear a gospel that sounds like this every Sunday and preach it in the midst of a world longing for good news?*

Mark 1:14 (Lent 1 B) registers the beginning of Jesus' preaching. "Now after John was put in prison, Jesus came into Galilee, preaching the good news of

God, and saying, 'The time is fulfilled, and the kingdom of God has come near; repent, and believe in the good news.'"

Luke 4:14–22 (Epiphany 3C) reports Jesus' inaugural sermon in Nazareth:

> Then Jesus, filled with the power of the Spirit, returned to Galilee, and a report about him spread through all the surrounding country. He began to teach in their synagogues and was praised by everyone. When he came to Nazareth, where he had been brought up, he went to the synagogue on the sabbath day, as was his custom. He stood up to read, and the scroll of the prophet Isaiah was given to him. He unrolled the scroll and found the place where it was written: "The Spirit of the Lord is upon me, because he has anointed me to bring good news to the poor, He has sent me to proclaim release to the captives and recovery of sight to the blind, to let the oppressed go free, to proclaim the year of the Lord's favor." And he rolled up the scroll, gave it back to the attendant, and sat down. The eyes of all in the synagogue were fixed on him. Then he began to say to them, "Today this scripture has been fulfilled in your hearing."

Matthew is packed with Jesus' preaching. Right after enduring his temptations, Jesus begins his public preaching. Matthew 4:17 (Epiphany 3A) announces: From that time Jesus began to proclaim, "Repent, for the kingdom of heaven has come near." From then on, it's unrelenting! Many scholars divide the entire Gospel of Matthew into **five discourses**, or sermons, from Jesus, each one concluding with "when Jesus had finished speaking": 7:28, 11:1, 13:53, 19:1, and 26:1.

The **Sermon on the Mount Matthew 5–7** Epiphany 4–7A, All Saints, Ash Wednesday ABC, Epiphany 8A, Proper 3A, Thanksgiving B, Epiphany 9A. Proper 4A is probably Jesus' most known and quoted sermon. It is the longest continuous discourse of Jesus found in the New Testament and has been one of the most widely quoted elements of the Gospels, holding forth the central tenets of Christian discipleship and community. The sermon on the mount includes the Beatitudes and the Lord's Prayer. To many Christians, the Sermon on the Mount contains the central tenets of Jesus' mission.

A second discourse, sometimes called the **missionary discourse**, is in Matthew 10 (Proper 7A; Proper 8A), Mark 6:7–13 (Proper 9B), Luke 9:1–6, Luke 10:1–12 (Proper 9C).

Appendix

The third discourse, in Matthew 13 (Proper 10–12A), is often called the **parabolic discourse.**

The fourth discourse is called the **discourse on the church,** Matthew 18 (Proper 18–19A).

The fifth discourse, in Matthew 25, is sometimes called the **discourse on end times,** with parables of the ten bridesmaids and the talents, and the story about the last judgment (Proper 27–8A; New Year's Day; Reign of Christ 34A; last Sunday of the Church Year, Christ the King Sunday; also Luke 21:5–36 Proper 28C and Advent I C, and Mark 13:5–37 Proper 28B and Advent I B). The coming destruction of the Jerusalem temple and an eschatological mood surrounding the coming of the reign of God are the setting. The stage is being set for a final exam waiting to test all Christians.

9. Jesus welcomes women and outsiders and calls us, in his name, to do the same/
How do women and outsiders fare in our congregations?

Year A, Lent 3 John 4.4–42 Jesus meets a Samaritan woman at a well, where Jesus has gone to rest on his way through Samaria. He says to her, Give me a drink. She wonders how Jesus, a Jew, is even talking to her, a despised Samaritan. Jesus says that if she even had a clue about the gift of God waiting for her, she would have asked for *living water.*

Year B Ordinary Year 8 Mark 5:21ff. tells a story about Jesus, on the way to perform a perfectly acceptable healing of the daughter of a synagogue leader, pauses to notice a strange sorrowful woman who has suffered bleeding for many years and is thus ritually impure.

The Gospels (Matthew 26, Luke 7, and John 12) tell the story about a woman with ointment who, seeming to grasp the path toward death Jesus is on, anoints him in advance.

In Luke 8, several women are in Jesus' entourage, who had been cured of evil spirits and infirmities, including Mary Magdalen healed of seven demons. Jesus welcomes their ministrations. In a story in Luke 13, Jesus heals a long-crippled woman and sets her free, and she stands up straight praising God. But the leader of the synagogue calls it sacrilege to heal on the Sabbath. The crowd rejoices!

John 8 depicts a scene in which a woman caught in adultery is thrust before Jesus by religious leaders to see if he will condone the penalty of stoning her.

Matthew 28.1–8/Mark 16:1–8/Luke 24:1–12/John 20:1–13 tell the story of the women at the tomb.

Matthew 28:9–10/Luke 24:10–11/John 20:14–18 Jesus appears to women.

10. Jesus teaches wisdom in parables that open up alternative realities in which God can appear/*Will we walk into that space and learn to live new lives in it?*

Christian disciples on this way station can evoke a wisdom that sees through constricting worldly assumptions and opens up space for the presence of God. The Gospels are replete with the parables Jesus told, and the Gospel readings assigned for every Sunday by the Common Lectionary reflect that as well. Luke contains twenty-four parables, with eighteen unique to Luke. Matthew contains twenty-three parables, with eleven unique to Matthew. Mark contains eight parables, with two unique to Mark. Sometimes what some readers call parables would better be called "sayings" that are pithy and brief. Beyond the two selections below, in the Common Lectionary, Matthew, Mark, and Luke are loaded with captivating parables.

Year A, Ordinary Year 17 Luke 13:20–21
Year A Ordinary Year 21 Matthew 13:33

11. Jesus rides into Jerusalem and challenges the religious and political establishment/*Do we dare to speak nonconforming truths as communities of resistance?*

Christians walking the stations may confront worldly power and religious corruption and, in response, commit to continuous reformation. Walking the stations during Holy Week is especially resonant, since the historic stations of the cross were riveted to Good Friday.

The Common Lectionary recognizes Jesus' triumphal entry into Jerusalem in the following Gospel readings:

APPENDIX

Palm Sunday in years A, B, and C: Matthew 21:1–11 Mark 11:1–11 or John 12:12–19, and Luke 19:28–38.

Matthew 21.12–16/Mark 11:15–17/Luke 19:45–46/John 2:13–17 cleansing of temple.

Mark 11:1–11 Triumphal entry into Jerusalem.

12. Jesus washes the disciples' feet, gives a new love commandment, and offers his own body to the world in his Last Supper/*Can we learn a servant discipline in this light?*

We are called to practice an obedient discipleship that reflects God's love with a place at the table for everyone, reflecting Jesus' "commensality." Many churches offer a Eucharistic liturgy every Sunday, with the Maundy Thursday service in Holy Week the mother of them all.

The Common Lectionary readings appointed for Maundy Thursday are Matthew 26:26–30, Mark 14:22–25, and Luke 22:14–23. In some liturgies the rather long passion narratives are read in their entirety as the text of the sacred drama of Holy Week. In John 13–17, Jesus' "Farewell Discourses" are unique and very extensive, but John 6:22–71, following the feeding of the five thousand, also offers an extensive discourse on Jesus as the very bread of life, the *bread from heaven*. Only in John 13:1–20 is there a story about Jesus washing the disciples' feet before the Last Supper. In 1 Corinthians 11 Paul offers a commentary on how Communion should be celebrated when the church gathers.

13. Jesus dies the most famous death in history/ *Can Christians see in it a messianic enthronement and their salvation in God?*

Sometimes the long narrative of Christ's passion in John is read in its entirety during Holy Week, or even dramatically reenacted, on Good Friday.

But each Gospel offers its own individual account: Matthew 27, Mark 15, Luke 23, John 19. All four Gospels have been described as elaborate passion narratives with a long preface in the life of Christ.

Although the apostle Paul passes on very little regarding Jesus' earthly ministry, he is very much a theologian of the cross. He discusses the cross of Christ in 1 Corinthians 1:13 (Christians belong to Christ because Christ was crucified for them); 1:18 (The message about the cross is foolishness to those who are perishing, but to us who are being saved it is the power of God); 1:23 (We proclaim Christ crucified, a stumbling block to Jews and foolishness to gentiles); 2:2 (I decided to know nothing among you except Jesus Christ, and him crucified); 2:8 (None of the rulers of this age understood this; for if they had, they would not have crucified the Lord of glory.) In 1 Corinthians 15:3–4, Paul writes: "I handed on to you as of first importance what I in turn had received, that Christ died for our sins in accordance with the scriptures, and that he was buried, and that he was raised on the third day in accordance with the scriptures." When Paul refers in Galatians 6:12–14 to "the cross of our Lord Jesus Christ," it is shorthand for the Christian's entire means of salvation, the source of a theology of a new creation.

In Luke's account in Acts 2:22–24, Peter preaches in his Pentecost sermon: "You that are Israelites, listen to what I have to say: Jesus of Nazareth, a man attested to you by God with deeds of power, wonders, and signs that God did through him among you, as you yourselves know—this man, handed over to you according to the definite plan and foreknowledge of God, you crucified and killed by the hands of those outside the law. But God raised him up, having freed him from death, because it was impossible for him to be held in its power." And further in Acts 2:36: "God has made him both Lord and Messiah, this Jesus whom you crucified."

Early Christians believed that Jesus' suffering was foretold, or prefigured, in the Old Testament, such as in Psalm 22 (which Jesus seems to be praying on the cross) and the suffering and humiliation of the Messiah in Isaiah 53.

14. Jesus rises from the dead and signals the triumph of God's love/*Do Christians spend their lives following in the train of their risen Lord?*

The resurrection of Jesus, or *anastasis*, is the Christian belief that God raised Jesus on the third day after his crucifixion, beginning or restoring his enthroned life as Christ and Lord. According to the New Testament writings, Jesus was firstborn from the dead, ushering in the kingdom of God. He appeared to several women and to eleven disciples after his resurrection, calling them to the Great Commission of proclaiming the Gospel of eternal salvation through his death and resurrection, and then ascended to heaven.

The early Christian missionary Paul, newly and dramatically called by Christ himself in a dramatic conversion experience on the road to Damascus, wrote to the Corinthians: "For I handed on to you as of first importance what I in turn had received: that Christ died for our sins in accordance with the scriptures, and that he was buried, and that he was raised on the third day in accordance with the scriptures. He appeared to the disciples and then to more than five hundred brothers and sisters at one time. Last of all, as to one untimely born, he appeared also to me."

Commentaries on the Bible, popular and scholarly, are never-ending. Especially in recent decades "proclamation commentaries" have attempted to coach preachers and teachers into understanding appointed New Testament lectionary texts as kerygma-saturated, the very Gospel that founds the church and brings liberating good news into the world. But textual preaching itself, unless deliberately rooted in the entire life of Jesus, often does not provide a fully adequate and memorable witness. Even preaching from the three-year lectionary does not necessarily call attention to Jesus' life/death/resurrection as an organic whole and a proper impetus for discipleship. Recently some churches have begun adopting a narrative lectionary, which, according to the tenets of narrative theology or the narrative quality of experience, works its way through entire Gospels, one by one. The congregation comes back Sunday after Sunday to follow the story. Nonliturgical preachers who never follow a lectionary cycle but preach series of sermons on relevant topics might find in the stations an optimal fourteen-week adventure. One can imagine user-friendly commentaries arising whose subject matter is a kerygmatic exposition of these fourteen stations—possible sequels to this book. Or campus ministry programs keyed to a semester.

Strategies for Christian teaching would be foolish not to build on stories deeply ingrained in the "oral tradition" of Christianity, learned and repeated since Sunday school. Just as hymn tunes and texts become *settled into the very bodies of Christian worshippers* over time, so does the hearing of well-known stories resemble children who over the course of an entire childhood keep saying, "Read it again." These stories are part of the church's preaching and teaching equipment, all the more important in an age when college students exemplify a remarkable biblical illiteracy. These fourteen stations in Jesus' life should be like family recipes handed down from generation to generation. They are the stories we repeat that anchor and define us, our stock and trade. They are the original texts of the Christian life that, when repeated, drive us deeper into the church's consciousness.

The resurrection of Jesus Christ from the dead is central to and indispensable for the Gospel accounts, the theology of Paul, the inauguration of early Christianity, and the historic course of Christian theology. This way station is the climax of Jesus' life, and Easter is central to Christian proclamation and celebration.

Bibliography

Barr, Beth Allison. *The Making of Biblical Womanhood: How the Subjugation of Women Became Gospel Truth*. Grand Rapids: Brazos, 2021.
Bauman, Christy Angella. *Theology of the Womb: Knowing God through the Body of a Woman*. Eugene, OR: Cascade, 2019.
Bolz-Weber, Nadia. *Accidental Saints: Finding God in All the Wrong People*. Colorado Springs: Convergent, 2016.
———. *Pastrix: The Cranky, Beautiful Faith of a Sinner & Saint*. Brentwood, TN: Worthy, 2021.
———. *Cranky, Beautiful Faith: For Irregular (and Regular) People*. Atlanta: Canterbury, 2022.
Bonhoeffer, Dietrich. *The Cost of Discipleship*. London: Macmillan, 1963. Original ed. 1937.
Borg, Marcus. *Meeting Jesus Again for the First Time: The Historical Jesus and the Heart of Contemporary Faith*. San Francisco: HarperOne, 1995.
———. *Jesus: The Life, Teachings, and Relevance of a Religious Revolutionary*. San Francisco: HarperOne, 2015.
Brueggemann, Walter. *Sabbath as Resistance: Saying No to the Culture of Now*. Louisville: Westminster John Knox, 2017.
Budde, Michael. *Beyond the Borders of Baptism*. Eugene, OR: Cascade, 2016.
Bunyan, John. *The Pilgrim's Progress*. Mineola, NY: Dover, 2003. Original ed. 1676.
Cavanaugh, William T. *Migrations of the Holy: God, State, and the Political Meaning of the Church*. Grand Rapids: Eerdmans, 2011.
Chaucer. *Canterbury Tales*. Overland Park: Digi Reads, 2015. Original ed. 1400.
Cobb, John. *Jesus Abba: The God Who Has Not Failed*. Minneapolis: Fortress, 2016.
Cone, James. *A Black Theology of Liberation*. Maryknoll, NY: Orbis, 2020.
———. *The Cross and the Lynching Tree*. Maryknoll, NY: Orbis, 2013.
Crossan, John Dominic. *The Historical Jesus: The Life of a Mediterranean Jewish Peasant*. San Francisco: HarperOne, 2010.
———. *Jesus: A Revolutionary Biography*. San Francisco: HarperOne, 2009.
Dante. *The Divine Comedy*. New York: Berkley, 2003. Original ed. 1321.
Dickens, Charles. *A Christmas Carol*. Mineola, NY: Dover, 1991. Original ed. 1843.
DuMez, Kristin Kobes. *Jesus and John Wayne: How White Evangelicals Corrupted a Faith and Fractured a Nation*. New York: Liveright, 2021.
Ehrenreich, Barbara. *Nickel and Dimed: On (Not) Getting By in America*. London: Picador, 2021.

Bibliography

Fiorenza, Elizabeth. *In Memory of Her: A Feminist Theological Reconstruction of Christian Origins.* New York: Herder and Herder, 1994.

Glaspey, Terry. *75 Masterpieces Every Christian Should Know: The Fascinating Stories behind Great Works of Art, Literature, Music, and Film.* Chicago: Moody, 2021.

———. *Discovering God through the Arts: How We Can Grow Closer to God by Appreciating Beauty & Creativity.* Chicago: Moody, 2021.

Gorny, Grzegorz. *Mary, Mother of God: In Search of the Woman Who Changed History.* San Francisco: Ignatius, 2023.

Grady, J Lee. *Ten Lies the Church Tells Women.* Lake Mary, FL: Charisma House, 2006.

Hauerwas, Stanley. *A Community of Character.* Notre Dame: University of Notre Dame Press, 1991.

Hauerwas, Stanley, and William Willimon. *Resident Aliens.* Nashville: Abingdon, 2014.

Harris, James. *The Year of Jubilee: Biblical Principles for Systemic Freedom.* London: Guru Jimmy, 2020.

Harris, Maria. *Fashion Me a People: Curriculum in the Church.* Louisville: Westminster John Knox, 1989.

Heinz, Donald. *After Trump: Achieving a New Social Gospel.* Eugene, OR: Cascade, 2020.

———. *Christmas: Festival of Incarnation.* Minneapolis: Fortress, 2010.

———. *The Last Passage: Recovering a Death of our Own.* New York: Oxford, 1998.

———. *Matthew 25 Christianity: Redeeming Church and Society.* Eugene, OR: Cascade, 2022.

Horsley, Richard. *Jesus and the Politics of Roman Palestine.* Columbia: University of South Carolina Press, 2013.

———. *Jesus and Empire: The Kingdom of God and the New World Disorder.* Minneapolis: Fortress, 2002.

Kazantzakis, Nikos. *The Last Temptation of Christ.* New York: Simon and Schuster, 1998.

Kinsler, Ross, and Gloria Kinsler. *The Biblical Jubilee and the Struggle for Life.* Maryknoll, NY: Orbis, 2003.

Knippa, Michael. "Concerned Citizens: From National Allegiance towards Heavenly Adherence." *Word and World* 37:4 (Fall 2017) 395–403.

Lowery, R. H. *Sabbath and Jubilee: Understanding Biblical Themes.* Des Peres, MO: Chalice, 2020.

Luhrman, T. M. *How God Becomes Real: Kindling the Presence of Invisible Others.* Princeton: Princeton University Press, 2020.

———. *When God Talks Back: Understanding the American Evangelical Relationship with God.* New York: Vintage, 2012.

Mason, Eric. *Woke Church: An Urgent Call for Christians in America to Confront Racism and Injustice.* Chicago: Moody, 2018.

McClaren, Brian. *The Great Spiritual Migration: How the World's Largest Religion Is Seeking a Better Way to Be Christian.* Colorado Springs: Convergent, 2017.

———. *We Make the Road by Walking: A Year-Long Quest for Spiritual Formation, Reorientation, and Activation.* Nashville: Jericho, 2015.

McLaughlin, Rebecca. *Jesus through the Eyes of Women: How the First Female Disciples Help Us Know and Love the Lord.* Austin, TX: Gospel Coalition, 2022.

Miles, Jack. *Christ: A Crisis in the Life of God.* New York: Knopf, 2001.

Moltmann, Jürgen. *The Crucified God.* Minneapolis: Fortress, 2015.

———. *Resurrected to Eternal Life: On Dying and Rising.* Minneapolis: Fortress, 2021.

———. *The Living God and the Fullness of Life.* Louisville: Westminster John Knox, 2015.

Bibliography

O'Grady, Ron. *The Bible through Asian Eyes.* New York: Pace, 1991.

———. *Christ for All People: Celebrating a World of Christian Art.* Maryknoll, NY: Orbis, 2001.

Pontifical Council for the Promotion of the New Evangelization. *The Parables of Mercy: Pastoral Resources for Living the Jubilee.* Huntington, WV: Our Sunday Visitor, 2015.

Schweitzer, Albert. *The Quest for the Historical Jesus.* Mineola, NY: Dover, 2005. Original ed. 1906.

Tan, Kim. *Jubilee and Social Justice: A Dangerous Quest to Overcome Inequalities.* Nashville: Abingdon, 2021.

Tisby, Jemar. *The Color of Compromise: The Truth about the American Church's Complicity in Racism.* Grand Rapids: Zondervan, 2020.

Thurman, Howard. *Jesus and the Disinherited.* Boston: Beacon, 1996.

Weaver, Denny. *The Non-Violent Atonement.* Grand Rapids: Eerdmans, 2011.

Williams, Terran. *How God Sees Women: The End of Patriarchy.* Independently Published, 2022.

www.ingramcontent.com/pod-product-compliance
Lightning Source LLC
Chambersburg PA
CBHW031427150426
43191CB00006B/427